ALONE

AGAINST

THE

NORTH

FELLOW, ROYAL CANADIAN GEOGRAPHICAL SOCIETY

ADAM SHOALTS

ALONE AGAINST THE NORTH

AN EXPEDITION INTO THE UNKNOWN

VIKING

VIKING

an imprint of Penguin Canada Books Inc., a Penguin Random House Company

Published by the Penguin Group

Penguin Canada Books Inc., 320 Front Street West, Suite 1400, Toronto, Ontario, Canada M5V 3B6

Penguin Group (USA) LLC, 375 Hudson Street, New York, New York 10014, U.S.A.
Penguin Books Ltd, 80 Strand, London WC2R 0RL, England
Penguin Ireland, 25 St Stephen's Green, Dublin 2, Ireland (a division of Penguin Books Ltd)
Penguin Group (Australia), 707 Collins Street, Melbourne, Victoria 3008, Australia
(a division of Pearson Australia Group Pty Ltd)
Penguin Books India Pvt Ltd, 11 Community Centre, Panchsheel Park, New Delhi – 110 017, India
Penguin Group (NZ), 67 Apollo Drive, Rosedale, Auckland 0632, New Zealand
(a division of Pearson New Zealand Ltd)
Penguin Books (South Africa) (Pty) Ltd, 24 Sturdee Avenue, Rosebank, Johannesburg 2196, South Africa

Penguin Books Ltd, Registered Offices: 80 Strand, London WC2R 0RL, England

First published 2015

2 3 4 5 6 7 8 9 10 (RRD)

Manufactured in the U.S.A.

LIBRARY AND ARCHIVES CANADA CATALOGUING IN PUBLICATION

Shoalts, Adam, 1986–, author
Alone against the north / Adam Shoalts.

Includes bibliographical references and index.
ISBN 978-0-670-06945-3 (bound)

1. Hudson Bay Region—Discovery and exploration.
2. Hudson Bay Region--Description and travel. 3. Discoveries
in geography. 4. Shoalts, Adam, 1986– —Travel. 5. Explorers—
Canada. I. Title.

FC3969.4.S56 2015   910.9163'27   C2015-901095-0

eBook ISBN 978-0-14-319399-9

Visit the Penguin Canada website at **www.penguin.ca**

Special and corporate bulk purchase rates available; please see
www.penguin.ca/corporatesales or call 1-800-810-3104.

To my fellow explorers, in spirit and deed.

CONTENTS

PROLOGUE

Here we have reached the remotest region of the earth …
a wilderness without a footprint.
—Aeschylus, *Prometheus Bound,* fifth century BC

A HEAD OF US LAY the pitiless expanse of frigid ocean known as Hudson Bay. Behind us lay countless miles of windswept tundra, trackless swamp, and impassable muskeg. Half-famished polar bears roamed the desolate coastline. It wasn't a place one should travel alone—or at all, really.

For the past two weeks my friend and expedition partner Brent Kozuh and I had been hacking and paddling our way across this still largely unexplored wilderness, battling hypothermia and insufferable clouds of mosquitoes and blackflies.

Once we reached the bleak shores of Hudson Bay, Brent finally cracked.

I had seen this moment coming—for the past few days he had fallen into a stupor, his resolve corroded by the millions of bloodsucking insects and the grimness of our journey. We were ankle-deep in icy water, dragging a heavily laden canoe behind us while staggering against fierce winds sweeping off the sea when Brent finally seized up altogether.

"Adam," he said mechanically, "I can't go on … I want to go home."

"We can't quit. We haven't reached the river yet," I replied.

"I don't care about the river. This is about survival. Let me have the satellite phone. I'm going to call a pilot and try to get him to land here."

The wind howled across the treeless tundra, biting into our bearded faces. For a fleeting moment, I thought about Brent's proposal to abandon the expedition. But as I stood there shivering in the salt water, I felt I would never be able to live with failure. I *needed* to reach the river we had come to find.

"No," I said shaking my head, "quitting isn't an option."

"What does it matter? We've done enough," Brent said.

"We've barely done anything."

Brent didn't reply. To him, the nameless river we were seeking wasn't some priceless prize, but just another subarctic river like all the others we had paddled since we began our journey. To me, however, this river represented something more—it was a mystery, and a promise of a pristine place untouched by the modern world, a river so obscure that no known person had ever previously explored it. That made it irresistible. But I could see that all Brent had in mind when he thought of another river was more discomfort, more cold, more swarms of mosquitoes and blackflies.

So I tried to appeal not to the explorer in him, but to the athlete. To quit now, I told him, would be to admit defeat. It would open the door for someone else to explore the river instead of us.

Brent slouched down against the canoe's oak gunwale. "No one in their right mind is ever going to do that."

"Someone has to do it," I replied.

Brent sighed, "It doesn't have to be me."

My feet were numb from standing in the cold water. With the sun sinking below the horizon, I was keen to get moving. "Let's push on a little farther. We'll make camp, get a fire going, warm up, and then you'll feel better."

Brent didn't budge. "I won't feel better until I'm home on my couch with a roof over my head."

"There's the rest of your life for that. This is a chance to do something different."

Brent just stared at the canoe. The wind continued to howl around us. We both shivered in the cold. Snow geese flapped across the sky. I scanned the tundra in either direction. There were no bears in sight.

"Each day feels like an eternity out here," mumbled Brent. "It's freezing, I'm hungry, tired, and wet. There are polar bears all over the place, and we've no idea what might be on that river."

"Things will get easier. We've just had some bad weather," I replied, but without much conviction, knowing that things would likely only get worse.

"Adam," Brent said slowly, "sometimes you're insane."

"I can't do this alone."

Brent shook his head, "I can't do this at all."

Clearly, appealing to Brent's competitive side would now get me nowhere. So I appealed to the one thing I thought he still valued: "If you quit now, you'll have to pay for the entire cost of the flight out of here. The Geographical Society won't cover any of it. It'll cost you a fortune."

"I'd gladly spend my entire life's savings to get out of here."

"You'd really leave me alone in polar bear territory?" I was grasping at straws.

"There's no reason you can't get on that plane with me."

"Not until we've succeeded."

Brent just kept staring at the frigid sea. I was sympathetic. I knew he was cold. I knew the truth of his words—a day can drag on endlessly when you're hungry, exhausted, and wet. When you have only the dimmest sense of what lies ahead. When polar bears are stalking you. I knew it must be hard to put one foot in front of the other if you aren't drawn magnetically toward your destination—as I was.

Brent tossed his hands in the air. "We can just lie about it. We can say we explored the river." His expression finally showed some life.

"Brent!"

"What?"

"We obviously can't do that."

"Who'd know?"

"*We'd know.*"

It became clear that nothing would convince Brent to push on deeper into the wilderness. His will was broken, his mind made up. Now I had to accept the inevitable. To argue any further while standing idly in the estuary would just give us both hypothermia. "All right," I said after a very long pause, "we'll head back to the old goose hunting shack and you can try to contact a pilot."

With that, we grabbed hold of our loaded canoe and dragged it back upriver, wading through frigid water and fighting our way up several sets of rapids to the relative safety of a dilapidated hunting cabin. The next day, I knew, the pilot would arrive for Brent ... but I wouldn't be getting on that plane with him. Daunting as I found the prospect, I would have to remain behind to somehow finish the expedition on my own.

As of tomorrow, I'd be alone against the North.

INTRODUCTION

I am tormented with an everlasting itch for things remote.
I love to sail forbidden seas, and land on barbarous coasts.
—Herman Melville, *Moby Dick*, 1851

I THINK I ALWAYS KNEW I was destined to become an explorer. Joseph Conrad, the great Victorian novelist and an experienced mariner, recalled that in his childhood he liked nothing better than to stare at maps and dream, as he put it, of "the glories of exploration." That was in the 1860s. My childhood consisted of much the same thing. Only, unlike Conrad, I was told that I was born in the wrong century to be an explorer. I was told that there was nothing left to discover and that if I had a passion for adventure and the natural world, I should look into a career as a park ranger or wildlife biologist. But whether from stubbornness or stupidity, I kept dreaming of exploring. The explorers I read about in history books loomed large in my imagination: they were heroic adventurers who undertook dangerous journeys sponsored by geographical societies to navigate wild rivers and map uncharted lands. I aspired to do precisely the same thing—no matter how improbable this goal seemed to

others. And succeed I did. By the age of twenty-five, I was leading an expedition to a river that was so remote it had never been
explored or even named. This book recounts that adventure and
my other expeditions to unexplored rivers for the Royal Canadian
Geographical Society.

PEOPLE OFTEN ASK ME how I became an explorer. They
wonder how I acquired all my wilderness survival skills. Did I
take the best survival course offered anywhere? Had I been the
most diligent of Boy Scouts? Was I an orphan who was raised by
some grizzled old-timer in a cabin in the backwoods? The answer
to all three questions is no. The truth is, developing survival skills
and learning about the outdoors was the easy part. There was
nothing to it: it was just an incidental part of my youth and a
logical consequence of growing up with a passion for the outdoors
in rural Canada. My backyard in Fenwick, Ontario, was a swampy
deciduous forest, and there I roamed with my fraternal twin,
Ben, and our dog from sun-up to sundown. My father, a wood-
worker who could make anything with his hands, taught us
how to fish, trap, track, and enjoy the mystery of the woods. The
hard part was figuring out how I could use these skills in a career.
After the bloom of boyhood enthusiasm and dreams of exotic
lands had worn off, I assumed that exploration was largely a
thing of the past—that the whole world had already been
explored. It was only when I started to study geography, history,
archaeology, and anthropology that I learned that the age of
exploration was far from over. This knowledge, rather than any
physical skill like rock climbing or canoeing, was the difficult
part of my journey to success as an explorer. I first had to

appreciate that the world still contained hidden gems waiting to be revealed.

Over the course of high school, I became disillusioned with my prospects. I remember watching someone on the Discovery Channel say that there was nothing left to explore in the world—that the entire planet had already been explored. Not knowing any better, I resigned myself to believing that this was true. After all, the source was the Discovery Channel. It was only when I entered university that I came to realize, from better books and wiser sources, that the world still contained unexplored areas. This knowledge was invigorating. It made me realize that my childhood dream was—if not yet within reach—at least theoretically possible. To my amazement, I learned that new species were still frequently discovered (such as the Lavasoa dwarf lemur in Madagascar and a species of toothless rat in the Indonesian rainforest), that some parts of the world are yet unmapped, that rivers exist that no one has ever canoed, and that mountains exist that no one has ever climbed. As incredible as it seemed, some Stone Age tribes were still living in isolation from the outside world, deep in the Amazon jungle. It seemed, then, that the adventures of the past were not over, and that it was yet possible to live the life of an explorer.

What intrigued me the most was looking at maps showing wilderness around the world—they indicated that the earth's greatest expanse of wilderness outside Antarctica happened to be in my own country: Canada. What a blessing to be born in a land of almost limitless wilderness. This vast area offered me the best prospects for exploration. Canada's desolate northern wild stretches across more than five thousand kilometres—from the

Alaskan border to the windswept shores of Labrador—and forms a wilderness region larger than the Amazon rainforest, the Sahara Desert, the wilds of Siberia, or the Australian Outback. Even today it's possible to travel through Canada's remote northern landscape for literally thousands of kilometres without ever crossing a single road. As I would soon learn first-hand, a person can journey for weeks into these wilds without seeing another soul or even any trace of humanity. There is nothing else like it on the planet. And this wilderness is even greater than Canada's political boundaries: it continues westward into Alaska, all the way to the Bering Sea; eastward across the ice and frigid seas into the immensity of Greenland; and northward to the Pole. It comprises over a dozen distinct ecosystems, including the icy barren lands of the Arctic, the subarctic boreal forest, the snow-capped peaks of the Rocky Mountains, the lush temperate rainforest of the Pacific coast, the swampy Hudson Bay Lowlands, and the rugged northern cordillera.

The population density of this enormous swath of wilderness is less than 0.09 people per square kilometre, meaning that most of it has no population at all. To put that in perspective, the population density of India is 390 people per square kilometre and the population density of Mongolia, the world's most sparsely inhabited country, is 1.76 people per square kilometre. In other words, Mongolia's barren landscape is approximately *nineteen times more populated* than the immense wilderness cloaking northern North America. On a global map showing population density, Canada's northern wilderness appears as one vast uninhabited wasteland—or a paradise, if your point-of-view is similar to mine. It's little wonder then that mapping and exploring this territory has taken centuries and is still not finished today.

Leaving aside the excursions of the Vikings and aboriginal people, Europeans first began exploring Canada in 1497 with John Cabot's voyage to the rocky shores of Newfoundland. In the centuries that followed, explorers gradually filled in the broad outlines of Canadian geography, mapping and exploring the major rivers, lakes, and coastlines. But this still left thousands of rivers and lakes as well as countless topographic features uncharted. In 1916, the Geological Survey of Canada estimated that the country still contained over nine hundred thousand square miles (almost one and a half million square kilometres) of unexplored territory that appeared as blank spots on the map. The Survey was founded in 1842 with the purpose of accurately mapping all of Canada, building off the work of early explorers stretching back to the time of Samuel de Champlain. But despite nearly seventy-five years of systematic fieldwork that involved dispatching parties of explorers to canoe rivers and map as much territory as possible, Canada is so vast that well into the twentieth century an aggregate area nearly the size of India remained virtually unexplored. Astoundingly, it was only in 2012 that the last 1:50,000 scale topographic map of Canada was finally finished, which completed the mapping of Canada at that scale—the standard scale for a topographic map. However, despite this accomplishment, considerable portions of the country's wilderness remain unexplored and, in some cases, aren't even accurately mapped. How is that possible?

Technology superseded actual exploration. By the 1920s, the Geological Survey began to rely on aerial surveys conducted with airplanes. With the newly invented planes (and later helicopters), surveyors were able to fly over remote stretches of Canada taking aerial photographs that could then be used to finish the process of mapping the country (safely, back in Ottawa). This type of surveying was a far cry from the traditional work of cartographers in birchbark canoes, trudging through wilderness with theodolites to painstakingly explore, map, and record the geography of unknown lands. Today, we have progressed to even more advanced methods with the use of satellites. But viewing the ground from high above in airplanes, helicopters, or satellites is no more like exploration than staring at the moon through a telescope in your backyard is akin to the *Apollo* moon landings. Deriving maps from satellite imagery and aerial photographs also ensures that some topographic features—such as waterfalls and islands—are occasionally missed. Ultimately, the only way to really know what's out there is to do things the old-fashioned way, by seeking out the rivers no one has canoed, the mountains no one has climbed, and the caves no one has entered. As far as this sort of actual boots-on-the-ground exploration goes, Canada still contains plenty of territory that has no record of any person exploring it. When modern explorers venture into these isolated places, it remains possible to discover topographic features omitted from the map, as I began to do myself soon after high school.

That brings us to what professional exploration has always been about: not the hair-raising adventures and narrow escapes that were the stuff of my childhood imagination, but the generation of new geographical information that adds to humanity's stock of collective knowledge. You could think of professional exploration like a grand mural, with each explorer as an artist who contributes a little more detail to the big picture. Historically, explorers' manuscripts and maps filled up the private studies and libraries of a privileged few in the capitals of Europe. Relics from explorers' journeys to the far corners of the earth bedecked aristocrats' wondrous cabinets of curiosities. Today, explorers' reports are more widely available, thus enriching not a privileged elite, but anyone who takes an interest in their revelations. Exploration has always been a two-step process: a physical journey followed by the publication or dissemination of new geographical knowledge. Without engaging in both steps, one is not truly engaged in exploration.

In my own small way, I try to contribute to our understanding of Canada's wilderness. I seek to add a few more brush strokes to the grand mural of Canada's topography by being the first to photograph, film, canoe, or make written descriptions of a particular river, lake, or area whose features are yet to be drawn.

At this point, you might be wondering how the nomadic hunter-gatherers of North America's past fit into the story of exploration. After all, didn't they at some point in time paddle or travel every inch of Canada's wilderness? While these nomads covered a lot of ground, aside from limited archaeological finds, we have no way of knowing exactly what areas they did or didn't visit. This is because they created no maps nor left any written records behind. Their journeys have vanished into the unknowable mists of time. In other words, though they were in some respects among the greatest travellers who ever lived (they made journeys that no modern individual could hope to equal), ultimately they made no contribution to the mural of Canada's wilderness. That is not to say that latter-day aboriginal people made no contribution—great aboriginal explorers such as the Chipewyan leader Matonabbee and the heroic Cree adventurer George Elson journeyed into isolated regions where neither they nor anyone they knew had previously ventured. Many European explorers could not have succeeded without the help and expertise of aboriginal people. But it's an error to equate hunter-gatherers—or for that matter, fur traders, adventurers, sport hunters, and wilderness campers—with explorers. Explorers are a different breed altogether.

Still, out of purely academic interest, you might be wondering whether humans have penetrated every corner of the country. Explorers and anthropologists occasionally declare that Canada is so immense that places remain in which no humans have ever set foot. For example, the celebrated wildlife artist Robert Bateman, who has an academic background in geography, made this claim when in 2013 he was awarded the Royal Canadian Geographical Society's prestigious gold medal, the Society's highest honour. Bateman, in his acceptance speech, recounted how in the 1950s he explored a remote section of Quebec's Ungava Peninsula with a pair of geologists and two Inuit hunters. The hunters informed them that they had never been into the area before, nor had any member of their community. Bateman stated that they were the first humans *ever to set foot there*. Two other eminent geologists and cartographers at that same event spoke of their experiences hiking in parts of Canada's wilderness where no humans had ever previously ventured. Ray Mears, a British survival expert and TV host, has similarly stated matter-of-factly that Canada's wilderness is so vast that places remain that have never seen a human footprint. Claims like these, if nothing else, fire the imagination and encourage one's appetite for adventure. But skeptics might well wonder if this is all just romantic wishful thinking. Perhaps it merely reflects some deep-seated human desire to believe that unexplored territory still lies beyond the horizon? An almost mythical untouched place where it is still possible to become the first human visitor? At any rate, that was my original impression on the matter as a young undergraduate. However, as I researched the topic more extensively, I was surprised to learn that most evidence favours the idea that the earth still has places no human has ever been (and not just in Antarctica). Some of these places are tucked away deep in the Canadian wilderness. To assume that each of Canada's three million lakes, infinite number of ponds, and tens of thousands of other waterways must have been visited by someone is rather naive. (In fact, Canada has so many lakes that no geographer has ever succeeded in counting them all—three million is the currently accepted best estimate.) North America is not Europe or Asia: it was never densely populated, has been inhabited for a much shorter period of time, and has always contained vast uninhabited regions incapable of sustaining significant human populations.

The most rigorous scholarly estimates for Canada's population before European contact put the number at a mere 200,000 to 300,000 people (compared with over 35 million today). That would give pre-contact Canada a population density of less than 0.03 people per square kilometre. With such an extremely low population density scattered over such a vast expanse of territory, it is exceedingly improbable, if not impossible, for humans to have covered all that ground in the fewer than 10,000 years most of Canada has been inhabited. Canada's foremost expert on aboriginal history and culture, anthropologist Diamond Jenness (himself a recipient of the Royal Canadian Geographical Society's gold medal), noted: "A quarter of a million people cannot effectively occupy an area of nearly four million square miles, and there were doubtless many districts seldom or never trodden by the foot of man, just as there are to-day." Jenness thus corroborated the view that Canada's wilderness is sufficiently vast to still contain territory unvisited by any person.

Jenness' conclusion is more credible when one considers that those roughly 250,000 inhabitants weren't evenly distributed across Canada. In pre-contact Canada, approximately two-thirds of all people lived in just two small areas of the country: the lush temperate rainforest of coastal British Columbia and the lower Great Lakes region of what is now southern Ontario. In the Pacific Northwest, the mild weather, abundant resources, and, above all, immensely plentiful salmon runs made it possible for a relatively large population to develop (though that population would be considered small relative to that area's current population). The territory around the southern Great Lakes, in contrast, supported agriculture, which allowed certain aboriginal groups with cultures based on farming rather than hunting and gathering to flourish. In these regions, the first European explorers found well-established villages, well-worn portage trails, and guides who could tell them about the surrounding country and how to get from one place to another. Elsewhere it was a different story.

Almost everywhere else, Canada was very thinly populated with huge empty stretches that were uninhabited and unknown even to aboriginal people. Explorers themselves often remarked on this fact. For example, Sir Alexander Mackenzie found that in British Columbia he could follow well-worn trails made by aboriginal people, whereas in the harsh subarctic wastes where survival was infinitely more difficult, there were plenty of places his native guides could tell him nothing about. The difference is one of environment: coastal British Columbia's more favourable geography could support a larger population, whereas the Canadian subarctic was sparsely inhabited, with a low life expectancy and periodic famines during harsh winters that could obliterate entire hunting bands. Indeed, archaeology informs us that life expectancy among pre-contact hunter-gatherers in the subarctic was extremely low, no more than mid-twenties. There were few elders to speak of. Thus, it was difficult for anything like detailed knowledge to pass from one generation to the next. Nomadic hunter-gatherers would certainly have possessed a good knowledge of the broad outlines of their hunting territories, the major rivers and lakes, heights of land, and watersheds. But within these immense districts were plenty of unknowns. Moreover, without any aid to memory in the form of a written language or maps, it was utterly impossible for any person to memorize the tens of thousands of different lakes and waterways in just one portion of Canada's northern wilds, let alone names for even a small percentage of these landmarks. That is why even to this day, most of these lakes and waterways still have no names. To name them all would be practically impossible—*several million distinct names* would be required.

Population scarcity also made the nature of exploration in northern North America different from exploration in Africa,

Asia, or further south, where Europeans could rely to some extent on local knowledge of an area's geography. In contrast, explorers in Canada's desolate wilds sometimes couldn't find any people at all, and those they did find were often unable to tell them much about the country beyond their own territory. Often, European explorers and aboriginal guides would venture together into unexplored territory that neither group had any prior knowledge about. The subarctic forests in particular were an area with limited human populations. These immense forests, consisting chiefly of black spruce and tamarack, possess meagre nutritious resources, scarce game, and long, harsh winters. Populations in these areas were usually confined to major rivers or other water routes.

Stray far enough from a major waterway in the subarctic wilds, and there is a reasonable chance that you may find yourself in an area previously unvisited by humans. Mind you, without a time machine and in the absence of archaeological evidence, we can't know with certainty what areas have and have not been visited by people in the distant past. That is why responsible explorers seldom make any claims on this front: they are impossible to verify and therefore meaningless. That is why, in the realm of exploration, records are essential. Just as science is about documentation and publication, exploration is similarly grounded in the publication and dissemination of maps, journals, scientific reports, books, and photographs. That is also why in explorers' terminology, an "unexplored area" is anywhere on earth where no records exist of human exploration.

One area that stands out as exceptionally sparse on people, even by the standards of Canada's northern wilderness—and which was soon to exercise a strange spell over me—is the massive wetland known as the Hudson Bay Lowlands. The Lowlands is one of the world's least-explored regions—a place where bears outnumber humans, maps are often inaccurate, and rivers are so remote that they have no names in any language. Stretching across 373,700 square kilometres of desolate muskeg, stunted forest, and windswept tundra, the Lowlands is North America's largest wetland—an Amazon of the north with the highest concentration of bloodsucking insects on the planet. The haunt of polar bears, wolves, wolverines, and other hardy animals, aboriginal people called the swampy Lowlands "sterile country" for its scant trees (only one-quarter of this gigantic wetland is forested) and harsh winters, preferring to remain within the confines of the boreal forest. As a result, the vast majority of the Lowlands is uninhabited and always has been. Archaeologist J.V. Wright noted that the Hudson Bay Lowlands "has produced very little evidence of prehistoric occupation by man." In other words, it wasn't a place anyone would choose to live.

What few hunter-gatherers there were in the Lowlands were confined to the major rivers, though it's unclear whether they made any sustained attempt to live within this dreary swampland until the arrival of European traders on Hudson Bay and James Bay in the seventeenth century. With the establishment of fur trading forts on the mouths of the major rivers draining into Hudson Bay and James Bay, family bands settled around the forts. Others made seasonal journeys to trade at the isolated posts by following the major rivers. However, the rapid introduction of Old World diseases by European traders resulted in a huge decrease in the already minuscule aboriginal population, producing a virtually uninhabited wilderness. The few survivors managed to eke out a difficult existence into the twentieth century as fur trappers. Because the land-to-person ratio was so overwhelming, they remained largely confined to the best waterways, namely the major rivers and their large tributaries. Beyond these familiar places lay a forbidding, mysterious wilderness that Cree mythology peopled with demons, monsters such as the dreaded wendigo, and evil spirits.

Early European explorers mostly passed the area over; much of it wasn't even mapped until the mid-twentieth century—and only then by the use of aerial photographs rather than ground surveys. This means that huge tracts of this bleak landscape, including dozens of its many thousands of rivers and creeks remain unexplored to this day. The terrain is nearly as tough as imaginable: trackless muskeg (the "quicksand of the north"); endless swamps of small, twisted spruce and tamarack trees; thousands of meandering, rock-strewn creeks and rivers; weedy lakes; impassable bogs; and millions of mosquitoes and black-flies. It is a land of mystery, where adventure beckons, nature remains unconquered, and endless wilderness stretches as far as the eye can see. So the world still does contain remote, unexplored territory and the age of exploration is not over … which is where I enter the picture. My vocation is to explore one of the world's last great wildernesses.

1

THE START OF AN OBSESSION

*We live only when we adventure and give expression to
the results of our adventure.*
—Lawren Harris, Group of Seven, *notebook*, 1920s

EXPLORATION BEGINS by figuring out what you don't
know. In the spring of 2008, I was sitting in my cluttered
room with a bunch of maps sprawled on the pine floor and draped
across the table in front of me, looking for somewhere that I could
explore. I had been there all morning sipping green tea, pondering the maps, making notes, and pacing around the room like a
caged bobcat. My bookshelves were crammed with explorers'
manuscripts, old adventure novels, and volumes on geography,
archaeology, history, and zoology. Well-used Ojibwa snowshoes, a
prized Gränsfors Bruk axe, assorted antlers, canoe paddles, waterproof Bushnell binoculars, a brass sextant, a Brazilian machete,
and a hickory walking stick occupied whatever available space
there was atop the bookshelves and between them. Miscellaneous
other expedition gear lay scattered about. My faithful companion,
a huge Rottweiler-Shepherd mix named Riley, was sleeping on a
rug in the corner, probably dreaming of rabbits.

From the maps stretched out before me, I had compiled a list of rivers in the Hudson Bay watershed—172 rivers in all, which excluded smaller streams and creeks. Then I began crossing rivers off the list if I could find anything published on them. The better known rivers, like the Missinaibi or Albany, could be stricken from the list at once. I would invariably discover—much to my disappointment—that others that seemed to hold brighter prospects had been the subject of some obscure surveying report, canoeing pamphlet, book chapter, blog post, or magazine article. I was beginning to wonder if I would ever find a single river large enough to warrant the name that had not been addressed in some medium or another. What I was after was a mystery—a hidden-away place on earth that I couldn't learn about simply by picking up a book or looking it up on Wikipedia. I wanted something as obscure as possible—an almost unknown river with no published record of anyone exploring it. If I could find such a river, I planned to go see it for myself—the sort of old-fashioned expedition boyhood dreams are made of.

Most people who canoe rivers select ones that have detailed guide books, specialized canoeing maps, or historic explorers' journals published about them. Such records make planning a wilderness journey—never the simplest of tasks—infinitely safer and easier. They usually allow canoeists to know what they are getting themselves into: how to access the river, how difficult it is to canoe, where suitable campsites are located, when to portage, and how long the trip should take. But people don't make a name for themselves by following in the footsteps of others, and the easy path is generally not the most interesting. My thirst for the unknown made me an explorer, and it is the business of an explorer to venture where few if any have gone before, regardless of the difficulties. Besides, things don't seem that difficult from the comfort of my room, with all my maps and books.

That morning, staring at the maps, I thought I had finally found what I had been looking for: a river that no one knew anything about. My fingers were tracing the vague outlines of dozens of rivers in the James Bay watershed when I hit upon one that was unlabelled on the map. The area appeared promising for an expedition: here were hundreds of waterways draining north into the brackish waters of James Bay, and then into the Arctic Ocean. The region is beyond the reach of roads and the urban sprawl-styled "civilization": the only settlements to speak of are a few Cree communities scattered around the windswept shores of James Bay. This nameless river that had excited my interest was easily overlooked on the map because it was obscured by the artificial Ontario–Quebec boundary line. However, I soon discovered that the river had an official name by examining some of my more detailed maps and matching them with the large-scale one. Rather curiously, it was labelled the Again River—curious because "Again" is neither an aboriginal word, a surname of an explorer, nor a descriptive term like "Trout River." How, I wondered, did this river get its name?

I scanned my bookshelf for Bruce Hodgins and Gwyneth Hoyle's *Canoeing North into the Unknown: A Record of River Travel*, hoping to find the answer. This indispensable encyclopedia lists every known expedition or canoe trip down Canada's northern rivers up to 1997, including nearly a thousand such journeys in all. Riffling through its pages, I was surprised to discover that the Again wasn't listed in the book. Next, I lifted another volume off the shelf, Jonathan Berger and Thomas Terry's venerable *Canoe Atlas of the Little North*. Published in 2007, with several dozen contributors, including geography professors, aboriginal elders, and veteran canoeists, I thought that it would surely have some information on the river. But I searched the atlas and found that this obscure Again River wasn't even mentioned. My curiosity piqued, I went through every likely book in my library on the subject, unable to find any hint of the Again River. Even Google generated nearly nothing on the river. Aside from the Canadian government's standard issue 1:50,000 and 1:250,000 scale topographic maps (derived largely from mid-twentieth-century black-and-white aerial photos), the only meaningful reference to the river appeared in one sentence on a government website, in a list of geographical names approved in both French and English: "Rivière Again or Again River." That did nothing to explain the origin of the name or reveal whether an expedition had previously explored the river. When I entered the name in the government's Geographical Names Data Base, the search results merely indicated that "Again River" had been approved in 1946, but offered no further clues. In contrast, the search results for other geographical names sometimes included an annotation explaining the name's origin—such as "Mackenzie River, named after the explorer Alexander Mackenzie"—but the entry for the Again was left blank. Promising as this all seemed, I understood that many archival documents had never been digitized and that I might still locate an account of an expedition to the river if I dug deeper.

Over the following days, I did some extensive sleuthing to see if I could uncover anything further. I visited several university libraries and searched through their vast databases. At my disposal were newspaper archives dating back over a century, magazines, geographical journals, Geological Survey files, and explorers' records. After searching through a multitude of documents, there was still nothing. Expanding my inquiry, I began to comb through tedious mineral exploration reports, which were unlikely to yield much information on the navigability of the Again River, but they might at least provide some clues to whether any expedition had ever ventured there. After a few weeks, I finally located a brief report on file with the provincial department in charge of mining that mentioned, in passing, the Again River. The geologist who had authored it had never been to the river himself. His small party had flown via helicopter to a lake southeast of the Again to do some prospecting work in 1983. But they did no canoeing, and their report contained no description of the river.

In spite of the scarcity of documentary evidence, I could be certain that some people had been to at least a few portions of the river. Fur trappers and occasional canoeists would surely have passed by its outlet on the much larger Harricanaw River. A few of them might even have ventured a short distance up its meandering course, fighting against the presumably swift current. The Harricanaw, while never a major trade route because of its shallow depth and many rapids, served as a minor fur trade river and is still canoed sporadically by wilderness enthusiasts. It would have been paddled by hunter-gatherers for centuries and was first explored by Europeans in the seventeenth century. Even the young Pierre Trudeau had paddled it in the 1940s. But these people had only canoed the Harricanaw and hadn't wasted their time attempting to fight their way up its rock-strewn, swift-flowing tributaries.

It was also evident that during the surveys of the Ontario–Quebec boundary, a small party of government surveyors must have at least criss-crossed the Again at the two points where the artificial boundary crossed the river. Locating these surveyors' records would offer me the best (and only) written clues as to what I could expect on the river and the extent to which it had been previously explored. But I couldn't find their records and neither could the archivists who were assisting me in my search.

So, having exhausted the published record and finding next to nothing, I resolved to explore this mysterious river, of which no one apparently knew much of anything. Whether someone had canoed the river and left no record of their journey was of course no concern of mine. My objective was simple enough: to make the first detailed exploration of and substantial published account on the Again River in history. The idea alone—the first in history—was positively intoxicating.

While there were no written records to assist me in my planned exploration of the river, maps and satellite images were available. These enabled me to plan a provisional route through half-a-dozen lakes, partially down a parallel river, up a nameless creek, and then overland to reach the Again's isolated headwaters. It was a circuitous and difficult route that would entail upstream travel and nightmarish portages through presumably impenetrable swamp forest. Of course, nothing less could be expected. Topographic maps, however, can still be inaccurate or incomplete. Waterfalls and rapids might be omitted; streams that are drawn on the map might not actually exist. This, I knew, could well prove the case with the Again River.

What I did know about the Again, on the basis of blurry, low-resolution satellite images and old topographic maps derived from black-and-white aerial photographs snapped in the late 1950s, was that it measured some 107 kilometres in length. It wasn't surprising that the Again had attracted little attention: it's too small and marginal to be of much interest to most wilderness canoeists, particularly since the Hudson and James Bay water-shed contains many dozens of larger, more navigable waterways. For example, the Albany, the longest river in the Hudson Bay Lowlands, extends over a thousand kilometres. I could be certain that the blackflies and other bloodsucking insects would be horrible, since the Again snakes across the southern reaches of the world's third-largest wetland, the Hudson Bay Lowlands. In terms of political geography, the Again meanders back and forth across the artificial Ontario–Quebec boundary, with a total of approximately 63 kilometres of the river within Ontario and 44 within Quebec. I could tell from the black-and-white aerial photos and topographic maps that I would encounter many rapids. The river might also possibly contain waterfalls, but how big and dangerous they were as well as their precise location were unknown.

My intention was to make the expedition as comprehensive as possible. The primary objective was geographical: I would make the first published description of the river, creating a canoeing guide of the sort that exists for other wilderness waterways. I would also keep a record of the wildlife I encoun-tered and, with luck, photograph them. There was also the mystery of the Eskimo curlew to consider, a rare bird believed to have gone extinct. The last confirmed sighting of this medium-sized brownish shorebird, a member of the sandpiper family, had been in the 1960s. But there had been an unconfirmed sighting in 1976 by an ornithologist in southern James Bay, an area I intended to pass through after exploring the Again. In terms of archaeological exploration, I would keep an eye out for any artifacts that could shed light on the unwritten history of the river. Ancient pictographs and petroglyphs—rock paintings and carvings—were a speciality of my academic research. Finally, I would make what inquiries I could in the Cree communities on James Bay concerning the existence of the Again River to ascertain as far as possible if any individuals there knew anything of it.

Finding this little-known river and exploring it was a chance for adventure and old-fashioned discovery, or so I hoped.

A FEW MONTHS LATER I was in a pickup truck, travelling along a bumpy gravel road, winding through monotonous boreal forest, heading toward the point where I would leave civilization behind and go to seek the Again River. In the passenger seat was clean-shaven Terry O'Neil, a, genial old-timer who made extra cash shuttling canoeists and hunters to various rivers and hunting camps across northern Ontario and Quebec. Driving was my father, who had decided—quite unexpectedly—to come along on my expedition. We were on the fringes of the northern wilderness heading some two hundred kilometres northeast of Cochrane, a small logging town located over six hundred kilometres north of Toronto.

My father, an engineer and woodsman extraordinaire, built canoes, among other things. He had countless camping trips under his belt, but he had never undertaken a true expedition: his preference was for idyllic paddles on picturesque lakes, not the gruelling ordeals through mosquito-infested swamps to unexplored rivers that I favoured. At forty-nine, he felt that this was perhaps his last chance to join me on one of my notorious expeditions. Notorious, because generally anyone who had ever accompanied me on an expedition swiftly arrived at the conclusion that—while proud to have done it—they would not readily subject themselves to such a discomforting experience ever again. While I too enjoyed leisurely canoe trips, they're not the stuff adventures are made of, the trailblazing expeditions into the unknown that I hungered for.

Back in Cochrane, Terry had taken down our information in the event that we didn't return from the wilderness. He had been under the impression that our objective was merely to canoe the Kattawagami River, a wild enough waterway, but one easily accessible via a remote unserviced highway that snakes northeast of Cochrane to an old gold mine—the gravel road we were travelling on. The Kattawagami attracts adventurers down its winding, rapid-filled course, but by my standards, it's well-explored territory.

"To tell you the truth," said Terry from the front passenger seat, as we drove along the road, "I don't like shuttling people to the Kattawagami. I prefer going other places."

"Why is that?" I asked.

Terry stared out the passenger window for a while at the passing spruce forest, then, clearing his throat, he explained, "Well, the last time I shuttled someone to attempt the Kattawagami, it was a young couple. Only one of them came back alive."

"Do you know what happened?"

"Their canoe upset in a rapid. The wife drowned. The guy survived. He was delirious when search and rescue found him. You don't get over something like that. He's in a mental institution now."

My father swallowed hard. "Terrible," he mumbled.

Later I found a newspaper article about it. In 2006 Zanna Marie Cruikshank and her husband Derek attempted to canoe the Kattawagami. Zanna, a nurse, was described as an "avid outdoor enthusiast." Their canoe capsized in a dangerous rapid; Zanna was killed. Her husband survived and managed to continue downriver for several more days, until he stumbled across a trapper's cabin. The trapper, according to the story, brought him to the nearest hospital—a considerable distance away in Moosonee, a small Cree community. Zanna's body was later found in a shallow bay on the river. Nor was this the only recent tragedy in the area—two months earlier, some hundred kilometres to the southeast, there had been a fatal bear attack. A woman had been mauled to death and her corpse partially consumed by a black bear outside an isolated hunting cabin.

"The Kattawagami's right up here," Terry pointed to the narrow bridge just up ahead.

"We don't want the Kattawagami," I said.

"You don't want the Katt?" Terry asked, surprised.

"No, we want a different waterway, a small creek. It's called Hopper Creek on the map. It drains into the Kattawagami. We want to explore it as a different route to reach the Kattawagami. Do you know it?"

"Ah, no. I've never heard of it. Where is it?"

"Just a bit farther, roughly another twenty-four kilometres past the Kattawagami." I knew this because I had measured the distance between the bridge over the Kattawagami and the creek via satellite image ahead of time, and then kept track of the distance on the truck's odometer once we had passed the bridge.

"Fellas, I don't know this creek, never heard of it. Not sure you guys should go down it. You should stick to the Kattawagami." Terry was uneasy.

But I had not come all that way to paddle the Kattawagami, a river plenty of other people had already paddled. The days when paddling something like it would satisfy me were long past. My father, on the other hand, had never canoed any northern river and was starting to become a bit alarmed at the sight of them, as we passed over each bridge on the road north.

"Maybe we should just do the Kattawagami?" he suggested.

I shook my head. "Let's stick with our plan. We're heading to the Again River."

"The what river?"

"The Again. Have you heard of it?"

"No." Terry shook his head.

As we drove deeper into the seemingly endless spruce forest, a wandering black bear crossed the gravel road in front of us. "This is God's country, I've never been this far down the road before," muttered Terry.

"Keep going," I said to my father behind the wheel, "everything will be fine." Fifteen minutes later, we reached a tiny creek shrouded in alder bushes and clouds of blackflies.

"This must be it," I said with excitement. My father and Terry looked appalled.

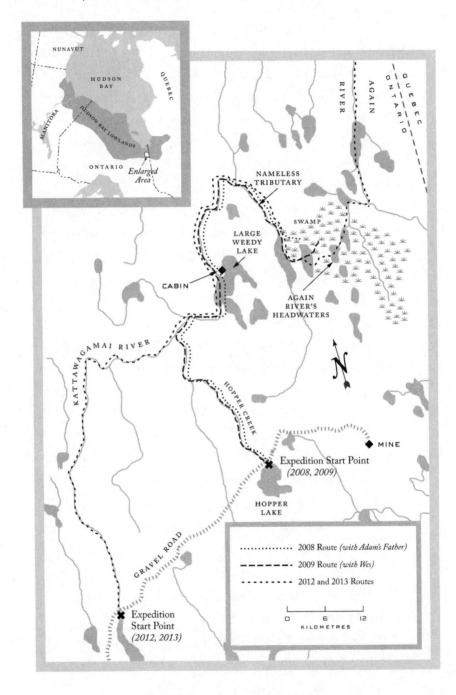

HUDSON BAY LOWLANDS

It was raining as Terry drove away in the truck, leaving us by the narrow stream packing a cedar-strip canoe my father and I had made. Shallow and rocky, the creek was only a couple of paddle-widths across, but with a swift current. Amid an onslaught of blackflies, we set off down the dark, swirling waters of the stream into the unknown. It proved barely navigable—choked with rock-strewn rapids that made wading necessary much of the time. Scrubby black spruces and lichen-draped tamaracks hemmed in the waterway, while granite outcrops and boulders as tall as us appeared in places along the banks. It might almost have been called pretty, if not for the swampy muskeg that lay just beyond the fringe of forest skirting the banks and the dismal hum of millions of mosquitoes and blackflies swarming us, enjoying our blood. A gruelling, day-long struggle down the creek brought us to where it joined the swift-flowing Kattawagami River. By nightfall, we reached the shallow waters of a large, weedy lake. On this lake, isolated as it was, stood a lonely, ramshackle hunting cabin that appeared to have been untouched in years.

For the next three days, we hacked, paddled, portaged, and waded through trackless alder swamps to leave the Kattawagami watershed behind. That was enough exploration for my father. He had nothing to prove to anyone—and to him, the Again River was just a meandering blue line on a map—not an ideal. As darkness fell on the third day, my father announced that he was calling it quits and wanted to turn around. I was disappointed but couldn't force him to continue. So I had to content myself with having explored Hopper Creek and a certain nameless tributary river that we had ventured up, as well as the alder swamps. My father, in contrast, was cheerful enough with a more leisurely form of exploration around our camps at night. He looked at the hardy trees growing in the acidic soil with an engineer's appreciation: "170 years old—remarkable," he would say in a sort of reverie, after having meticulously counted the rings on another black spruce that had toppled over. In his notebook, he compiled a list of all the flora he found growing along the riverbanks.

When we eventually returned to the isolated mining road, our legs were scraped and cut from the jagged rocks and fallen trees hidden beneath the swift waters, through which we had laboriously dragged the canoe against the current. Our faces were swollen and cut with blackfly bites. My father resolved not to go on any further expeditions, but my determination to explore the Again River remained as strong as ever.

THE FOLLOWING SUMMER, I returned to the area for a second attempt: this time with a friend, Wesley Crowe. Wes and I had been fast friends since our days on the playground of E.W. Farr elementary school. We had shared in many adventures together—canoeing rivers, braving storms, spearing fish, sleeping under the stars—and the summer after our high school graduation, we had embarked together on a journey as deep into the wilderness as we could go. Sturdy, resolute, and as close to fearless as it is probably prudent to be, he remained my first choice whenever I was in need of an expedition partner. Wes, tied down with a construction job, had been unable to accompany me the prior summer but was now free to join me. He had spent the last seven months living with his girlfriend in Australia, but had just arrived back in Canada and was burning for an adventure. However, his older sister's upcoming wedding in mid-August meant the expedition had a fixed end date. Naturally, I had presumed that missing his sister's wedding to explore an obscure river was eminently understandable—but I was made to appreciate that this was not the case.

Wes and I retraced my route from the previous summer down the tortuous course of Hopper Creek, dragging and wading with a canoe through shallow rock-strewn rapids and then paddling down a section of the Kattawagami River. Soaking wet and exhausted, at dusk on the first day we arrived at the decrepit log cabin on the large, weedy lake. The cabin looked like it hadn't been touched since my father and I had been there the previous year. I was content to set up our tent on the shore and sleep there, but asked Wes if he cared to spare the trouble of unpacking and just sleep in the old, musty cabin.

"This place reminds me of *Deliverance*," he replied.

"There are no hillbillies around here," I said.

"If you say so," Wes looked suspiciously at the surrounding trees, "let's sleep in the cabin, then."

We pulled the canoe onshore—it was an old fibreglass vessel that its previous owner gave me, thinking it was worthless. The battered fourteen-foot canoe was nearly forty years old and had several holes in its hull, which I had repaired as best I could. I would have preferred a sturdier vessel for this kind of expedition, but Wes and I didn't have the funds for one. We unloaded the canoe, strapped on our backpacks, and headed up the gravelly beach toward the cabin in the fading light.

"Watch your step," I said, motioning to a bed of nails protruding from the crude porch in front of the cabin. The nails were intended to serve as a bear deterrent. Black bears, adult males of which can weigh over five hundred pounds, sometimes break into cabins if food is stored inside. We gathered some firewood and lit a fire in the cabin's rusted cast-iron stove to cook soup and make tea. It was dark by the time we finished supper. Exhausted from the struggle along the creek, down the Kattawagami River, and across the large, choppy waters of the lake, we were soon asleep in the cabin's wooden bunks. But sometime in the night, our slumber was disturbed by a loud crash immediately outside the cabin door.

"What was that?" Wes whispered, sitting upright in his sleeping bag and staring into the darkness toward the door.

"A bear," I whispered, fumbling for my hatchet, then my flashlight.

We remained silent, straining our ears to detect any sound from outside the thin walls. After a brief silence, we could hear something lumbering through the thick brush.

Wes and I sprang to our feet. Breathing rapidly, we moved as quietly as we could toward the door. Wes seized a rusty old axe that was propped up against the wall. We both peered out the windows toward the lakeshore, but saw no movement.

"Let's check it out," I whispered, switching on my flashlight and slowly opening the door.

"Watch out for the nails." I shone the light toward the bear trap.

"Maybe that's what we heard—a bear stepped on the nails." Wes crouched down to inspect them.

"See anything?"

"Hmm … I don't see any blood or fur," replied Wes as he looked over the ranks of nails that guarded the cabin's door. I circled the light around the front of the cabin, looking into the spruces and poplars to see if I could catch sight of anything. It was a cold, starry night.

"Well, I guess if it was a bear, it's gone now," I concluded.

"I think it had to be a bear," said Wes standing up. "What else could have made a noise like that?"

"A lonely hillbilly," I offered.

Wes laughed. We returned to the bunks, switched off the flashlight, and slept with our axe and hatchet handy, in the event that anything else should disturb us.

OVER THE FOLLOWING WEEK, Wes and I fought our way down the Kattawagami River, dragged our fragile canoe up a nameless tributary that I had explored the previous summer, and then set about the arduous process of trailblazing our way overland to the Again's isolated headwaters. We had neither a GPS nor satellite phone and relied mostly on the sun for navigation, aided at times by map and compass. The sun, with a bit of practice, can be more easily relied upon to keep a steady course than a compass, especially in dense forest where both hands need be kept free to blaze a trail. We were making good progress until the sixth day of our expedition, when we encountered some difficulty crossing a vast swamp. It was uncertain if we would make it back in time for Wes' sister's wedding if we proceeded any further.

"I'd say we have at least a fifty-fifty chance," I concluded.

Wes stroked his scrubby black beard. "Hmm ... that's not good enough. I'd need a one hundred percent assurance we'd be back in time, or else my family will disown me."

I sighed, disappointed. After a few moments of silence, I reluctantly said, "Well, in that case, we should turn around. With nothing to guide us, we can't be certain how long it will take us to reach the Again and then get down it." It was a bitter pill—so close only to have to turn back. For the second summer in a row, I wouldn't reach the Again River.

Wes nodded, "All right, so now what?"

I pulled out the crude sketch map from my pocket. "We turn around, retrace the trails that we made, portage back to the Kattawagami, then paddle down it to tidewater at James Bay. Cross James Bay to the Moose River, head up the river until we reach Moosonee, and then catch the Polar Bear Express train south to Cochrane."

"How long will—" Wes swore and slapped the back of his neck. Several dozen mosquitoes were feasting on him, "that take us?"

"About ten days," I replied. Of course, stormy weather on James Bay—a body of water with a fearsome reputation for drowning canoeists and boaters—could delay us for days on end. But since the weather was beyond our control, I didn't mention this detail.

"Okay, sounds like we have nothing to worry about."

"Right," I cheerfully replied.

But by the time we fought our way back to the banks of the Kattawagami—through impenetrably thick forest, across mosquito-infested swamps, and over several pristine lakes—we had to concede our canoe had heard its death knell. The old fibreglass vessel was nowhere near as strong as the cedar-strip canoe my father and I had made, which had survived the punishing rapids and jagged rocks without a single leak. But that beautifully hand-crafted canoe was a real work of art, and I was reluctant to subject it to the punishment of another expedition— preferring to save it for gentle trips on calm water. So I had acquired this old fibreglass canoe, which was now leaking like a strainer as we attempted to paddle it. The canoe had sprung numerous leaks on our return journey down the shallow creek, which was filled with sharp rocks. With spruce gum and duct tape, we repaired the leaks well enough to keep the vessel afloat, but not enough to make it withstand the damage that hundreds of whitewater rapids would inflict upon it if we paddled the Kattawagami all the way to the sea. Our only choice was to try to make it back to the remote mining road where we had started out.

"You know, it's sort of ridiculous that we do these crazy expeditions with the gear we have," Wes observed.

I shrugged.

"Most people wouldn't attempt this sort of thing without a satellite phone or GPS, or the best canoes and Gore-Tex clothing," Wes continued.

"Maybe one day we'll have sponsors who give us that stuff."

"It'd be nice to have a canoe that didn't leak." Wes bailed a pitcher of water overboard.

"You're going soft," I joked while trying to paddle the half-sinking canoe from the stern.

Wes and I could travel at great speed when the occasion called for it—sinking canoe or not—and with only one of us paddling and the other constantly bailing, we made it back to the isolated mining road in four days. Just as we emerged from the

shadowy, moss-draped forest onto the narrow roadway—soaking
wet from sitting in a canoe full of water—the dark sky above us
began to rumble.

"That doesn't sound good." Wes glanced skyward.

We headed for the shelter of a big spruce. The next instant,
a hail storm of near biblical proportions descended upon us,
furiously pelting us with golf-ball-sized ice. We photographed
the gigantic hail, thinking no one would believe us otherwise.

Battered from the hailstorm and drenched by pouring rain,
Wes and I huddled under the shelter of the thick canopy. We
were stranded—after dropping us off at Hopper Creek, Terry
O'Neil had driven our vehicle back into Cochrane and parked it
at the train station for us—some two hundred kilometres away.
We didn't relish the thought of walking the long, lonely road all
the way back into town. I suggested hitchhiking, half as a joke.
We had no idea when anyone might pass by.

Wes raised an eyebrow. "But who'd pick us up? A couple of
scruffy guys decked out in army camouflage who don't smell very
nice and just appeared out of nowhere. We look like bandits out
to rob the gold mine up the road."

"Right, well let's try to look charming."

But no opportunity to use our charm appeared for over an
hour as we huddled in the rain as night fell, the steady drip of
rain filtering down between the spruce boughs. Finally, we could
hear the sound of a truck coming down the narrow road. As we
emerged from the woods, a black Chevy pickup came into view.
Wes and I stuck out our thumbs, and the truck slowed to a halt.
Behind the wheel was a middle-aged aboriginal man who looked
rather surprised to see us.

We thanked him for stopping and explained our situation. It turned out that he was hired by the gold mine to keep the road open by trapping beaver. Beavers, when left to their own devices, were inclined to build dams, which would flood out the road. His job was to make sure that didn't happen. Just now he was coming from Cochrane on his way to the mine. He offered to drive us to the mine, where we could try to find a ride back to town. This arrangement seemed generous to us, and we thanked him profusely.

"You got to ride in the back," he smiled sheepishly and gestured to the box. "I've got a little too much stuff in here."

"Sure," I replied happily, though I sensed the real reason was because the trapper believed that two men who appeared out of nowhere around these wild parts might not be people you wanted in your truck.

Wes and I, having left our backpacks, gear, and the canoe concealed in the forest, jumped into the back of the pickup, only to quickly regret it. The driver put his pedal to the metal and we were soon flying along at over a hundred kilometres per hour down a wet gravel road in fading light. Terry, the old-timer who shuttled our vehicle back to Cochrane, was adamant that he wouldn't drive this road after dark or even at dusk because of the bears and moose ("swamp donkeys," as he called them) that frequently cross it—a deadly hazard for drivers. A collision with a moose has about the same effect as a collision with a backhoe. Even in daylight, Terry sternly complained when I was driving if he noticed the speedometer creep above sixty. Wes and I held on for dear life in the truck, flying up in the air with every bump on the gravel road and holding on as best as we could when we took turns at terrifying speeds.

"Is this guy trying to kill us?" Wes shouted in my ear as the trees swirled passed us in a blur of dark green.

"I think so," I said, pressing myself down in the truck. We were quite literally in greater danger now than at any time on our expedition—though Wes had stepped on a nail at the old cabin and busted his middle finger on a bad fall while wading in the treacherous, slippery rocks of Hopper Creek. After a wild fifteen-minute ride in the fading light, the driver suddenly slowed down. An oncoming transport truck was returning from the gold mine. Our driver motioned the trucker to stop.

The trucker peered down suspiciously from his cab at the three of us. Our driver spoke, "These guys here are looking for a ride into Cochrane. Can you take 'em?"

The trucker boasted an Abraham Lincoln–like beard and shoulder-length hair tucked under a grimy old ball cap. After a pause, he said gruffly, "I only got room for one in my truck."

This was a little bewildering—Wes and I thought both of us could fit in the truck. But the trucker insisted there was only room for one of us. I was curious to see the gold mine, so I suggested to Wes that he take the ride—he could drive back to the mine and get me once he had retrieved our vehicle from town. So I remained in the back of the pickup while Wes climbed up into the rig.

While he rode into town along the winding road that sliced through the vast forest, I was heading in the opposite direction toward the mine.

It took three hours to reach Cochrane, where Wes retrieved our pickup truck from the train station, refuelled it, and then prepared to drive another three hours to meet me back at the mine.

At the gold mine, flood lights illuminated the haul trucks, hydraulic shovels, and grey construction trailers that littered the landscape. Exploratory work was being conducted in the area to see if it was profitable to re-open the mine, as it had lain abandoned for decades. The high price of gold made the prospect of mining here potentially feasible once again.

Beside the construction camp, what greeted my eyes was a deeply unsettling sight: where once had been verdant forests was now a barren moonscape, devastated by strip-mining. It was a bleak, apocalyptic-looking place destroyed by machines and riddled with dark chasms that led deep into the earth. It filled me with dismay that society could permit the wanton destruction of wilderness—earth's true gem—in the pursuit of shiny stones. But my opinions reflect a life spent seeking untouched, hidden-away places.

The workers were gathered in the common room of a temporary building erected on the site, watching television. I met most of them as well as the man in charge. Only a few dozen people were at the mine because it wasn't yet fully operational. I was a little concerned, irrationally so, that one of the workers would recognize me as the explorer who penned articles arguing against mining in the Hudson Bay Lowlands. Yet they seemed to regard me as just some sort of eccentric who liked canoeing rivers no one had heard of. I chatted with them and asked if any of them knew of the Again River. None of them had ever heard of it.

My escort in, the aboriginal trapper, with whom I talked the most, had likewise never heard of the river. A thoroughly modern trapper, he was eager to fetch his laptop and have me show him the river on Google Earth. I did so, pointing out to him the blurry little black ribbon that snaked through emerald green forest on the low-resolution images. He nodded and affirmed he knew nothing of that river. As we talked, I learned that he was originally from Moosonee, a Cree community on the mouth of the large Moose River, near James Bay, and the northern terminus of the government-owned Polar Bear Express railroad. He had grown up fishing, hunting, and trapping there, before drifting south to Cochrane. He didn't much care for Moosonee anymore and told me he wouldn't move back.

Since he had proved helpful, and I had both enjoyed our conversation and was grateful that Wes and I had not been killed on the ride he generously provided—I decided to pay him as best as I could for the ride. I had little money, but offered him my old canoe, telling him it needed repairs but was his if he wanted it. He happily accepted my offer.

It was getting on near midnight, and all the workers and the trapper soon disappeared off to bed for the night. I had been given a room of my own to sleep in while I waited for Wes to return, as well as a dry pair of wool socks to replace my soaking wet ones. It wasn't until 3:00 a.m. that Wes finally arrived. I met him outside the makeshift buildings erected on the site.

"What took you so long?" I asked, half asleep.

"I drove slow. It's pitch dark and there's moose and bears crossing the road. I was terrified I'd hit one."

We decided not to stay at the mine—though we had been offered the room for the night—and instead drove back to where we had stowed our canoe and gear beside the creek. We spent the night there; then departed in the late morning for our drive home, so that Wes could make it to his sister's wedding. Before we left, we hauled the canoe out beside the road, leaving it there for the trapper to pick up.

"Well, we didn't get to explore your river," remarked Wes as he drove us south.

"No, but that's all right," I said a little ruefully, "the river will still be there next summer."

2

PLANS AND PREPARATIONS

Geographers ... crowd into the edges of their maps parts of the world which they do not know about, adding notes in the margin to the effect that beyond this lies nothing but sandy deserts full of wild beasts, and unapproachable bogs.
—Plutarch, *Plutarch's Lives*, first century AD

MUCH OF THE HISTORY OF exploration is the story of failures. Christopher Columbus, after all, wasn't looking for North America when he made landfall in the Bahamas in 1492. He was attempting to sail around the world to Asia—more precisely, the East Indies—hence the Italian mariner's mistaken belief that the people he met with were "Indians." Sir Alexander Mackenzie, perhaps the greatest of North America's land explorers, had the misfortune to journey over two thousand kilometres in the wrong direction in his attempt to reach the Pacific Ocean. The eccentric genius Sir Richard Burton, among the most celebrated of African explorers, failed in his famous quest to find the source of the Nile. And then there was Sir Ernest Shackleton, widely considered a gifted leader and polar explorer par excellence, who never succeeded on any of his expeditions in reaching his objective. I took solace in these facts over my failure to explore the Again River two summers in a row. While I had not reached the Again,

I had a consolation prize in that I had still explored a nameless river (a tributary of the Kattawagami, a map of which I created) and together with Wes blazed kilometres of new trails into unexplored territory. More importantly, my resolve to explore the Again remained undiminished.

It would be necessary to wait until the Hudson Bay Lowlands' long winter ended and the ice melted before another attempt could be made to canoe the Again River. I felt certain that the summer of 2010 would be when I'd finally explore it—in fact, restless as always, I was growing impatient to free myself of the mental hold the Again was exercising over me and move on to other challenges. While the desire to reach the Again remained, haunting me like some sort of spectre, I hurled myself into other undertakings. I ventured to Lake Superior to search for ancient pictographs on that majestic body of water's rocky shores and to explore its many mysterious caves. I wandered off into remote parts of the Rockies, crossing paths with black bears and elk. On the wide open grasslands of the prairies, I slept under the stars and collected mule deer antlers. And in Manitoba, I paddled azure lakes while fishing for pickerel. In fact, I roamed all around Canada's wilderness from the rocky inlets of the Atlantic to the temperate rainforests of the Pacific. My life devolved into a restless search for one adventure after another—a desire "to escape from the commonplace of existence," as Sir Arthur Conan Doyle put it.

When the summer arrived, I was impatient to attempt the Again once more. However, a wrench was thrown in my plans when Wes informed me that two weeks was all the time that he could afford for exploration. Financially, Wes found himself in difficult straits (I was no better off), and the practical man that he was, he was attempting to save money in order to buy a house with his girlfriend. For Wes to take an unpaid leave from his construction job to go exploring wasn't economical. Until that time, I had mainly financed our expeditions the same way most explorers had paid for their work since the Victorian era—through writing and public lectures. While these speaking engagements and articles allowed me to eke out a living as an explorer and had made me something of a local celebrity in our small town, it wasn't going to buy any house.

But things got even more complicated when in July, Wes gloomily informed me that a week was now all he could offer me.

"But a week isn't enough time to explore the Again River," I scoffed.

"That's all I can afford to take off," Wes explained.

"Yes, but just think, if we make this sacrifice now and succeed, it will pay off in the long run."

"We need sponsors," replied Wes, unimpressed.

"We'll get sponsors by doing expeditions and making a name for ourselves."

"We need them now, though."

"We have only a few weeks, it's not enough time to get any."

"Then find a way to explore it in a week."

Disheartening as this revelation was, I wasn't going to abandon my quest to explore the Again that easily. As much as I disliked the thought and dreaded the increased financial cost to myself, I entertained the possibility of chartering a helicopter or float-plane to fly us as close to the river as possible, which might, under the best of circumstances, permit us to complete the expedition in eight or nine days.

However, this approach wasn't without considerable draw-backs: inevitably it would entail exploring less territory, which would diminish our accomplishment. It felt as if half the point of the expedition—exploring the area fully from the ground—would be unfulfilled by doing things in this manner. Still, if this was the only way Wes could join me, I'd consider it. Since a heli-copter was beyond my financial resources, I made inquiries with bush pilots about taking us, our gear, and our canoe to one of the lakes in the upper part of the Again River's watershed. The response wasn't encouraging.

The chief bush pilot in Cochrane, who made his living flying hunters and fishermen to remote wilderness lakes, had never heard of the Again River and wasn't familiar with any of the lakes in its watershed. By now, I was familiar with this response. The bush pilot was uncomfortable flying to a lake he didn't know—it might after all prove too shallow or rocky to land on—and suggested that we fly to one of the lakes he did know and content ourselves with paddling some other river. As far as our purposes were concerned, he proved unhelpful—he wouldn't fly us where we wanted to go, so that option was quickly dropped. There was no way then—given Wes' time constraints—to explore the Again that summer. Since I had come to regard the Again as the special shared ambition of Wes and me, it didn't seem right to explore it without him. With much regret, I resigned myself to waiting another year to explore it.

Wes and I had to content ourselves with some minor adven-tures and exploring of a different sort—such as searches on the wooded hillsides of our rural countryside for giant puffballs, an oversized mushroom that resembles a volleyball (or as I like to say, a dinosaur egg), which we collected and ate. But the failure to explore the Again left me restless and more eager than ever to hurl myself into new challenges. Perhaps I was compensating for failure, but, regardless, I needed more adventures, more quests— to live a more satisfying existence. That autumn, I worked on my survival skills in the northern woods. I also made arrangements to spend the winter in Ottawa writing articles and doing research for *Canadian Geographic* magazine and the spring in the Amazon rainforest on a scientific expedition. These new challenges, which broadened my horizons, actually helped dissipate my interest in the Again. I half told myself to forget about that obscure river and to turn my attention elsewhere. The Amazon had long exercised a spell over me—rare is the explorer who isn't interested in exploring its exotic, otherworldly jungles, where species unknown to science remain to be discovered and Stone Age tribes still live. I also longed to explore the Arctic and the northern reaches of the Hudson Bay Lowlands, the home of earth's largest land carnivore, *Ursus maritimus*, the polar bear. The Again, in contrast, was in the southern part of the Lowlands, outside the range of the great white bear. I was eager to undertake bigger expeditions farther afield and convinced myself that the cursed Again had become a sort of millstone that was weighing me down. I told myself that one day I would undoubtedly explore it, but that it could wait for the time being.

That winter, Wes and I were snowshoeing and tracking wolves north of Lake Huron when he suggested that we canoe the Florida Everglades. Such an adventure sounded like a suitable warm-up for the Amazon jungle, so I started making plans for an Everglades canoe trip as soon as we returned from the wilds. But just days before we were to depart, Wes abruptly cancelled. He had decided instead on a trip with his girlfriend to a resort in the Caribbean. I was disappointed—considering the time that I had invested in making arrangements for the Everglades—and began to wonder whether his thirst for adventure was drying up. It certainly seemed like he was becoming domesticated. I shuddered with horror at the thought of such a thing ever happening to me.

ON MY FIRST DAY at *Canadian Geographic*'s head office in Ottawa, I attended an editorial meeting. On the wall opposite from where I sat was a glorious collection of old charters for the magazine's publisher: the venerable Royal Canadian Geographical Society. The Society, modelled on Britain's Royal Geographical Society, was founded in 1929 by the explorer Charles Camsell and other like-minded individuals. Besides publishing *Canadian Geographic*, the Society sponsors expeditions, produces the *Atlas of Canada* and other maps, promotes geographical education, and bestows awards and honours on explorers and geographers. I had held the institution in holy reverence ever since my grandparents had given me a subscription to *Canadian Geographic* as a child for my birthday. I dreamed of carrying the Society's blue flag, emblazoned with its crest—a white, eight-point compass overlaid with a red maple leaf—on an expedition of my own one day.

Beside the old charters hung an antique Asian-looking sword with a golden hilt and decorative scabbard. With this curious artifact directly in my line of sight, it wasn't long before I lost the thread of the editorial discussion and started pondering the sword. Beneath the sword, a plaque mounted on the wall read:

Presented to The Canadian Geographical Society by Sir Francis Younghusband, guest-lecturer, at the inaugural meeting of the Society in Ottawa. January 1930. This Tibetan sword was presented to Sir Francis Younghusband by the Chief of Bhutan in 1904.

Sir Francis Younghusband—now here was a true adventurer and explorer. He had lived a life so extraordinary that it seemed like he was straight out of the imagination of some adventure novelist. Younghusband was born in 1863 in the British Raj, or what is now Pakistan, where his father was stationed on military service. He was sent to England to receive an education and attended the Royal Military College, Sandhurst. But it was as an explorer, not as a soldier, that Younghusband would make his name.

In 1886, Younghusband participated in an expedition journeying from India to Manchuria. Impressed by his abilities, his superiors then dispatched him to explore the vast Gobi Desert of Mongolia and northern China. With only a few guides, he set off from Beijing on a journey through unknown territory, successfully crossing the Gobi Desert and then making his way over the Himalayan Mountains into India. For this remarkable journey, at age twenty-four, he was elected the youngest ever Fellow of Britain's Royal Geographical Society. Next, Younghusband explored the border regions between India, China, and Russia, and the Hindu Kush mountains of Afghanistan, entering remote lands that time seemed to have forgotten. He wrote about these adventures in his book *The Heart of a Continent*.

In 1903, he was tasked with leading an expedition to Tibet, one of the world's least known and most mysterious countries. Tibet's isolated location high in the snowy Himalayas and its policy of keeping out all foreigners made it something of an adventurer's dream—an enchanted kingdom hidden in the clouds. Younghusband became one of the first Europeans to enter Tibet's ancient capital, the Forbidden City of Lhasa. But the dream became a nightmare when Younghusband's troops massacred Tibetan militia. The bloodshed and lofty mountains left a deep impression on Younghusband, and he underwent a spiritual epiphany. He became a mystic, contemplating founding his own religion and writing numerous books on the subject. Younghusband even mused about fathering a "god-child" who would become a prophet of the new religion he dreamed of creating. Regardless of his eccentricities, he was elected president of the Royal Geographical Society, and in that capacity began promoting an expedition to scale Mount Everest. In 1930, by then an explorer of legendary stature, he arrived in Ottawa with a memento from one of his expeditions, a sword from the chief of Bhutan. Younghusband presented it to the newly founded Canadian Geographical Society, and perhaps by doing so hoped to inspire the same sense of adventure and wanderlust that drove his life. Whatever his claims as a mystic, he succeeded in bewitching me. Staring transfixed at his sword on the wall, I felt myself seized by an irresistible urge to explore distant lands.

As a result, I spent only three months in Ottawa working at *Canadian Geographic*. More importantly, during this time, I also submitted a detailed expedition proposal to the Geographical

Society's Expedition Committee, which approved and sponsored expeditions. I proposed to explore a remote, nameless river in the northern reaches of the Hudson Bay Lowlands that, like the Again, was all but unknown and had nothing on it in the published record. I planned to mount the first expedition to canoe this far-flung river with Wes. To reach the river would entail a long and difficult journey, preceded by an expensive flight north by bush plane. As far as I could ascertain, the Geographical Society had never previously sponsored a journey to the blackfly-infested Lowlands—which would give me the distinction of leading the first-ever Society expedition into North America's largest wetland. But a response from the Expeditions Committee wouldn't be forthcoming for some months, leaving me to pursue other projects.

In April, I was back home in Fenwick, working with my father to build a birchbark canoe for a local museum. In the swamp forests beside my family home, we found a large white birch that was straight with few branches and knots, which made it suitable for our purposes. With a knife and chisel, I climbed a maple sapling growing beside the birch and delicately peeled off the bark to a height of six metres. Not wanting to waste anything, we later chopped down the tree for firewood (my parents heated their house with wood in the winter). In a stroke of fortune, a windstorm struck the area in the following days, toppling over several big spruces. I dug up their strong and supple roots for lashing, while my father fetched some basswood bark for additional lashing. We felled a white ash for the canoe's gunwales and thwarts, as well as for paddles. The only tree we needed but couldn't find in our forests was eastern white cedar—the cedar's flexible wood we wanted for the canoe's ribs. Instead, I went to the local farmers' co-op and bought some cedar fence posts, which my father and I split and bent to form the ribs. After working only intermittently for four weeks, we finished the thirteen-foot canoe (which was as large as we could make it, given the limited size of the birch we felled) and tested it in our pond. It handled well and, unlike the old fibreglass vessel Wes and I had paddled, didn't leak at all. I penned an article for *Canadian Geographic* about it then boarded a plane to Ecuador, to set off into the Amazon rainforest.

ONCE I ARRIVED at a base camp deep in the Amazon jungle, a written test was placed before me by the scientists there, asking me to identify sundry species by their Latin names. I hadn't done much biological fieldwork since my time working for Ontario's Ministry of Natural Resources as a student, but I had spent the last eight months reading Amazon zoology books in my spare time. I have always been blessed with the capacity to memorize large amounts of data, and while rote memorization may not be much of a skill, my visual memory is one of the best assets I possess as an explorer—it has invariably saved me from losing my way, since I can always remember where I have been. The scientists seemed satisfied when I got a perfect score on the test, correctly identifying each species by its scientific name and all of the tropical bird calls they played on a tape recorder.

Soon I was hacking my way through the jungle with a machete, helping to carry out biological inventories and in the process acquiring a fine collection of ant bites. There was no electricity at our base camp in the rainforest, but after five weeks in the jungle I paid a visit to the nearest village with an internet connection to check my email. It proved a moment of triumph: I learned that the Geographical Society's Expedition Committee had endorsed my proposal and was sponsoring the expedition to the Hudson Bay Lowlands.

A WEEK AFTER that I was back in Canada—eager to begin the greatest adventure of my life. Not even the "hangover" from the Amazon could dampen my enthusiasm. My legs were covered with insect bites, and I had pinched a nerve in my back when doing some heavy lifting in the jungle. I would have to continue my daily doses of malaria pills for another four weeks, and as a precaution I was prescribed a course of antibiotics because of a tick bite on my leg. But I had escaped any serious illness or inconvenience—some of the scientists had contracted leishmaniasis, dengue fever, and other tropical diseases. I came back feeling impatient to plunge into the subarctic wilderness.

Upon my return from South America, I expected Wes to be primed for our expedition, which we planned for the end of July. It was, after all, just over five weeks away and the adventure that we had dreamed of since childhood. But to my dismay, I found him noncommittal about whether he would even accompany me at all. He wanted to come, he told me. But he had to think about his job, his girlfriend, and saving money.

"But Wes, this is a dream to have the Geographical Society sponsor us to explore a wild river with no name," I said in disbelief.

"It is a dream," replied Wes, "but it's your dream."

Several weeks passed while Wes procrastinated over whether he would quit his job and accompany me on the expedition. In the meantime, I couldn't be idle: over the winter I had made arrangements for my own intermittent employment as an occasional wilderness canoeing guide in Algonquin Park. I soon found myself guiding a short trip there with some German and Australian tourists. Still taking my malaria pills each morning, I was hiking and paddling around the wilds of Algonquin. When I returned home, I was greeted with the news I had been dreading. Wes told me that he couldn't go through with the expedition. This was a huge blow—to me it felt something like Clark abandoning Lewis on the eve of their journey into the uncharted American West in 1804. Trying to pull off the expedition without Wes would be difficult, if not impossible. I certainly couldn't do the expedition alone. I would have to find a replacement for him. I needed someone with Wes' skills and experience whom I could rely upon. But more than that, Wes had been my friend since childhood; to do the expedition without him would be a deep disappointment.

That evening, melancholic from having received Wes' unwelcome news, I took a lonely walk in the woods, accompanied by my dog Riley. He was a magnificent animal—he stood nearly three feet at the shoulders, weighed a trim 138 pounds, and had a handsome black and tan coat highlighted by a patch of white fur on his muscular chest. For eight years he had been my closest companion, a beloved and faithful dog that shadowed my steps through the woods.

As we passed through some maiden-hair ferns growing beneath a big swamp oak, I turned to him and said, "Well, Riley, Wes may have quit on me, but I know you never will."

He wagged his tail and looked up at me, his big brown eyes full of understanding.

As we walked on through the woods, I noticed that Riley didn't leave my side. At first I imagined that was only because he had missed me while I was away in the Amazon. But I sensed something wasn't right—he didn't have his usual lightness of foot and was curiously uninterested in the rabbit trails we were passing. The following day, I took Riley to the veterinarian. I was informed that he had an inoperable tumour, that there was nothing for it, and that all my love couldn't save him. I was stunned. For the first time, I no longer cared about unexplored rivers. All I cared about was saving my best friend—the dog that I had shared countless adventures with. Refusing to believe the veterinarian's diagnosis, I drove Riley to a specialist outside Toronto. But I was told the same thing. Riley had to be put down. He died in my arms. Heartbroken, feeling as if I had lost a part of myself, I buried his kingly body beneath a maple tree that he had always loved to sit under.

I HAD BARELY OVER THREE WEEKS to find a replacement for Wes, get him up to speed, and take care of all the planning and logistics for the expedition. It wasn't going to be an easy task. I knew, from past experience, that my options for finding a suitable substitute for Wes—in fact finding any substitute—were not good. I learned quickly that wilderness exploring didn't hold the same deep appeal for everyone that it did for me. While most people might enjoy a weekend spent leisurely paddling around tranquil lakes, a gruelling, hazardous expedition deep in the nightmarish Lowlands—where far more time would be spent carrying and dragging the canoe through thick forest and muskeg than ever paddling it—came across as decidedly unappealing.

Typically, when I broached the subject of joining my expedition, the response was initially enthusiastic—until I explained the details of the horrendous portages through trackless swamps filled with millions of bloodsucking insects and the deadly hazard posed by half-famished polar bears looking to devour anything foolhardy enough to stray into their domain. Suddenly, that enthusiasm would dissipate.

After two weeks of interviews, I still hadn't found anyone to replace Wes. The first people I had turned to were a couple of my cousins. Both experienced outdoorsmen who had in the past roamed around the wilds with me, neither of them (prudent people that they are) wanted to step up and accompany me to the Lowlands. My twin brother was equally uninterested—he positively despised portages and couldn't fathom the over one hundred kilometres of it I was planning on doing, all of it without a trail. Next, I fired off a message to a friend of mine who was serving in the army. Unfortunately, so he told me, he had used up all of his leave for the year and wouldn't be able to take the time required for the expedition.

In the midst of these hectic preparations, chance brought across my path an old friend, a gifted all-around athlete named Brent Kozuh. He was one of the most skilled hockey players our small town had ever seen and was equally adept on the tennis court and soccer field. It was thought by some that he might have gone pro in some sport. That is, if not for his Achilles heel: like many extraordinarily talented athletes, Brent found training, hard work, and old-fashioned grit beneath him. He liked to boast, with peculiar pride, how in high school he had been such a slacker that he had failed even his career studies course—and that he had literally slept through economics, finishing with a grade of seven percent. At age twenty-five, he was unemployed and still living at home with his parents. His life, so he proudly told me, consisted of getting by with the minimal level of effort. Since Brent had been on a few easy canoe trips with me in the past and because we unexpectedly crossed paths, I jokingly asked if he might like to join me on an expedition to the subarctic.

To my surprise, Brent took an immediate interest and said that he had always wanted to do a serious expedition. Perhaps, I wondered, he did have some iron buried in his soul—or maybe he just wanted to prove his doubters wrong. He didn't exactly seem to be an ideal candidate for a gruelling wilderness journey. Despite his athletic physique, he was still an inveterate slacker. But I was fresh out of candidates and Brent, unburdened by a job, leapt at the chance to join me. If Brent really wanted to complete an extreme wilderness journey, I had no doubt he had the physical skill to do it. He did, in addition to a few canoe trips, have a passion for animals and the natural world—albeit largely limited to watching the Discovery Channel.

Desperation breeds hope, and with the expedition only a couple of weeks away I was desperate. I needed a partner—*any* partner. To go alone into polar bear territory was unthinkable. What gave me some hope that Brent would cast off his laziness and prove himself a capable expedition partner was his tremendous prowess as an athlete. Paradoxically, while anywhere outside a sporting match he was paralyzed by an all-consuming listlessness, when he was "in the zone," he transformed into a fierce competitor. Whatever the sport, Brent was the kind of player for whom dominance came naturally. If his team was down in the third period, he'd single-handedly strip the opposing team of the puck and even the score. But after the final buzzer, it was as if a switch flipped off in his brain that caused him to transform back into an incorrigible idler who struggled just to carry his hockey bag to the parking lot. I figured that if I could get Brent to see an expedition as a sport—a physical challenge to be won—he would snap out of his habitual indolence and exert himself with all his superb skill.

Immersed in the preparations for the expedition, Brent showed an uncustomary keenness in helping (which was promising). He began to accompany me on my daily errands obtaining supplies. One of those errands was the important task of acquiring a suitable firearm. My arsenal consisted of only two guns—a .22 calibre rifle and a 1930s-era twenty-gauge shotgun—neither of which would deter a polar bear. My preference was for bows and arrows rather than firearms. I had grown up using a fibreglass longbow and had once fashioned my own bow from the wood of an osage orange tree, the finest of all North American trees for bow making. But government policy was to carry twelve-gauge shotguns in polar bear territory—nothing less was considered safe. So, Brent and I paid a visit to the local gun shop on the main street in our small town. We parked outside the wood-shingled building and entered a storeroom crowded to the rafters with firearms and mounted animal heads. The proprietor, a man in his mid-eighties who had been in the gun business since shortly after the Second World War, stood behind the counter, rows of rifles mounted behind him.

"We need something for polar bears," I explained.

The old clerk nodded solemnly at my question, as if he had expected as much. "You hunting them?"

"Uh no, it's just for a worst-case scenario. We're going on an expedition and need some protection."

"I got just the thing." He reached behind the counter and produced a mean-looking shotgun. "Winchester Defender, twelve gauge, pump action, the perfect expedition gun. The short barrel will let you get it up in a hurry," and with a rapid movement that belied his age, the clerk jerked the gun up to his shoulder, feigning a bear attack.

"Excellent," I said.

"You'll want rifled slugs. Nothing else will stop a polar bear," he said as he reached behind the counter and produced a box of shells.

"Great," I replied.

"And I'll tell you what. I'll throw in some birdshot, should you find yourself in an emergency like a plane crash and need to kill something for food."

Brent stared wide-eyed at the accumulating arsenal on the counter.

"Perfect," I said.

"And some target shot for practice shooting."

"Wonderful."

After completing the purchase (at a rather steep price) and the required paperwork, we exited the store with our new hardware. Brent, feeling hungry, suggested that we pay a visit to the Subway down the street.

"All right, then we'll have to head to the map library at Brock University to get the topographic maps," I said, glancing at the time. I had a hundred things on my mind, having to plan every detail of our journey down to the last food ration. As we entered Subway, there was one more thing on my mind: my friend's notorious habit of misplacing things. Brent would lose his car keys pretty much daily, his phone regularly, and his TV remote habitually. My concern was that in the wilderness, his careless- ness could have serious repercussions were he to leave behind some vital piece of equipment.

"God, I love meatball subs," said Brent, between mouthfuls.

"Yes. Did you find your cellphone?"

"No," said Brent, pausing to think, "must have left it at the bar the other night."

"You know, when we're on the expedition, it will be critical not to lose anything. We can't afford to forget something at a campsite or misplace the satellite phone."

"Don't worry," Brent gave a dismissive wave of his hand, "I won't lose anything."

We finished our subs and got up to leave. Just as we were walking out, the young woman who had served us spoke up. "Hey, I think one of you guys forgot your wallet." She pointed to a black leather wallet at our table.

"Oh, my bad," said Brent, as he sheepishly retrieved it.

I couldn't help but feel a little uneasy about my new part- ner. He admitted that he had lost his wallet twice before that summer. This didn't inspire a lot of confidence for our long journey ahead.

IF THERE IS ONE LESSON that can be gleaned from the history of exploration, it's that nothing ever goes according to plan. Therefore, I had made a point of devising alternative plans for our expedition in the event of any unforeseen difficulties. From the very beginning, when I was preparing the expedition proposal back in Ottawa, I had made sure to keep my plans flexible. I zeroed in on two rivers in the northern reaches of the Hudson Bay Lowlands that I was interested in exploring, both apparently nameless. It didn't much matter which of the two rivers we ended up exploring, as they were similar. The larger of the two was situated some forty kilometres east of Cape Henrietta Maria, and it appeared on maps as a nearly 150-kilometre-long nameless tributary of the isolated Brant River. This, however, as is so often the case when dealing with obscure geography, wasn't entirely clear: other maps labelled the tributary as the Brant River itself. Consulting various maps from different government agencies only compounded the problem: there was no agreement on which of the upper forks in this river was the Brant and which was unnamed. Since the basis of my expedition proposal to the Geographical Society was the exploration of a nameless river in the Lowlands, I was loath to go to the effort of exploring this river only to have someone later claim that it was the fork which was properly known as the Brant. Government scientists, ornithologists, and others had flown via helicopter and bush plane to the Brant and explored portions of it. But no one, insofar as was known, had ever canoed the river from its headwaters to the seacoast. I spoke on the phone with the superintendent of Polar Bear Provincial Park, a reserve whose boundaries on the ground are indistinguishable from the surrounding wilderness. She was unable to tell me anything about these rivers or their names, except to say that she knew of no one who had ever attempted to canoe them.

In contrast, the other river that I had my eye on was more obscure and had no name on any map. This fact made it seem almost perfect—except that it wasn't quite as long as the other waterway, measuring only a hundred kilometres. Thus, the choice was between the more obscure smaller river or the bigger, but somewhat better known, waterway that might or might not have a name.

I eventually resolved, having absorbed the lessons of past explorers, to keep our plans flexible. The presumed tributary of the Brant River would remain our primary objective, with the more obscure nameless river serving as an alternative should, for whatever reason, we fail to reach the first one. In any case, I planned to eventually explore both rivers over the course of several expeditions. If I had the funds and a willing partner, I might have attempted both in a single season—yet Brent affirmed that forty days was the absolute maximum amount of time he would spend in the wilderness.

As things stood, there were plenty of obstacles to undertaking any exploring that summer. I had originally imagined that the backing of the Geographical Society would open doors and make our preparations straightforward. This wasn't the case. An almost soul-crushing plethora of problems and obstacles arose in the weeks leading up to our departure. Things were already complicated by the last-minute lineup change from Wes to Brent, which put the entire burden of making preparations on my shoulders, as I dared not delegate anything to Brent— knowing him as well as I did. Time was of the essence: my hasty arrival back in Canada from the Amazon coupled with my work as a guide had severely compressed our preparatory time into a few hectic weeks. Everything needed to be in order by the end of July. Besides the annoyance of my lingering Amazonian recovery, there were serious logistical problems. My old car, our means of transportation to the northern town where we would board a bush plane, was pronounced unfit for the road by my mechanic. And Brent's vehicle was no better. To add to our difficulties, it was a hot, dry summer in the North—the Ministry of Natural Resources fire report indicated that 109 forest fires were burning across Ontario's wilderness, a serious hazard. I kept an eye on them via satellite updates, apprehensive that one might sweep across the area we were headed into. And if these concerns weren't enough, I was informed by the Geographical Society's president that the other expedition sponsored that year, to a river in Labrador, had failed to materialize. This news doubled the pressure for our expedition to succeed.

Most problematic of all was the common bane of an explorer's existence: a shortage of cash. While I was accustomed to performing expeditions with limited resources—I put my faith in traditional skills and knowledge rather than flashy gear—this was a Society expedition, so I couldn't take the risks I normally did, and all sorts of expensive equipment, such as a satellite phone and a GPS, had to be obtained. But even with the Society's generous funding, we had to cut some corners.

This put us in good company: most of history's greatest explorers were impoverished. Columbus set the template for many Renaissance-era explorers by spending years shifting between royal courts seeking a patron who would sponsor his proposed voyage across the Atlantic. The famed Victorian explorer of darkest Africa, Sir Henry Morton Stanley, was so embarrassed by his threadbare funding that he felt compelled to wildly inflate his expeditions' budgets in his books. Despite his fame, Stanley was reduced to all sorts of cost-saving measures and once had to sell his watch for food. His contemporary, David Livingstone, wasn't much better off. Livingstone had difficulty raising two thousand pounds in 1866 for his African explorations, complaining that even that amount was "wretchedly inadequate." Sir Ernest Shackleton struggled almost as much in the drawing rooms of imperial London to raise funds for his expeditions as he ever did in the howling wastes of Antarctica. Unable to raise the necessary funds, Shackleton's 1907 expedition to the South Pole left him deeply in debt. Seven years later, for his epic and unprecedented attempt to cross Antarctica, the Royal Geographical Society offered him a paltry thousand pounds, which would comprise only a tiny fraction of his budget. To make up the difference, Shackleton was forced to plead with wealthy private sponsors as well as a British government preoccupied with the looming conflict on the continent.

Legendary explorer Percy Fawcett was a beggar at the Royal Geographical Society's coffers, chronically short of money for his expeditions. On his quest in the 1920s to find the ruins of a lost civilization deep in the Amazon jungle, Fawcett received no salary, and the funding provided by the Geographical Society proved insufficient. But it took a certain flare, even genius, to mount expeditions with limited funds, and explorers like Fawcett who could do it were highly prized by underfunded geographical societies. Sir John Keltie, secretary of the Royal Geographical Society, noted:

It is quite true that [Fawcett] has a reputation of being difficult to get on with, and has a queer manner in many ways, being a mystic and a spiritualist, but all the same he has an extraordinary power of getting through difficulties that would deter anybody else.

While Fawcett did succeed time and again against great odds, eventually he vanished without a trace in the Amazon.

I now found myself in a similar financial situation: the Society's generous grant of 5,500 dollars was inadequate to cover the entire expedition, which I estimated at around 10,000 dollars if we stuck to just the bare essentials. So, like Stanley, Livingstone, Shackleton, and Fawcett, I did the necessary trimming. We couldn't afford bear spray, so that was dropped. We couldn't afford watertight canoe barrels, so I improvised some of my own (in addition to one that I already possessed). We made a road trip to the United States to purchase a GPS, but couldn't afford the mapping software that went with it—so we had to content ourselves with a GPS that had no maps but could at least give us our coordinates. Freeze-dried meals proved too expensive—so pasta, rice, and oatmeal would be our staples. Expensive waterproof Gore-Tex clothing was out of the question, as was a new canoe. Any sort of tripwire system or electric fence for protection against polar bears proved beyond our budget. Hiking boots and other miscellaneous gear were all old stuff that I had worn for years. Brent, having no money of his own, was outfitted entirely from my own closet: he was wearing my shirt, cargo pants, jacket, hat, bandanna, boots, and belt knife the day we left. Wes, meanwhile, lent Brent his backpack, sleeping bag, and a waterproof liner. By

2011 standards, our expedition was woefully under-equipped, but it was still the best outfitted expedition I had ever mounted—and besides, I reasoned, we were better provisioned than any of our historic predecessors. I took heart in those explorers who had done the seemingly impossible with what limited geographical society funding they had possessed. I resolved that, like Fawcett, we would find a way to get through all difficulties—be they pinched nerves, tick bites, malaria pills, a broken-down car, inadequate gear, raging forest fires—or anything else fate might have in store for us.

[3]

INTO THE WILD

Exploring is delightful to look forward to and back upon,
but it is not comfortable at the time, unless it be of such
an easy nature as not to deserve the name.
—Samuel Butler, *Erewhon*, 1872

FROM THE CO-PILOT'S SEAT of a bush plane, I peered through cloud and rain at a reddish and green patchwork of bog, sphagnum moss, and isolated clusters of stunted spruce and tamarack trees. It was about as gloomy and forbidding a landscape as I could imagine.

The night before, Brent and I had arrived in the small frontier logging town of Hearst, Ontario, which is nestled on the fringes of the great northern wilderness. The thirteen-hour drive north had been complicated by my injured back, which caused me considerable pain to the point where I was literally choking from back spasms as I drove. But the car didn't let us down, despite my mechanic's grave prognosis, and we arrived without much difficulty.

Bright and early the next morning, we met our pilot on a lake outside of town. His plane was a 1960s-era single-engine DHC-2 Beaver, the standard bush plane of Canada's North.

We weighed our gear to ensure it was under the limit for the long flight to the Hudson Bay Lowlands: it measured in at 165 pounds. Our canoe, which weighed 52 pounds, we strapped onto one of the plane's aluminum pontoons.

We would have to fly more than five hundred kilometres due north across vast wilderness to reach our expedition's starting point, an isolated lake situated some seventy kilometres south as the crow flies from the shore of Hudson Bay. The roar and vibration of the plane's engine rattled us inside the cockpit; talking was only possible through the headsets. Brent, who was sitting behind me, complained that the noise of the engine was giving him a headache and kept his head down and ears covered for the duration of the flight.

From the co-pilot's seat, I was taking in the vast wilderness below us. Immense boreal forest, interspersed with meandering black rivers and island-studded blue lakes, dominated the first stretch of the flight. Gradually, as we flew farther north, the landscape began to change: trees became sparser and smaller as the boreal forest thinned out into the open muskeg and innumerable ponds and beaver meadows of the Hudson Bay Lowlands. I knew all too well that every one of those waterways made excellent breeding ground for mosquitoes. Sandy eskers, an elevated ridge of gravel and sand left by retreating glaciers thousands of years ago, occasionally snaked across the landscape. But mostly it was a dreary swampland of stunted trees and countless small ponds, lakes, and rock-strewn creeks. The rainy weather we were flying through served to make the swampland below appear even drearier.

We were headed to Hawley Lake, named after explorer and geologist James Edwin Hawley. From there, Brent and I would

veer off into unexplored territory. I had read Hawley's dry
report from the 1920s on the geology of the area, as well as
reports by the handful of other Geological Survey explorers from
the late nineteenth and early twentieth centuries who had been
active in the Lowlands. Those explorers had come here in search
of mineral wealth. But, until recently, virtually no mineral extraction had been undertaken anywhere in the Lowlands, leaving it
a nearly untouched wilderness. That changed in 2006 when
De Beers, a South African diamond conglomerate, began mining
for diamonds near the Attawapiskat River. The controversial
project was vehemently opposed by the few environmentalists
who knew of the plans. They argued that it was a travesty to put
an open-pit mine in the middle of pristine wilderness. But the
project was approved, ostensibly on the grounds that it would
generate prosperity for the province and particularly for the
community of Attawapiskat, a small, impoverished Cree reserve
situated some ninety kilometres downriver from the mine site.

"We're going to pass near the diamond mine on the
Attawapiskat River soon," mumbled the pilot into his headset a
few hours into the flight.

We didn't pass near enough to see the mine; the thick
cloud cover and rain prevented us from spotting it in the distance.
That was fine by me: I had no real desire to see another environmental tragedy inflicted on Canada's wilderness for limited
short-term material gain—especially on a river I had once
paddled. Wes and I had canoed together on this very river as
teenagers after high school. Despite the mine, the vast majority
of the Lowlands remained untouched and unexplored by the
modern world—a fact amply illustrated by the countless acres

of wilderness passing beneath us. The mine, though a travesty for the Attawapiskat area, was but a pinprick in what remained an immense wilderness.

The landscape below us was as flat as a pancake—a poorly drained lowland that seemed more water than land. At times it was impossible to spot a single patch of solid ground. When R.M. Ballantyne, a fur trade clerk, first laid eyes on the desolate Hudson Bay Lowlands from the decks of a nineteenth-century ship, he noted, "Though only at the distance of two miles, so low and flat was the land, that it appeared ten miles off, and scarcely a tree was to be seen." While almost all of the Lowlands is marshy, like what Ballantyne saw from his ship, near its northern fringe lies a series of spectacular ridges that tower several hundred metres above the surrounding swamp forest. Known as the Sutton Ridges, I had selected this unique area as the drop point for our expedition. One of these towering rock escarpments runs across Hawley Lake, forming a large canyon, or gorge. We would land near there to begin our journey.

To my surprise, the pilot had never previously flown to Hawley Lake and while in mid-air had to cautiously check his fold-out maps on several occasions. He was new, he explained, to the bush pilot business. After about four hours of flying, the grey outlines of the distant Sutton Ridges suddenly loomed into view, rising above the swamps like small mountains. The pilot circled the plane around in a wide arc to land on the long shimmer of navy blue water that was Hawley Lake, just north of the tabletop ridges. From the air, the surrounding country through which we would have to portage appeared fairly promising: it seemed relatively well-drained and elevated, and at places there were sandy hummocks left by glaciers and what looked like ancient beaches from long-vanished shorelines. Beyond the waterways, the country was sparsely treed—forest fires had charred some stretches. On Hawley Lake itself, I could see near its northwestern shore several small cabins, a dock, and some overturned boats on the grassy banks. The pilot brought the small plane down steeply toward the lake, which for a moment made us feel like we were on a roller coaster. We bounced along the water on the pontoons as the plane gradually coasted to a halt near the wooden dock.

"I guess this must be the place," said the pilot.

"Yes, it is," I replied, recognizing it from my research.

"It's cold," complained Brent.

The three of us sprang from the plane onto the bobbing dock. Brent and I wasted little time in unstrapping the canoe from the pontoon and unloading our assorted gear: two bulky expedition backpacks, a plastic canoe barrel, two watertight buckets placed inside old worn packs, two fishing rods, three wood paddles, and the shotgun. The pilot, meanwhile, was busy refuelling the plane from a steel oil drum and half a dozen red plastic jerry cans—the low fuel light had flashed on as we were flying in.

"Good luck," mumbled the pilot. He waved a hand, leapt back onto the pontoon, and hopped into the cockpit.

"Hmm, he seems eager to leave," Brent observed. "I wonder why ... Fuck!" Brent slapped at his ears and waved his arms furiously. "Fuck! I'm getting eaten alive!"

"Put your bug net on," I said, as I swiftly donned my own. Unlike Brent, I had grown up in swampy forests, so I never much minded mosquitoes, though blackflies are a torment to anyone.

"This is horrible," groaned Brent as he pulled the mesh net over his short black hair.

"Don't worry, once we get paddling out on the lake, the breeze should keep the bugs away," I said. "Let's quickly check out the cabins, then head out."

The lake appeared much the same as it had a hundred years earlier when D.B. Dowling of the Geological Survey had arrived in the area. Dowling had explored the lakes—then known as the Sutton Mills Lakes, since renamed Sutton and Hawley Lakes—in 1901. However, unlike in Dowling's day, the log cabins were now mostly used by wealthy fishermen who came here to catch brook trout. The more adventurous sorts would occasionally paddle down the Sutton River, where near its mouth they would be airlifted out by float planes. The camp was maintained by a Cree family, the Chookomolins. The closest community, Peawanuck, a tiny Cree reserve of some 237 people, was situated nearly a hundred kilometres to the northeast on the large Winisk River. These northern Cree, or *Omushkego* as they call themselves, were the descendants of the hunter-trappers of the fur trade, and a few still engaged in trapping. No one was at the cabins, so we returned to the dock and the delicate business of packing our canoe.

I had hoped to acquire a new canoe for the expedition—ideally, one made of either strong, lightweight Kevlar or heavier but virtually indestructible Royalex ABS. But the price tag for such a vessel was beyond our budget, and I was forced to find something for less than eight hundred dollars, second-hand. After weeks of searching, I despaired of ever finding anything adequate and thought we might have to paddle one of the cedar-strip canoes my father and I had crafted. But at last I found an acceptable, though far from perfect, canoe within our limited price range. It was only thirteen feet long and very shallow, which would limit its utility and safety in whitewater or when facing big waves. But, crucially, given the portages we would face, it weighed only fifty-two pounds. While this wasn't light by the standards of expensive Kevlar canoes, which weigh as little as thirty pounds, it was an improvement over my other canoes.

It had been necessary to make some modifications to the vessel. I replaced the seats with lighter ones that I made myself and fastened nylon rope for lining to both ends. My father carved an ash centre yoke to replace the existing steel one, which would enable us to carry the canoe on our shoulders. I didn't think much of the oak gunwales the previous owner had added and wished to replace them, but time constraints made it impossible to do so. The canoe's small size, while an asset for the gruelling overland travel through forest and muskeg, was a drawback on the water. But such compromises were necessary; if explorers insisted on perfect gear, not much would have been explored.

Brent and I set off and began paddling up the lake. Meanwhile, the bush plane droned off into the distance, disappearing from view into cumulus clouds. As the sound of the engine faded away, we were left in the profound silence of the northern wilderness. Hawley Lake was beautiful; its clear blue waters were surrounded by a rocky shoreline and mature forests of cedar, poplar, spruce, and tamarack. Low hills sloped gently up from the lake. If not for the bugs, it seemed like an oasis in a wilderness of swamp.

The great size of the lake, however, made paddling in our heavily laden little canoe rather risky. As it was, the oak gunwales were riding only a few inches above the waterline, and as we paddled toward the distant south end of the lake, the wind whipped up four-foot swells. I steered the canoe from the stern delicately into each wave, riding over them without much difficulty. But eventually some of the bigger waves lapped over the bow, splashing Brent.

"Whoa! These are big waves," Brent said as he drew a stroke of his paddle.

"At least the wind has taken care of the bugs."

The situation was actually quite dangerous. If we swamped in the lake, it would be a long and difficult swim to shore. My heart leapt as another big wave plowed into us and increased the water accumulating in the bottom of the canoe. There was no way around it. We had to head to shore and wait for the waves to die down. I cautiously steered the canoe toward the eastern shore.

While we waited onshore for the wind to die down, I taught Brent how to load and fire the twelve-gauge shotgun, which wild edibles were around us, and how to make a fire. The wind, meanwhile, showed little sign of slackening, so we ate a simple lunch and I next showed Brent how to operate our hand-held water purifier. Several hours passed while the waves remained as fierce as ever. Brent, never patient, was growing fidgety and restless to press on. He had the intense look in his dark eyes that I had seen years before when we were hockey teammates. He was "in the zone" and primed for a challenge. Buoyed by his enthusiasm, I agreed to his suggestion that we risk battle with the waves.

"All right," I said. "I think we can manage it if we can get away from the shore, out of the breaking surf where the waves are the worst."

Brent nodded, took a moment to tighten the grey bandana wrapped around his head, and then grasped his ash paddle, much as he would his hockey stick before some on-ice heroics. The waves were noisily pounding against the pebble beach we were standing on and a light rain was falling—a reminder of how quickly the weather could change here.

"We're going to have to get our feet wet," I said. "We'll have to wade out a bit, then jump in and paddle as hard as we can away from shore." Even though we were ready for action, I was under no illusion about how grim the struggle actually would be: as soon as we edged the bow into the water, the waves slammed it sideways and threw the canoe back onto shore.

"We'll have to be quicker," I said, "or else the waves will capsize the canoe."

Brent and I grabbed hold of the shallow vessel like it was a surfboard, wading with it into the cold water, pushing it into the waves. Brent leapt into the bow and swung his paddle into an oncoming wave, while I gave one last push then leapt into the stern. But just as I did so, a wave jarred the canoe sideways, causing my knee to come down hard on my thumb, crushing it against the sharp edge of the oak gunwale as I landed in the stern of the canoe. A surge of pain shot through my hand. I had to ignore it and focus on paddling and steering the canoe; keeping the vessel right-side up as the waves jostled us about. Some water surged over the gunwales, but Brent performed well in the bow, keeping cool as I guided us away from shore. We soon escaped from the breaking surf and continued heading south along the lake, now untroubled by the waves, which we rode over harmlessly.

Meanwhile, my thumb was bleeding profusely and throbbing with pain. There was a gaping cut on the outer side of my thumb, near the nail. Thrilled as I was that we had beaten the waves, I thought little of my hurting thumb at the time—I quickly bandaged it, then resumed paddling. By evening, the rain had ceased and a warm glow of orange sunshine bathed the lake as the sun sank into the horizon.

"Let's paddle to the end of the lake, where the canyon is. That should be a good place to camp for tonight," I said. I was eager to see the Sutton Gorge; there was nothing else like it in the Lowlands.

We paddled for another two hours to reach the rock cliffs of the Sutton Ridges, which dominate the end of the lake. D.B. Dowling's 1902 Geological Survey report of his visit to the area described the scene:

> The rocks at the narrows of the lake ... are cliffs one hundred and fifty feet in height of trap [igneous rock], capping beds of probably Animikie age.... Those rocks protrude through the clay plain in rounded oval ridges.... In the narrows the cliffs are broken down and the debris has filled the channel.

We made camp for the night in the shadows cast by towering rock cliffs. Beneath the black spruce trees grew a carpet of caribou lichen that resembled delicate ocean coral, thick mats of green sphagnum moss, blueberry shrubs, and Labrador Tea shrubs (whose leaves are traditionally used to make tea). Brent set about making a fire inside a circle of rocks we quickly assembled, while I headed down to the lakeshore to gather water and clean my injured thumb. When I returned to our sheltered camp in the forest, I was surprised not to see any smoke rising. The teepee of carefully arranged dead sticks was sitting as I had left it—nothing was burning. Brent, head down and draped in a mosquito net, was sitting on the ground a few feet away in apparent despair. A cloud of mosquitoes and blackflies swarmed about him.

"Why didn't you start the fire?" I asked, puzzled.

Brent looked up slowly, "It's no use. I tried. It won't burn."

This surprised me. Despite the brief rain earlier, here in this sheltered patch of thick forest everything was bone dry. Merely tossing a smouldering ember would be enough to start a forest fire. "What do you mean? Did you try lighting the tinder?"

"The sticks won't burn."

"You need to light the tinder first and let it catch. Then the smaller sticks will burn," I explained as I bent down beside our unlit fire. With a match from my pocket, I lit some dead spruce needles, and in less than a minute had a blazing fire—to Brent's amazement.

"Oh," he muttered glumly.

"You just need more practice." I stood up and searched for some bigger sticks to toss on the fire. "Before we reach Hudson Bay, you'll be making fires in the pouring rain with your eyes closed." I said this as cheerfully as possible, though inwardly I was a little alarmed by Brent's inability to start a fire. He probably could have made one if he had merely shown some patience and concentration—but patience and concentration had never been his strong suits, and hordes of biting insects did little to improve this.

That night, I found it impossible to fall asleep, given the pain in my thumb. Painkillers were in the first aid kit stashed in my backpack outside the tent—but I long had an almost superstitious dread of anything, painkillers included, that dulled the mind. Plus it was cold outside. After two hours of lying there, I was still wide awake. Finally, I relented and crawled outside our tent into the cold darkness to fetch some painkillers, on the grounds that I needed a good night's sleep for the hard journey that awaited us.

THE NEXT DAY DAWNED warm, sunny, and windless, which made the blackflies and mosquitoes doubly atrocious. My mangled thumb felt as if someone had crushed it with a sledgehammer. The mantra "mind over matter" was my only comfort. After a quick breakfast of oatmeal—which I had to convince Brent to eat after he explained that as a rule he never ate breakfast—we set off to explore the towering canyon on foot. The lower slopes were a chaotic jumble of grey boulders and loose rocks that rose steeply to a vertical cliff face—the perfect terrain for twisting an ankle.

Brent stared wide-eyed at the imposing rock cliffs and offered his appraisal: there was no way we could scale those rocks.

I told him it would be easier than it looked. Brent was unconvinced.

"Well, we'll know soon enough," I said as we picked our way amid the boulders and loose rocks up the slope toward the rising precipice.

"It looks like Mordor," said Brent in a low voice, invoking his beloved *Lord of the Rings*.

I carried the blue flag of the Royal Canadian Geographical Society. The summit of the gorge seemed better than any place I could have imagined to be photographed with the Society's standard. We found an opening in the cliff face that wasn't quite vertical and managed to cautiously scramble our way up to the tabletop summit of the gorge. Straggly black spruces crowned the windswept summit. We hiked over to the edge of the gorge; far below a tiny stream trickled into Hawley Lake from Sutton Lake, which was on the southern side of the ridge. In all directions, we were surrounded by unbroken wilderness that stretched to the horizon.

Then we made an unexpected discovery. We spotted a huge mass of sticks perched on the interior wall of the gorge. With excitement, I realized that we were looking at a bald eagle's nest. According to the field guide I had stashed in my backpack, we were north of the bald eagle's range, but there was no doubt that eagles were around. I soon identified another nest on a ledge in the canyon. Brent thought that climate change might have pushed the eagle's habitat farther north. What was more likely, though, was that the field guide was simply wrong. That tends to happen with the exact ranges of birds, especially in remote parts of the world.

We photographed the eagles' nests with the intention of submitting a report to the Society of Canadian Ornithologists. Then we took the obligatory photographs with the Society's flag—carefully balancing our camera on a spruce branch in order to get one of us together. The blackflies on the summit, however, were extreme, so we soon cautiously climbed back down the cliffs to the forest below.

"Now what?" asked Brent, half out of breath.

"We portage around the gorge to Sutton Lake on the south side. It shouldn't be too difficult. The portage is only four hundred metres. We'll have to make three trips: one with our backpacks, then the food barrels, and finally the canoe. So, counting doubling back, we've got two kilometres to do."

"I guess that doesn't sound too bad," said Brent.

But the blackflies and mosquitoes were so intense that it proved a miserable ordeal that took the wind out of Brent's sails. He complained fiercely and, growing impatient with the heavy loads we carried under the hot sun, he carelessly tangled up our fishing rods while ducking under branches, struggling through thick forest. I was left to untangle the fishing lines, which was no pleasant task given that my face, neck, and hands were consumed by biting flies while I did so. As always, the blackflies not only attacked our necks, faces, and behind our ears, but also crawled up our shirts and bit our bodies. In 1743, English fur trader and naturalist James Isham furnished one of the best descriptions of the torments caused by the Lowlands' clouds of blackflies, which he knew as "flesh flies":

> Flesh flies are still more troublesome and offencive [than mosquitoes], they taking a piece wherever they Bite … these are Very troublesome to the beasts … the poor creatures running as … [if] persu'd by a much more formidable Enemy … into the water, where they Lay themselves Downe, under the Surface of the Water, to Keep these Vermin from Destroying them.

Fortunately, we were soon on the water again, away from the "flesh flies," paddling south along Sutton Lake.

The little canoe, however, was so tightly packed with our gear that there was little room for us, and none to stretch our legs. Within a few hours of paddling, our legs were sore to the point of numbness. I promised Brent that I would somehow devise a better way to pack our gear in the canoe so that we wouldn't be so cramped. At any rate, I assured Brent that after today, we wouldn't have much paddling to do for the next two weeks, as I anticipated mostly overland travel and portaging.

"Two weeks of portaging?" gasped Brent, horrified. In silence he stared off into the dark forest on the distant shore. I kept paddling.

Sutton Lake appeared much the same as Hawley Lake, a gem in a wilderness of gloomy swamp. It was about thirty-five kilometres long and over two kilometres across at the widest point, gouged out by a glacier some ten thousand years ago. Our plan was to hug the eastern shore for a distance of five or six kilometres, at which point we would begin our trek overland, commencing the long and laborious process of blazing our way to the headwaters of the river we had come to explore. We made camp that evening on the lake's eastern shore.

Once we had pitched the tent, we still had several hours of daylight, so I suggested to Brent that we head back out to scout the way forward and blaze a trail, which would save us time the next day. Brent agreed.

In the recesses of the forest, the mosquitoes and blackflies were twice as bad as in the open near the lakeshore. Therefore, we gave ourselves an extra dousing of bug spray and pulled our mesh bug nets over our heads. I tucked mine in beneath my faded brown fedora. As a rule, when confronted with some looming challenge, I always anticipate the worst, which usually allows me to remain unflappable in the face of any difficulty, since it is never as bad as what I had expected. With map and compass, I led the way into the gloom of the moss-draped woods. The ground near the lakeshore was soggy and uneven, but soon the country began rising and we were heading up a sparsely treed slope where a forest fire had burnt through some years before. Charred black spruces and tamaracks dotted the landscape, while juniper bushes and other emergent shrubbery cloaked the ground.

We had to maintain a course due east in order to find the nameless lake we were seeking. Aided by the setting sun, I navigated with my brass surveyor's compass. Meanwhile, Brent followed behind, blazing the straggly trees to mark a crude trail. The blazes were critical for when the time came to undertake the actual portage—the backbreaking labour of carrying our heavy backpacks, food barrels, and finally the canoe through the forest. I knew all too well that when struggling under heavy loads, swarmed by hordes of biting insects, staggering through at turns thick brush and open swamp, battling both physical and mental fatigue, only a few missteps would be sufficient to make us lose our way. For that reason, large blazes were essential.

"Remember, Brent, blaze the trees front and back. We have to be able to see them from both directions," I said, wiping sweat from my brow.

As we plunged onward, Brent began to tire—though more from lack of enthusiasm than physical exhaustion. His blaze marks were feeble and indistinct—we would never be able to spot them. Despite my gentle cautioning that he needed to make them bigger, Brent kept up with his timid hatchet strokes. Reluctantly, I took over with the hatchet, hacking four inch slices of bark off the tamaracks and spruces while still navigating with the compass. Navigating in the monotonous woods demanded considerable concentration, but I found myself having to multitask still further given the low state of Brent's morale. It was essential to keep his spirits high so that he would stay engaged in the journey—to that end, while swatting flies, hacking trees, and orienting with the compass, I kept up a cheerful banter on Brent's favourite subjects, trying to buoy his spirits. For a while it seemed as if we were making fine progress; we were on schedule, and the terrain wasn't as difficult as it had been in the Again River watershed. But as I continued to trudge along, slicing at the trees, I no longer heard Brent behind me. I turned around, and he was nowhere in sight.

"Brent? Where are you?" There was no reply. I retraced my steps and came upon Brent standing statue-like behind a cluster of black spruces, a dumbstruck expression on his face.

"What's wrong?"

Brent snapped out of his reverie and looked at me. "Adam," he said slowly and with emphasis, "this is totally insane. There is no way in hell we can portage through this."

I tried to laugh it off. "Of course we can. It's not that difficult. Wes and I have done worse."

"There is no way we can carry the canoe through this. Just portaging around the gorge was hard enough. Doing this would be *impossible*."

"Everyone feels like that at the start of any big expedition. It's natural. It takes a while to get used to the routine. Once you get broken in, you'll find it much easier," I said, trying to hide my exasperation.

"Adam, there's no way I'll ever find this easy. It's too far. This is far worse than I imagined." Brent paused. "I want to go home."

"Brent, you listened to my stories, saw my pictures, you knew what it was like. And we're committed now, we can't quit. We have no choice but to continue."

"I never imagined it would be this bad. I have to quit. I'm dead serious. I want to go home. This is awful. I'm sorry, but there's no way I can stay here." It didn't help that just then the blackflies were thick as storm clouds around us.

"You can't quit. It'll get better, I promise. We can go back to camp and rest, and start again tomorrow. You'll feel better then."

"No, I won't. Even at camp there's no comfort. Everything about this is terrible."

"Brent, no matter what, I won't quit. If you won't go on, I'll just leave you here," I said firmly.

"Adam!"

"I'm serious, Brent. Your only choice is to follow me."

"Where's the satellite phone? I want to call a pilot to come back and pick me up."

"That'll cost you a fortune; the pilot will charge you an arm and a leg for that."

"I don't care. I have to get out of here."

"Brent, pull yourself together. We've barely done anything and you already want to quit," I said angrily. "Don't you have any pride? Everyone will think less of you if you quit."

"I don't care. They have no idea what it's actually like. They would all quit too if they were here—any normal person who valued their life would."

"You're just freaking out because of how raw this feels to you. It happens to lots of people when they're exposed to hardship for the first time. Even Wes wanted to quit on our first expedition. It takes time to get used to things, especially since you've never done anything like this before."

"I can't do this."

I was now furious at Brent's poor effort and his obstinate refusal to push on. We returned through the forest to our camp on the lakeshore, where we continued arguing. Brent insisted that I take him back to the cabins on Hawley Lake and leave him there until we could find a pilot to fly him back to civilization. To do so would mean the end of the expedition and the abandonment of my dreams and what I had strived for years to achieve. Tension between us was at the breaking point when out of the corner of my left eye I noticed something lumbering up the lakeshore.

"Look over there," I said in a hushed whisper of excitement. A large caribou was trotting along the lake in our direction. It had a huge rack of antlers and was the finest specimen I had ever seen. It looked like it could have been the model for a royal coat of arms. The caribou paid no heed to us and nonchalantly wandered right past our camp, no more than ten metres from where we sat.

"It has no fear of us," said Brent, staring transfixed at the magnificent animal.

Our unexpected visitor seemed to have raised his spirits a little, and it cheered our mood. If I handled the situation adroitly, I figured I could convince Brent to carry on. With that aim in mind, I kept up the conversation on caribou and other wildlife, as Brent loved animals, while building a heartening fire to keep the bugs away and cook supper.

That night, as we ate Kraft Dinner, I did my best to inspire Brent with stirring stories of adventure. The conversation drifted from Greek mythology to *The Lord of the Rings*, history and legend, great men and great deeds, of "immortal longings" and why we had to find the strength and fortitude to carry on. In other words, I pulled out all the stops. In the flickering light of our campfire, I could see the fire return to Brent's brown eyes; my words were gradually winning him over. He became steadily more animated as I talked of overcoming whatever dangers and difficulties lay in our path, and how a few weeks of hardship is worth it for a lifetime of proud reflection. Somehow I succeeded in building up his spirits again. We went to bed that night feeling better. Brent said he would sleep on it and decide in the morning whether to quit or continue.

WHEN WE CRAWLED out of our nylon tent into the cool, misty morning, Brent's spirits were again low. He looked miserable. In the hopes of encouraging him, I quickly made a fire, cooked some oatmeal, and put on a pot of tea. "How did you sleep?" I asked.

"Horrible," replied Brent.

An awkward silence followed while I finished preparing breakfast for us. It was demoralizing knowing that all the work of building up Brent's spirits had seemingly come to nothing. He appeared as lacklustre and shaken as ever. When I could bear the silence no longer, I asked him how he felt.

"I still want to quit. I can't sleep in the tent. The ground is hard and uncomfortable, and it's freezing at night. Without sleep, I have no energy. The bugs are unreal, worse than I could ever imagine. The work is too hard and dangerous. I want to go home."

"You'll get used to it. I promise."

"I don't think I could ever get used to this. I'm not made for this sort of thing."

"You are what you make yourself," I said. It was my personal motto.

We argued for some time, more gently and reservedly than the night before, but Brent finally broke down and wept.

"I'll never make it. I'll die. I know it. I want to go home."

As angry as I was, it was impossible not to pity Brent—he didn't have an ounce of pride left. He was afraid and made no secret of it. To push him any further seemed not only cruel but certain to cause him to experience some sort of breakdown. I couldn't force him to undertake the gruelling portage. There was nothing for it. Reluctantly, I agreed to retrace our route back to the cabins on Hawley Lake, some thirty kilometres away. I hoped that on the journey back I could somehow build up Brent's confidence and willpower enough to continue. After all, Brent was new to expeditions and needed time to adjust to life in the subarctic Lowlands.

"All right, we'll head back to Hawley Lake," I said.

We packed up our camp, loaded the canoe, and then launched it back into the clear blue waters of Sutton Lake. We had to perform the portage around the rocky gorge a second time.

Brent, eager to return home, displayed considerably more zeal portaging back than he had the day before when we were headed in the opposite direction. Thinking that some fresh fish might help fortify him, after we had finished the portage I cast a line in the lake. It didn't take long to land a good-sized northern pike.

"This will make for a great lunch," I said happily. I set the pike down in the bottom of the canoe, where it flopped about. Unsheathing my old belt knife, which had once belonged to my father, I reached down to fillet the fish.

"Adam—" Brent suddenly spoke up from the bow of the canoe, "look at it. We can't kill it. Don't you feel sorry for it? Poor fish. Let it go."

"Are you serious?"

"Just look at how helpless it looks." Brent's eyes were full of pity for the pike. He wasn't joking.

Not wanting to upset him, given the fragile state of his already deflated spirits, I reluctantly released the pike unharmed back into the lake. It bolted off into the weeds as soon as it touched the water. In all the years I had known Brent, he had never expressed the slightest interest in becoming a vegetarian. His objection to killing the fish was sentimental rather than philosophical. Regardless, we resumed paddling up the lake without the benefit of any fresh protein.

Another wandering caribou trotted along the shore. A pair of loons swam in the blue waters ahead of us, hunting for fish, and making what Theodore Roosevelt, a keen ornithologist, described as "the unholy laughter of a loon." As a child I had learned how to imitate the loon's haunting call by whistling through my hands. It was a skill I found useful for impressing tourists in Algonquin Park. Meanwhile, on the sparsely treed eastern shore of Hawley Lake, something was moving up the rising slope. It was too far off to make out clearly.

"Brent, look—do you see something on the far shore there?" I pointed out the dark objects.

Brent squinted. "Yeah I do, what is it?"

I fetched the binoculars from my backpack. "Two black bear cubs," I said, having focused on them.

"That's what I thought!" said Brent excitedly.

"I wonder where their mother is," I replied, still with my eyes pressed against the binoculars. The velvety black cubs looked less than a year old, but they soon disappeared from view into the brush. We continued paddling along Hawley Lake; the abundant wildlife seemed to raise Brent's spirits. I suggested that if he stuck around, we might even see a wolverine or pack of grey wolves. This seemed to encourage him. When we reached the north shore of Hawley Lake, opposite the squalid little hunt camp, the time came for a decision. Like any explorer worth his salt, I hadn't come this far without formulating contingency plans. We could still explore the alternative nameless river, which wouldn't involve much portaging. I told Brent about it.

"We would have to travel upriver, against the current, wading through the water and dragging the canoe behind us for about a hundred and twenty kilometres."

"Drag a canoe against the current *for over a hundred kilometres?* That sounds horrible. We'll die of hypothermia."

"Well, it's either that or portage."

"I can't portage. Nothing in the world could make me go back into those awful woods."

There was a third option—but it was so dangerous that I was reluctant to mention it. Still, since Brent wouldn't consider the other two options, I now sketched it out: "I suppose we could try another way. We could paddle down the Sutton River to Hudson Bay, then try to canoe along the coast of Hudson Bay to the mouth of the Brant River, then work our way on foot up the Brant to the nameless tributary. We can probably walk along the shore, its open tundra, and drag the canoe behind us easily enough. Then we'd canoe the Brant's tributary back to the coast, before canoeing along Hudson Bay to the mouth of the Sutton to finish."

Actually, this route wasn't much easier than my preferred one—but it would entail a relatively simple week while we canoed down the Sutton River. I figured this time might prove ample to build up Brent's spirits and adjust him to life in the wilderness, after which he could endure the real bushwhacking and exploring.

Brent hesitated for a while, weighing his options. I wasn't sure whether he understood what the plan I had sketched out involved exactly—and I was in no mood to explain it. It was well after dark when he finally came to a resolution. Sitting by the crackling fire in the quiet of the night, Brent spoke at last. "I'll see it through. I won't quit. I'm not entirely useless, you know. If we stick to this new plan, I'll keep going," he vowed solemnly.

"Excellent," I replied. "I knew you wouldn't quit."

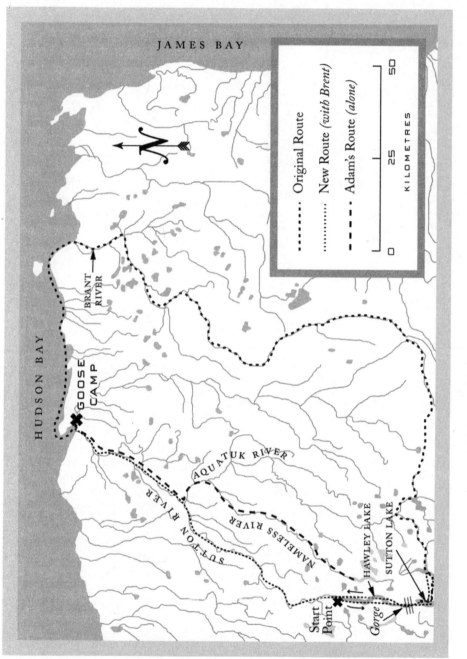

NAMELESS RIVER EXPEDITION ROUTES

JAMES BAY

HUDSON BAY

BRANT RIVER

GOOSE CAMP

AQUATUK RIVER

SUTTON RIVER

NAMELESS RIVER

HAWLEY LAKE

SUTTON LAKE

Start Point

Gorge

KILOMETRES

0   25   50

Original Route
New Route (with Brent)
Adam's Route (alone)

[4]

DOWNRIVER

There is nothing—absolutely nothing—half so much worth doing as simply messing about in boats.
—Kenneth Grahame, *The Wind in the Willows*, 1908

S UNBURNT FROM THE LONG DAY spent canoeing through the lakes, the following morning we began our descent of the Sutton River, which drains Hawley Lake, flowing northward some 133 kilometres to the salt water of Hudson Bay. In his expedition notes, D.B. Dowling had referred to it as the "Trout River" and made no mention of canoeing it. The river was too small and shallow to have served as a historic fur trade river—in places the water was less than ankle deep—but Cree trappers had travelled it for generations. Its waters were rich with brook trout, and no major rapids were on its winding course. We would paddle it out to Hudson Bay—and hopefully by the time we got there, Brent would be a new man—hardened and prepared for the real work of the expedition.

The Swampy Cree, or *Omushkego*, had survived here for centuries. They were described in the 1930s by anthropologist Diamond Jenness as "adventurous hunters and warriors who had traversed half the Dominion" in their heyday. They had ranged farther than almost any other aboriginal group in North America, across much of the boreal forest and onto the Great Plains, waging war against such distant enemies as the Chipewyans, Assiniboine, and even the Inuit. Despite his admiration for their prowess, Jenness had spent too much time immersed in the northern wild to romanticize their hard lives. He noted that historically among the Cree, "Old people who could no longer keep up ... were abandoned to starve or killed at their own request." Nor was this custom confined to the Cree—it seems to have been common among most northern hunter-gatherers. It was, as author Jack London put it, "the immutable law of the northland." But these same unforgiving conditions made the Cree such intrepid travellers. One individual I had long admired was George Elson, a half Cree, half Scottish explorer who had grown up near James Bay in the southern part of the Lowlands.

Elson had spent his youth honing his knowledge and skills when, in 1903, he was recruited by a couple of American explorers—Leonidas Hubbard and Dillon Wallace—for an expedition into the heart of uncharted Labrador. Elson was asked to meet his new companions in New York City. Despite never having seen a city before, Elson travelled over sixteen hundred kilometres to reach New York City alone, and arrived unfazed in what was, to the James Bay Cree, unexplored territory. Like his European counterparts, he too would return to his own community with new knowledge of strange places and peoples. With Hubbard and Wallace, Elson set out for the interior of Labrador—a place equally mysterious and unknown to all three men. In the mountainous interior of Labrador,

Elson emerged as the real leader of the expedition. Wallace wrote of him: "I do not believe that in all the north country we could have found a better woodsman. But he was something more than a woodsman—he was a hero." Conditions in Labrador proved to be so difficult that even with Elson's superb skills, the trio faced a grim death from starvation as the winter closed in on them. Hubbard eventually succumbed, while Wallace grew too weak to move. With almost superhuman strength and against great odds, Elson managed to stagger back through snowdrifts to reach Grand Lake in central Labrador. Ever resourceful, he built a raft to traverse the lake and reach the nearest trapper's cabin, finding help for the ailing Wallace. As if this adventure hadn't been remarkable enough, two years later, Elson returned to Labrador with Hubbard's iron-willed widow, Mina, who insisted on finishing the expedition her husband had died attempting. Together, they triumphantly finished what Leonidas had started. Afterwards, Elson returned to James Bay, married a Cree woman, and lived out his days as a hero of exploration.

The Sutton River was as beautiful a stream in the Hudson Bay Lowlands as I had ever seen—much prettier than the swampy waterways I had been navigating the past number of years. Its shallow waters were clear as crystal. The upper stretch had high sandbanks, which looked like dunes one would expect on a beach rather than a subarctic river. Waterfowl was everywhere: ducklings and goslings swam in procession after their parents, while terns, gulls, and plovers hopped along the muddy, pebbly shorelines. Perched in the spruces and tamaracks growing along the grassy banks were enormous bald eagles, which feasted on the river's abundant brook trout. At first glance, it appeared to be a pristine wilderness untouched by humans. But upon closer inspection, signs of human use were evident. There were past campsites on favourable river bends, even a few old cabins built by Cree trappers, and the attendant litter from these sites. This was something I had learned years ago—that generally speaking, a river, no matter how far-flung, if used by humans, will retain signs of their presence. I could only wonder if on the nameless river we were seeking we would find any evidence that people had been there previously. Of course, whether someone had or had not been there before was only of consequence to me personally; it had no bearing on our objective for the Geographical Society, which was to record the river through photographs, film, mapping, and a detailed written description.

The Sutton River, for most of its course, was about eighty metres wide. Small rapids, little more than undulating swifts of rushing water around boulders, appeared in the river with increasing frequency as we journeyed onward. Just as we neared the first sizable rapid, a caribou dashed through the shallows near the far shore. For a moment, as we drifted into the white-water, it looked as if this rather pugnacious caribou had a mind to charge us.

"Do caribou charge people?" asked Brent, staring suspiciously at the animal's impressive antlers.

"Not to my knowledge," I replied, while steering the canoe around an oncoming boulder.

"This one looks like it might want to," Brent said anxiously. The big caribou was directly facing us, no more than thirty metres away, standing in ankle-deep water.

Suddenly the canoe banged into an unseen boulder beneath the surface, jarring us sideways in the current. "Oh! There's a rock!" exclaimed Brent, turning from the staring caribou.

"I noticed."

"My bad," replied Brent. As the bowman, it was his job to keep an eye out for rocks, while I piloted us around them from the stern.

The caribou remained watching us as we drifted closer to the shallows near the river bend it occupied. I cautiously paddled us forward. Then, just as the caribou appeared ready to charge through the shallow water at our canoe, it pivoted sideways and struck a pose. It stood statue-like in the water, looking rather vainglorious.

"I think it's interested in pursuing a modelling career with *Canadian Geographic*," remarked Brent. We photographed the caribou for several minutes while it stood striking poses in the river. Then abruptly it dashed off along the river's edge, before disappearing into the alder bushes onshore.

We soon stopped on a treeless, grassy island in the river to gather tiny but delicious wild strawberries. The intensity of the blackflies, which only breed in running water and which the Sutton amply provided, prevented the moment from becoming too idyllic. As well, unfortunately Brent was sick with a cold he had been battling for a few days before we arrived. And I now felt I was picking up his illness: my throat was sore, my nose was stuffed up, and I was developing a headache. But my love of wilderness—my delight at discovering what lay beyond each river bend—the expectation of glimpsing another eagle swooping down to capture a trout or duckling in its talons or a beaver slapping its tail on the water to warn others that intruders were approaching—kept my spirits high. Brent too, despite his cold, seemed to be enjoying himself and took readily to photographing wildlife. The journey thus far wasn't overly difficult: paddling the river was fairly easy—though my back was still sore and my mangled thumb ached horribly. Frequently we were forced to get out of the canoe and wade through shallow stretches. This, however, was no real danger even this far north, so long as the weather remained warm and sunny. Otherwise hypothermia, which kills more people in North America's wilderness than all deaths by wild animals combined, could prove a hazard. As it was, our first few days canoeing the Sutton were as tranquil as could be expected in the Hudson Bay Lowlands.

Indeed, seldom in the history of exploration has anything proved as bleak and deadly as the inhospitable Lowlands was to early explorers. If even aboriginal people regarded the Lowlands as "sterile country," unfit for permanent habitation, one can only imagine what the first Europeans made of the place. Mortality rates on early expeditions to the Lowlands were astoundingly high. The first European explorers had reached the Lowlands by ship. They sailed across the North Atlantic, through Hudson Strait, into the uncharted immensity of Hudson Bay, and worked their way down to what is the Bay's southwestern coastline. They had come seeking a northwest passage to Asia that wasn't to be found.

The first of these pioneering mariners was the English navigator Henry Hudson, who arrived on the body of water that now bears his name in the spring of 1611 on-board his ship, the *Discovery*. He wintered on the more hospitable eastern shore of James Bay, which unlike the Lowlands of the western coast is not swampy and therefore has much better stands of timber, essential for surviving long winters. The following spring, however, Hudson's crew mutinied when he announced his intention to push on westward. Hudson, along with his son and seven other loyal retainers were cruelly set adrift in a tiny lifeboat on James Bay. They were never seen again and probably perished somewhere on James Bay's windswept coast. Of the thirteen mutineers, only eight made it back to England alive.

Eight years later, in 1619, the resourceful and talented Scandinavian explorer Jens Munk sailed into Hudson Bay in the service of the Danish king, with sixty-three men under his command. They wintered on the bleak coastline near the northern reaches of the Lowlands, building squalid shelters to survive in. As the unforgiving winter dragged on, men began to drop like flies from scurvy, a horrendous disease brought on by a lack of vitamin C. No aboriginal people were to be found anywhere—though on a trek inland, Munk and his men found a pictograph drawn on a rock that depicted what they thought was the devil. Truly, it must have seemed as if they had strayed into some northern hell. By the time the ice melted in spring, only three of the original sixty-four men were left alive. Incredibly, Munk, who had survived the punishing winter along with two other weakened crew members, managed to sail his ship home to Denmark, an astonishing feat of seamanship.

For aboriginal people, the Lowlands was a place where starvation was a fact of life. English explorer Charles Bayly, who sailed into James Bay in 1674, reported starvation among "Indians" near the mouth of the Ekwan River, on the Bay's western shore. Bayly observed that the natives seldom ventured into the Lowlands and spent the winters far in the interior, away from the swamps. Other explorers, when they chanced to encounter anyone at all, witnessed similar cases of starvation. Life in the Lowlands was, as Bayly's contemporary Thomas Hobbes would have put it, "nasty, brutish, and short." Making conditions even more extreme during this era of exploration was the so-called Little Ice Age, a climatic anomaly that saw the northern hemisphere's average temperature drop several degrees from the fourteenth through the mid-nineteenth centuries. Even the Lowlands' brief summers brought no relief—many explorers found the incessant attacks of mosquitoes and blackflies worse than the torments of winter. The bloodsucking insects literally drove men mad. Suicide was common at the fur trade forts built at the mouths of the Lowlands' major rivers, namely the Severn, Albany, and Moose.

ONE EVENING, after a week in the wilderness, preoccupied with rigging up a tarp between some stunted spruce trees to keep off the rain, I dispatched Brent to gather firewood. He took my hatchet and headed off into the shadowy forest that sprang up some twenty metres beyond the treeless, grassy riverbanks. Off in the woods, I could soon hear him chopping up a storm. "Well that's good," I thought to myself. "Brent seems to be getting the hang of this."

A good fifteen minutes later, Brent emerged from the woods, triumphantly dragging a sizable tamarack tree behind him. In despair, I saw that he had chopped down a live tree.

"Brent," I said incredulously. "That's not a dead tree, it won't burn."

"Oh, it *will* burn," replied Brent confidently.

"No," I said quietly, "green wood doesn't burn." Though I said nothing more, I was mystified by how Brent, after a week in the wilderness, hadn't absorbed the simple lesson that only dry, dead wood goes into a fire. He had, after all, seen and to some extent helped me make fires and cook our meals twice a day for the past week. Sensing his frustration at having exerted himself pointlessly, I tried to soften his disappointment.

"You did do a good job chopping down that tamarack," I said light-heartedly. "Maybe we can use it as a pole to help hoist up that side of the tarp."

"I'm useless here," Brent mumbled, discouraged.

"Not at all," I said. "You've been doing well in the canoe. You have excellent balance, and you paddle as well as Wes."

"Really?" Brent shrugged modestly. It was one of his most likeable traits that even when he had been the best player on our hockey team, he never boasted of his talents. He was invariably self-effacing.

We headed back into the swamp forest to look for some proper firewood, pushing past tamaracks and black spruce.

"It's so quiet here, it gets on my nerves," Brent whispered as he stared at the crooked, moss-draped trees. He was experiencing what Theodore Roosevelt referred to as "the perfect silence so strange and almost oppressive to the novice" that comes with northern wilderness.

"At least, we're from the countryside," I said as I stripped some dead branches from a spruce. "Imagine how much of a shock it'd be for someone from a city to be out here. Whenever I go to a city, I can't get over the noise."

"You say that as if a city is the most horrible thing in the world."

"To me it is," I shuddered. "Nothing horrifies me more than the thought of a place without wilderness."

"Nothing horrifies me more than wilderness," Brent muttered.

When I looked at the forest, I saw a fascinating place full of enchantment and wonder. Brent saw only a grim, alien environment.

That night, as we lay huddled in our sleeping bags inside the tent, a growling noise arose from somewhere in the darkness. I bolted upright and reached for my knife. My heartbeat quickened. Brent was asleep next to me.

"Brent," I whispered, nudging him. "Did you hear that?"

He mumbled inaudibly.

"Brent, I heard something growl outside."

"What?" he hissed back, now awake.

"Yeah, it—wait, there it is again."

Brent looked over at me. "That's my stomach."

"What?"

"That growling is my stomach."

"Are you kidding me?"

"No. That macaroni and cheese isn't cutting it for me anymore. Do we have any midnight snacks?"

As a rule, we never kept food inside the tent. Any food, even the wrapper of a granola bar, could attract black bears, which have a remarkably keen sense of smell. While plenty of black bears were around, we were still outside the nominal range of polar bears, which typically remain near the seacoast. I crawled outside the tent in the darkness to fetch one of our plastic food containers, in order to find some granola bars for Brent. Against my better judgment, I allowed him to eat them in the tent, since he complained that it was too cold to get out of his sleeping bag. Thinking his borrowed sleeping bag wasn't quite as warm as mine, I gave him my extra sweater. At night, the temperature had been dipping down to about two or three degrees Celsius.

Later that night, our sleep was again disturbed. A crashing noise came from the forest behind us. I grabbed my flashlight and knife, unzipped the tent door, and cautiously stepped out to investigate. The noise continued for a moment—then abruptly ceased. The gloom of the flashlight failed to illuminate anything but the vague shapes of contorted trees swaying in the wind.

"Probably just a caribou," I told Brent as I crawled back inside the tent. Exhausted from the long hours spent paddling, we soon fell back asleep.

SINCE BRENT SAID that he was hungry, I insisted that we resume fishing, regardless of his objections to killing anything. No matter what his state of mind, I could no longer restrain myself from casting a line for the river's delicious brook trout. Thinking to cheer Brent a little, when we stopped to rest at midday, I prepared the fishing rod for him and encouraged him to try a cast in a deep pool at the foot of a rapid.

"All right," said Brent, "but I have no talent for fishing."

"That's not true. I remember you caught a nice smallmouth bass on that canoe trip we did back in high school."

"Oh, that's right. I forgot about that." Evidently feeling more confident with the memory of what, I believe, was probably the only fish he ever caught, Brent boldly grasped the fishing rod and cast it toward the pool. The lure landed in the branch of a spruce tree near the bank. "Damn," muttered Brent.

"That's all right … happens to the best of us," I said as I untangled the line from the tree. I encouraged Brent to try again. This time, he landed the lure right in the pool. Just as he began to reel it in, a fish struck. It was a beautiful four-pound speckled trout. His next cast brought in another trout of equal size.

"Two fish on only two casts," I said, impressed.

"Three if you count the cast that landed in the tree," Brent corrected.

That night we feasted on trout, blueberries, and raspberries, and drank hot chocolate before rain forced us to take cover in the tent. On the bright side, Brent so enjoyed the fresh fish that I heard no more objections to catching them.

THE NEXT DAY, as we were canoeing, the sky turned dark grey with alarming swiftness. Flashes of lightning appeared. "We have to take shelter," I said from the stern. I didn't want to risk paddling out in the open in a storm.

"Can't we just ride it out?" asked Brent. It was a quirk of his that, despite his habitual laziness, once we started on a day of paddling, Brent didn't generally like to stop for anything.

"No. It's too risky. We can't be out in the open on the water like this with lightning." I counted the intervals between the bursts of thunder and the lightning flashes. The storm was close and getting closer. We headed for the river's grass-covered shoreline. We couldn't risk sitting under any trees to take refuge from the rain. But with our paddles as a frame, I quickly rigged up the tarp for us to shelter under. Brent curled up in the mud, out of the rain yet visibly dejected.

"This is horrible," he moaned.

"It will pass soon enough."

The wind blew so hard off Hudson Bay that the storm was over shortly, though the rain continued. We launched the canoe back into the river and resumed our journey. As we snaked our way farther north along the windy river, the trees grew smaller and more sparse. Soon we caught our first glimpses of open, windswept tundra. With no trees here to block the wind, we were at the mercy of the elements. We came to a straight section of river, where it proved impossible to make any headway against the fierce wind and lashing rain. The wind was so strong that it felt like we were paddling upriver.

"This wind is unreal!" shouted Brent above the gale.

"Let's paddle hard until we reach the next bend!" I shouted back.

We dug our paddles furiously into the waves, trying to fight our way against the billowing wind to no avail. My teeth were chattering in the cold.

"Man," I heard Brent mutter, "my legs are fucked. They feel asleep."

Brent's words snapped me into action. "Your legs aren't asleep. We're starting to get hypothermia. We're losing feeling." I couldn't feel my legs either, drenched as they were from wading through the shallows and from the steady rain.

"What do we do?" asked Brent.

"Head for shore," I replied, paddling furiously.

The muddy shoreline had high, treeless banks that rose to a height of nearly ten metres. We reached the shore in short order, but stumbled like drunkards as we tried to stand on our numb legs in the mud. Staggering about, I led Brent up the steep embankment into the scruff of stunted forest.

"We have to find a big tree to shelter under," I said, trying to keep Brent engaged as we struggled on. We were lucky to come across a big spruce, which protected us from the wind and rain.

"Try jumping around and waving your arms to keep warm as I make a fire," I told Brent.

Most of the wood was wet, but from the dead inner branches of the spruce I stripped enough dry wood to build a teepee of sticks. Hypothermia in the subarctic is nothing to fool with. I knew that Brent's life, and my own, depended on getting a fire going in the rain and wind. I crouched down around the teepee of sticks, trying to shelter it from the elements, and instructed Brent to do the same. With a match from my pocket, I lit some old man's beard, a type of lichen that grows on tree branches, and dry spruce needles, which I had stored inside a zip-lock bag in my pocket for just such an emergency. Ever so slowly, with numb fingers and chattering teeth, I built up the fire.

"I didn't think it was possible to make a fire," mumbled Brent.

"I can always make a fire," I said, tossing on more sticks. Though in truth I had been a little alarmed by the prospects, given the rain, wind, and lack of forest cover. "Keep adding dry branches from this spruce," I said, showing Brent the ones to break off.

"Where are you going?"

"Back down to the canoe," I said, feeling chilled to the bone, "we need to make some hot soup to warm up. Stay by the fire."

My legs were still wobbly as I jogged awkwardly through the scrub forest back to the embankment and our beached canoe. Out in the open once again, I was soaked by the rain, though my army rain jacket kept my torso and arms dry. I stumbled over to the canoe and with trembling hands unfastened the metal ring of one of the food barrels, which kept it watertight. I quickly dug out the pot for boiling water, two packages of Mr. Noodles soup, bowls and spoons, and stainless steel mugs for a hot drink. The pot filled with river water, I staggered back to where I had left Brent.

"It's fucking freezing," said Brent. In my absence, the fire had nearly gone out. Setting the pot of water down, I rapidly built the fire back up with more spruce branches.

"Keep rubbing your hands for warmth," I said. I set the pot over the fire and kept working to build the blaze up as big as possible. In ten minutes, the water had boiled, and our soup was ready.

"How are your legs now?" I asked.

"Much better. I'm good to keep going."

"Let's wait for the rain to stop and make some tea in the meantime." I didn't want to risk a second bout with hypothermia, especially since I knew the prospects of finding dry wood would continue to dwindle as we headed farther north. I broke off some green spruce twigs and tossed them in the pot. Spruce tea, a traditional drink among woodsmen, is rich in vitamin C. In terms of concentration, spruce contains more vitamin C than orange juice. If only Jens Munk, the Danish explorer, had known this his crew might well have survived the ravages of scurvy that plagued their expedition.

"What would you have done if you couldn't start a fire?" Brent wondered aloud, sipping his spruce tea.

"I can always start a fire," I replied. While at home, I made it a habit to cook my lunches over fires on rainy days, in order to keep my skills sharp.

"But what if you couldn't?"

"Body warmth would be our only option."

"Body warmth?"

"Yeah, we would have to strip naked and huddle together in the tent."

"Oh God!" cried Brent.

HUDSON BAY

To take up great resolutions, and then to lay them aside,
only ends in dishonour.
—Snorri Sturluson, *The Saga of Olaf Tryggvason*, twelfth century AD

O N THE FOLLOWING DAY, we reached the tundra proper, leaving behind the comparative comforts of the scrubby coniferous forest. The vast expanse of almost treeless, green tundra looked strangely like the grasslands of Saskatchewan. Here the permafrost—ice beneath the ground that never melts— prevents trees from taking root in the soil. The wind howled across the open plain. In the river ahead, we could see two caribou swimming across a deep pool, while another lay languidly onshore. The day before we had encountered our first moose on the expedition, finding it standing in the river behind a small island. Ducks and geese remained plentiful. The young ducklings and goslings would flee the river as we drew near, running off into the bushes while their parents feigned injuries to distract us. Not that this was necessary, as Brent and I weren't interested in killing anything other than the occasional fish. Hunting for pleasure had never appealed to me. My inclination was not to kill anything unless doing so was strictly necessary—and we had packed ample food rations, supplemented with fish and wild berries. The shotgun that we were carrying was strictly for protection against polar bears.

Brent's enthusiasm for our journey was fading. I made all the fires, did the cooking, set up the tent, packed our backpacks and the canoe, took care of navigating, and performed most of the paddling. At times, Brent seemed to slip into an almost comatose state, as if the incessant bugs and dreary weather had left him shell-shocked. Wrenched from the cozy, work-free life he had been living, Brent was finding the rigours of our daily routine a tough adjustment.

Yet we seldom became angry with each other. After all, not for nothing had we been friends for eighteen years. The history of exploration had taught me that camaraderie and good interpersonal dynamics were crucial to success. It was a lesson that Sir Ernest Shackleton took so seriously that he often selected men for his Antarctic voyages less on their knowledge and skills and more on their ability to crack a joke, play an instrument, or laugh off any difficulty. Many an expedition had floundered or ended in tragedy because its participants couldn't stand each other. On John Franklin's horrendous expedition through the heart of the Canadian subarctic in the 1820s, tensions among his men came to a breaking point: Dr. John Richardson, a tough, scholarly type, pulled out his pistol and shot a voyageur, accusing him of having been behind the death of another member of their party. Since Brent and I were together all day and slept side by side in a tiny six-by-four-foot tent with a shotgun and an assortment of knives between us, it was essential that we remain on good terms. Brent's self-deprecating humour, his love of animals, and our collective reminiscing about our high school days and hockey teams made getting along surprisingly easy.

"Remember our grade eleven biology class?" asked Brent.

"Of course," I replied, "I did a project on the eastern cougar."

"I didn't do any projects," said Brent proudly.

"I remember, your final mark was a forty-eight."

"Forty-seven," corrected Brent.

"Except we made sure you passed."

Brent laughed. With the assistance of Wes, who had acted as a sentry in the hallway, Brent and I had logged onto our teacher's computer while she had left the classroom on an errand. We adjusted his marks so that he would pass the course, with none the wiser. Alas for Brent, he didn't have Wes and me in all his classes and ended up—from sheer laziness, not lack of intellect—failing enough to force him to do an extra year of school.

By day ten of the expedition we were nearing the mouth of the Sutton River on the bleak coast of Hudson Bay. The tundra was all around us now, though clumps of spruces, willows, and alder bushes served to break up the landscape. Soon I would discover whether the week canoeing downriver had been enough to fortify Brent for the real travails that lay ahead.

"There's an old cabin, a goose hunting shack built by natives from Peawanuck, on an island near the mouth of the river," I said, drawing a stroke of my paddle.

"How do you know that?" asked Brent from the bow.

"I read it in the journal of some geographers and explorers who canoed the Sutton ten years ago."

Brent convinced himself that this old cabin was probably quite accommodating and built up his expectations that we would soon have a respite from sleeping in the tent, which he despised.

"It was ten years ago, Brent. The cabin is probably an abandoned ruin today," I cautioned.

"I bet it's actually quite nice," said Brent confidently.

Excited to reach the cabin, Brent paddled with renewed enthusiasm. We were now within the haunt of polar bears and had to be extra cautious of them. It was the most dangerous time and place to be in polar bear territory—summer on the shore of Hudson Bay. All the sea ice by this time had melted, forcing the bears, which normally remain on the ice hunting seals, to come ashore and fast until the return of the ice in the fall. During this time, a hungry bear will kill anything: caribou, walrus, humans— the males will even cannibalize smaller bears. The shotgun rested in its case behind my seat in the canoe.

Brent was breathtakingly naive about the dangers posed by polar bears—he seemed to regard them as harmless and misunderstood plant-eaters. But I knew better. A passage I had once read in biologist Jerome Knap's classic *Canadian Hunter's Handbook* was seared in my mind: "Hunting polar bears ... is sport for big game hunters who want to experience maximum thrills and danger. It is not for the physically frail and soft. The polar bear is not afraid of man. It recognizes no enemy." Ranking as the earth's largest land carnivore, the biggest polar bear ever recorded weighed a staggering 2,209 pounds and stood over 11 feet tall on its hind legs. These monarchs of the north are so powerful that they can effortlessly break through cabin doors and even plow through electric-fenced compounds, which one did in 2013 in a remote part of northern Labrador. A group of seven hikers was camped inside an electric fence they set up around their campsite, when one night a polar bear burst through the barrier and severely mauled one of the group. In fact, at the same time Brent and I were en route to Hudson Bay, a polar bear attacked a twelve-person expedition in Svalbard, shredding through a tent in the night and mauling one of its occupants to death. In one particularly horrifying incident in 1990, a bear chased down a man in broad daylight in Point Lay, Alaska, killed him, and consumed his corpse on the town's main street.

It was understandable why government policy recommended nothing smaller than a party of four adults, all armed, when travelling in polar bear territory—and why scientists study the bears via helicopter or from within electric-fenced compounds. Travelling by canoe or on foot in polar bear territory is not for the faint-hearted. American canoeist and wilderness traveller Cliff Jacobson, a veteran of many Arctic trips, recorded his experience with polar bears while canoeing in northern Manitoba in 1992:

> July 20 [1992]: Coming around a bend, my partner Joanie points and says: "Hey, Cliff, look at that mountain goat up there!" Seconds later the goat materializes into a full-grown male polar bear, which slides down the bank and swims straight toward our canoe.... Soon as the boat touches land I'm out, rifle in hand and praying I won't have to shoot. Seconds later Dick and Finette arrive,

sheet white … everyone massed in a tiny group, scared as hell, me clutching the half-cocked Marlin while Dick drops shotgun slugs into the sand and Tom gropes for a pack of shells…. We've arranged tents like a fort. Perimeter teams have capsaicin (bear mace). I served everyone double shots of Pusser's rum…. Twenty miles from Hudson Bay we came upon Doug Webber's hunting cabin. The windows were heavily barred and huge spikes protruded from the door—testimony to the destructive power of polar bears. We saw another cabin on Hudson Bay … which had been invaded by curious bears. Everything … had been torn to shreds. We climbed onto the roof … and promptly saw two more bears. After that no one went out without a gun.

Jacobson concluded:

Polar bears are not like other bears. They can swim faster—even through rapids—than I can paddle my canoe. You can't outrun a polar bear, and there are no trees on the tundra big enough to climb…. A charging polar bear can cover 100 yards in about three seconds, which is faster than most people can fire an accurate shot.

When I told Brent this story, it seemed to have a sobering effect on him. Staring at me from the bow of the canoe, he asked gravely, "Did we bring any Pusser's rum?"

Jerry Kobalenko, an accomplished Arctic explorer who has done several expeditions for the Royal Canadian Geographical

Society, by his own admission immediately opened fire on a polar bear he found outside his tent one night on Ellesmere Island. Not much of a shot, Kobalenko missed the bear and hit himself in the face from the recoil of the blast. Clearly, even hardened Arctic explorers are terrified of white bears. Few things seemed more repulsive to me than the idea of killing such a magnificent animal. I vowed to myself that I would never fire on a bear unless it was an absolute matter of life and death. Of course, vowing to myself was one thing—how I, or anyone else, would actually react when faced with an aggressive, growling polar bear could not be predicted.

As we rounded a bend in the river, I caught sight of a man-made structure jutting above a thicket of alder bushes on an island. It was the old goose hunting shack. We beached the canoe on the island's pebble shore and hopped out, our legs sore from having spent the day cramped in the canoe.

"Let's load the shotgun first, before we head off," I said. Anything could be lurking in the alder bushes, which cloaked the island and stood nearly as tall as us.

"All right," said Brent.

Cradling the gun, I led the way into the labyrinth of alders, heading toward the centre of the island. At every step I half-expected a snarling polar bear to materialize. After a short hike, we emerged from the alders at the cabin. Brent sighed from behind me—it wasn't what he had envisioned. The shack was really that—a dilapidated shack cobbled together from spruce logs. The door was missing and several logs had fallen out from the walls. Rubbish lined the interior, which was dark and windowless. It had a rusty cast-iron stove with no chimney, a few decaying chairs, and some metal bed frames with no mattresses. The setting sun shone through cracks in the thin walls and several holes in the roof were plainly visible.

"Well," I said, "would you prefer to sleep in here or set up our tent by the shore?"

"In here," Brent replied dejectedly.

We needed a good night's rest—tomorrow we would head out to meet our dreaded foe, the merciless expanse of frigid salt water and desolate seacoast known as Hudson Bay. Our little canoe would be at the mercy of enormous waves while polar bears would be roving the tundra. It was a cold night; the temperature dropped close to freezing. Brent, foolishly, had run out of dry socks. I had warned him to always keep an extra dry pair just for wearing at night around our camps. But he had insisted upon putting on a dry pair each morning on the journey downriver, though he knew they would be wet the second we plunged into the river. Fortunately, I had saved two pairs of dry wool socks, and now gave him my extra pair. Stretched out on the comfortless metal bed frames, Brent found it too cold to sleep. A storm struck in the night, pounding the cabin with lashing rain while deafening bursts of thunder shook the land. The wind was so fierce that I feared the cabin might collapse on us. As it was, we had to stumble about in the dark, dragging the bed frames to dry spots, trying to avoid the accumulating pools of water. With duct tape and a flashlight, I patched the holes in the roof as best I could. The bitter cold forced us to press our beds together for warmth and drape our emergency blankets over us.

When the morning dawned, the wind was just as fierce. "There's no way we can set off into Hudson Bay in this wind.

The waves will swallow us up," I said, looking out the open door frame of the squalid cabin. "We'll have to wait until the wind dies down before we can leave. We need calm weather to cross the bay."

Brent nodded in agreement. He was alarmed by the prospect of our shallow canoe doing battle with the sea.

We waited all day for the wind to die down, which it refused to do. Given the wind and scarcity of wood, making a fire to cook breakfast on the island was a tiresome chore. Yet, there would be even less wood along Hudson Bay—and nothing at all to shelter us from the winds. Finally, by five in the evening, the weather had calmed enough for us to take our chances. We put on our warmest clothes and wool toques, packed the canoe carefully, and then pushed off from the island. Flocks of snow geese and tundra swans swam in the river, drifting along with the outgoing tide. The water near the river's mouth was salty, which would further complicate our crossing of Hudson Bay. We would have to travel inland to fill our water bottles with freshwater or else collect rainwater. Several sets of rapids confronted us as we paddled toward the sea. We ran them without much difficulty and continued northward to the river's mouth. It was a wide tidal estuary filled with countless sandbars, shoals, and grassy islands. It was low tide, and the estuary soon proved too shallow to paddle.

"What do we do?" asked Brent, jabbing his paddle into the sandy bottom that the canoe was resting upon.

"We'll have to wade and tow the canoe behind us." This was highly dangerous, given our brush with hypothermia earlier. But we had no other choice, save to wait for high tide and attempt paddling then. Yet if we did that, we would have to battle large waves, which our canoe wasn't built to sustain. I preferred to take our chances with wading. We would just have to try to move as fast as possible to stay warm.

Over a hundred years earlier, the explorer D.B. Dowling had commented on sailing alongside Hudson Bay's flat, marshy coastline: "In sailing along this coast, it is impossible to know which way to steer so as to run parallel to the land as nothing is to be seen ahead by which to shape one's course." The English explorer Luke Foxe, who had explored Hudson Bay in 1631, summed it up even better: "A most shoald [sic] and perilous coast, in which there is not one Harbour to be found."

We pushed on for an hour, dragging the canoe through frigid salt water. Fortunately, it was only ankle-deep. The wind, however, soon picked up, and we were once again battling a stiff headwind sweeping off Hudson Bay. Brent and I crouched low in the water, pulling with all our strength to drag the canoe slowly onward, trying to maintain our balance against the fierce winds. As far as the eye could see was the most desolate stretch of harsh, unforgiving wilderness imaginable—with barely a tree in sight. Making a fire, assuming that we could even find wood to burn, would be nearly impossible with the strong winds. And, I was keenly aware that hungry polar bears were roaming the seacoast all around us.

The sun was already setting and we hadn't made much progress. For the first time I found myself doubting if we would make it at all. I now cursed Brent inwardly for having made me abandon the original route through the swamp forests. It would have been extremely gruelling and nightmarish as far as hordes of bloodsucking insects went, but a much safer way to seek the nameless river. Stumbling onward in the water against the wind, my back aching, my thumb still painful, my sinuses and head sore with a cold, I found myself earnestly wishing that Wes hadn't backed out of the expedition. For the first time I felt the need for a sturdy, capable partner that I could rely on. Pushing these thoughts out of my mind as best I could, I turned around to see Brent standing still in the shallow water—gazing toward the frigid ocean on the horizon with undisguised horror.

"Adam ... I can't go on," he said solemnly.

WE TALKED THE MATTER OVER at some length. Unlike when Brent first attempted to quit, I didn't argue much this time. It was clear he was unequal to the task, that his spirits were broken, that the wilderness had vanquished him. I did, however, propose that we consider abandoning Hudson Bay in favour of seeking the alternative nameless river. I made no illusions about the difficulties and dangers this plan would entail: it meant travelling up various rivers, against the current, roughly 153 kilometres in total. Challenging as this would doubtless be, if the weather wouldn't cooperate, traversing Hudson Bay was even more hopeless.

Brent looked at me with horror. "Adam, there's no way I'd ever do that. I don't want to explore any rivers. I'll die happy if I never see a canoe again. All I want to do is go home."

Reluctantly, I agreed to return to the old goose hunting shack, where we could attempt to reach a pilot with our satellite phone. It was dark by the time we fought our way back to the shack, having been forced to drag the canoe upriver.

That night, as we huddled inside the decrepit cabin for warmth, another storm struck. It was downright demoralizing.

Water poured in through the leaky roof, unchinked walls, and open door. The satellite phone couldn't be allowed to get wet and only worked with a clear, unobstructed view of the sky. That meant we had to wait until the next day to make arrangements to get Brent out.

Brent and I slept little that night in the storm. He was now mostly over his cold, whereas I was just coming down with the worst of it. I spent the night coughing and turning restlessly on the metal mattress frame, trying to steel my mind for the morning.

In the dark I heard Brent whisper, "Adam, are you awake?"

"Yes," I coughed.

"I can't sleep. It's freezing."

"You'll be home soon enough."

"I feel guilty."

"Don't quit then."

"Quit with me."

The storm howled frightfully outside the thin walls, while the whole cabin shook. A burst of thunder erupted from above— the flicker of lightning revealed Brent huddled up in his sleeping bag, a grim expression on his face.

"I fear for my life," he whispered.

"I promise nothing bad will happen if you stay," I said.

"You can't make promises like that. What happens out here is beyond anyone's control, even yours."

THE MORNING DAWNED DISMALLY: the sky remained overcast, a light drizzling rain was falling, and the wind was strong. It took several hours before Brent and I could cautiously set up the satellite phone and pick up a signal. Brent explained the situation over the phone to the pilot. The pilot said that he'd attempt to fly in at once, and hopefully arrive in about seven hours.

Brent looked at me. "What will you do?"

I paused. "What I set out to do. Find the nameless river and explore it."

"But you never set out to explore the river alone. You were supposed to do it with Wes, and he's not here. And neither is anyone else."

I didn't answer.

"No one will think less of you if you come with me," said Brent.

"But I'd think less of myself."

Brent shook his head in despair. Not knowing what else to do, I told him the story of Sir Ernest Shackleton's harrowing Antarctic expedition, in which nothing went according to plan. Shackleton's ship, *Endurance*, was crushed by pack ice and sank. He and his crew survived on floating ice for weeks, then sailed in tiny, open lifeboats to a miserable rock island. They knew that if they remained on the uninhabited island for long, all would perish. So Shackleton loaded up one of the lifeboats and, with five other men, pushed off into the sea to seek help, leaving the rest of the crew behind. After enduring massive waves and furious gales, they came ashore on another desolate, mountain-ous island. On the far side of this island was a whaling station. Shackleton, along with two of his men who could still stand, staggered off into the mountains, crossing them to reach the whaling outpost. Unwilling to rest until he rescued his crew, there Shackleton rounded up another ship and wasted no time sailing off to retrieve his men—saving them all. The Shackleton family motto, which had formed a great impression upon the explorer, and from which he derived his ship's name, was "By endurance we conquer."

Brent was so taken by this story that he unfolded his pocket knife and carved "By endurance we conquer" on the wall of the cabin. For a moment I thought he might be newly inspired to carry on.

"Does that mean you're not going to quit?" I asked after he finished carving.

"Hell no!" he exclaimed. "I just like the motto."

I set about making preparations to press on alone. Everything that was superfluous had to be discarded: this included Brent's half of the food rations. Going upriver alone meant it was essential that I travel as lightly as possible: otherwise, with only myself to pull the canoe, I'd never make much headway. Since bears were much more likely to stalk a lone traveller than two people, I loaded the shotgun and slung it over my shoulder. I sharpened my hunting knife and stuck it in my leather belt. I placed dry tinder in a waterproof bag and stashed it inside my jacket's breast pocket. I pulled up the collar on my old, torn jacket, over which I wore a lifejacket. With a bandana tied around my neck and my fedora pulled over my dishevelled brown hair, I felt ready for anything.

Bad weather hindered the pilot's flight and delayed his departure. He didn't arrive until ten hours later, landing a short distance down from the cabin on a wide stretch of unobstructed river. This time, the pilot was a grizzled old-timer who had spent decades flying in the north.

We paddled the canoe, loaded with the gear Brent was to take back with him, toward the bobbing float plane, while the pilot brought the plane to the pebble shoreline so we could load it up. The sky was overcast and the sun was sinking below the horizon. It remained as windy as ever.

The old pilot had misunderstood Brent's conversation on the phone—he thought we were both leaving with him. I explained that I was staying behind.

"But you can't stay here alone," he said gruffly.

"I have to."

"There's more bad weather headed this way. I saw it on the radar."

"I'm prepared for anything."

"It's too dangerous to stay here alone," insisted the pilot. I could see the fear in his grim face, thinking no doubt as he did that it was his responsibility to dissuade me from almost certain death.

"I have work to finish."

"What work is worth risking your life for?"

The pilot's words had no effect on me: I had made up my mind to stay. I trusted in my own abilities and told myself that my best asset was my mind: as long as I remained calm and level-headed, I could overcome any situation. Seeing that I was determined to stay, the old pilot nodded his head and shook my hand.

"Well, you're a brave man. Good luck to ya." He glanced at the darkening sky. "We've got to get going. Another storm is on the way."

Brent, looking a bit ashamed, mumbled "good luck" to me, then wasted no time climbing into the plane. The pilot climbed in after him and started the engine. He then had to manually start the propeller, whirling it until it spun into a blur. He glanced down at me, standing on the pebble shoreline, waved a last farewell, then got back inside the cockpit. I took a few steps back from the roaring plane: the pilot steered the craft out into the middle of the river, rapidly building speed. It skidded along the water and in a few seconds became airborne. The plane disappeared into the overcast sky as the roar of the engine faded into a faint buzz, like a big mosquito, and then after a few more moments, all was silence.

I was alone.

[6]

ALONE

The Canada that lies back of your civilization, the wild, fierce,
land of desperate struggle and untold hardship ... is ...
the heritage of the born adventurer. In this austere and savage land
men are sometimes broken, or aged beyond their years.
—Grey Owl, *The Men of the Last Frontier,* 1931

M UCH WEIGHED ON MY MIND as I paddled back to the
old goose hunting shack in the fading light. Pitting
oneself alone against the northern wilderness wasn't a challenge
to be entered into lightly. Virtually none of history's great explorers operated alone—many in fact did comparatively little of the
hard labour involved in exploring. Henry Morton Stanley, like
most explorers of Africa, always had porters and servants to carry
his baggage and equipment, cook his meals, make his fires, and
pitch his tents. On his journey through the Canadian subarctic,
John Franklin required voyageurs to paddle his canoes, start fires,
and take care of the hunting and fishing. Samuel Hearne, strong
and resourceful as he was, relied on his native guides to provision
him with food, shelter, and fire. Rare was the explorer who did an
expedition single-handedly, and even aboriginal people as a rule
travelled in groups. Huddled by my campfire that night, I racked
my brain to think of a solitary explorer for encouragement.

I remembered what Bill Mason, a veteran wilderness canoeist, had said of solo travel:

> I would be irresponsible in encouraging people to canoe and camp alone if I didn't also point out the dangers. I have always been aware that any mishap that renders me immobile will almost certainly lead to my death unless I am on a well-travelled route.

Here in the blackfly-infested Lowlands, I definitely wasn't on any well-travelled route. Mason had admonished those who would risk a solo trip to:

> Think about the possibility of injury even from routine actions, such as picking up and carrying the canoe over a muddy trail, chopping wood or running rock-studded rapids. Close your eyes and imagine yourself pinned helplessly between your canoe and a rock in the middle of a rapid…. When you are chopping or splitting your firewood, imagine sinking the axe into your foot."

I did what Mason suggested and envisioned these scenarios—none of which seemed terribly encouraging. Mason had concluded: "Six is just about the right number of people…. It is also considered the safest number for travelling on a remote wilderness river."

Those who dared to take on the North Country alone usually did so only after months of careful planning and preparation—psyching themselves up for the rigours of an absolute and all-encompassing solitude. I had no such luxury—I was thrown into the situation. Regardless, I had made up my mind to press on for the sake of the Royal Canadian Geographical Society, and more than that—my keen sense of curiosity to know what was out there inexorably led me on.

THE MORNING OF MY FIRST DAY ALONE dawned with a thick fog engulfing the river. It was impossible to see more than a few feet ahead. Having spent another unpleasant night in the shack, I was eager to be off. Before me lay 153 kilometres of upriver travel, most of which would have to be done by wading through the water against the swift current, dragging the canoe behind me with rope. The river bottom would be treacherous, full of rocks and crevices. To slip and hit my head would be a death sentence. As it was, it would be a race against time upriver; my only hope of avoiding hypothermia was to travel as fast as possible, without interruption. I put on my warmest sweater and replaced my fedora with a toque. As for polar bears, there was little to be done except to sleep with one eye open and keep the gun close. My thumb still ached terribly, but despite feeling sick and knowing that I now had to do alone what was supposed to be done with a partner, I remained confident.

What buoyed my spirits partially was the knowledge that other explorers had overcome greater odds. As far as impossible odds went, nothing could rival what legendary mountain man Hugh Glass endured in the American West. Described by a contemporary who had travelled with him as "bold, daring, reckless and eccentric to a high degree," Glass was, he went on to say, "a man of great talents and intellectual as well as bodily power.

But his bravery was conspicuous beyond all his other qualities."
In 1822 Glass, then a hardened woodsman in his forties, joined
an expedition ascending the Missouri River. Scouting ahead of
the main party one day in late summer, he was attacked by a
grizzly bear. Glass managed to get off a rifle shot before the bear
pinned him down and began mauling him. Not one to surrender,
the mountain man repeatedly stabbed the enraged grizzly with
his knife. Two of his companions arrived just in time to finish off
the wounded bear with their guns. Glass lay unconscious on the
ground with injuries that were so severe—his rib cage was
exposed through a gaping wound in his back, he had a deep gash
on his head, and his leg was broken—that any hope of his survival
was given up. Two men volunteered to remain behind until he
died. They wrapped Glass' body in a makeshift shroud then divided
his gun, knife, and other possessions between themselves, leaving
him for dead.

But incredibly Glass came to, finding himself alone,
unarmed, without provisions, and suffering from a broken leg
and festering wounds. The nearest outpost of civilization—Fort
Kiowa—was well over three hundred kilometres away. A lesser
man would have given up. Not Glass—furious that he had
been abandoned, he set his own leg, patched up his wounds as
best he could and—unable to walk—began to crawl. For six
weeks, he dragged himself onward, living off roots and berries,
until he reached the Cheyenne River. Glass then cobbled
together a crude raft to drift with the current, eventually reaching the fort. There he vowed vengeance on the men who had
abandoned him. After a lengthy recovery, Glass succeeded in
tracking them down, but in the end he proved as magnanimous

as he was indefatigable. He spared their lives and took no action against them.

I TOOK MY FIRST solo wilderness trip at thirteen. After some pleading, I had succeeded in convincing an uncle I was staying with to take me to the nearest wilderness and allow me to strike off alone. I didn't sleep a wink that night, thinking a bear was going to devour me. As I grew older, I moved on to solo trips canoeing rivers and snowshoeing across frozen lakes. One night on a wintery sojourn north of Lake Huron, a pack of wolves followed my trail over an ice-covered lake. Despite the minus-thirty-degree-Celsius temperatures, I was soundly asleep, buried under several layers of blankets in my sled when howling shattered the silence. Thrilled and excited, if a little alarmed, I grabbed my axe and built up my fire. Then with a birchbark torch, I struck out onto the lake, catching a spellbinding glimpse of the wolves as they disappeared into the night like phantoms. But none of these adventures could compare with what I reckoned would be at least another three weeks of not seeing another human being. I had always been a bit of the solitary sort, but this was pushing it.

I set off from the alder-covered island into the thick mist, paddling as hard as I could upriver. Within about twenty minutes of my departure, the swift current grew too strong for paddling. So, reluctantly, I wedged my paddle inside the canoe and plunged over the side to begin towing the vessel. Leaning on the canoe for balance, I splashed my way up to the bow in knee-deep water and took hold of the rope fastened to the canoe. Every step was precarious—the river bottom was lined with slippery rocks. To maintain warmth, I dared not stop once started, pushing onward as best I could. Fortunately, the sun, which we had seen little of over the past few days, began to peek through the clouds, warming my chilled frame. A short distance upriver, on an eroded bank I noticed a large burrow in the soil—the home of a wolverine or possibly an arctic fox.

My plan was to penetrate some forty-four kilometres up the Sutton River until I reached a fork where a tributary stream, the obscure and little-known Aquatuk River, joined the Sutton. Then I would branch off up the Aquatuk, following its meandering course some thirteen kilometres until coming upon the mouth of a nameless tributary that drained into it. This nameless tributary was the river I was seeking—the plan was to explore its hundred-kilometre-long course, dragging my canoe if necessary the whole way to its headwaters. Once there, I'd turn around and paddle with the current back to the Aquatuk, then onto the Sutton, and finally out to Hudson Bay again, where a pilot could land. Aside from near the mouth of the Sutton, the rivers themselves were too shallow and rocky for any float plane to land on.

The first day travelling upriver progressed slowly. At times, the current slackened enough to allow for hard paddling or "poling"—that is, jabbing my paddle along the river bottom to propel the canoe forward. At a few straight sections of river, I experimented with hiking onshore while dragging the canoe with rope through the water. None of this proved practical for very long—only wading in the river and dragging the canoe behind me could make substantial headway. The worst was when rapids had to be navigated—several times I nearly lost my balance, dangerously stumbling in the rushing torrent.

Early on, when rounding a bend, I caught sight of something white moving off in the distance. Thinking I was about to glimpse a polar bear, the binoculars revealed only a couple of tundra swans swimming in the shallow waters. But soon I encountered the real thing: passing some islands, which had obstructed my view of the eastern shore, a large white mass out on a vast expanse of tundra suddenly loomed into view. Instinctively, I froze as a rush of adrenaline surged through me. It was a polar bear, luckily a long way off, lumbering along the tundra. The distance between us made me feel reasonably secure. But not secure enough that I wanted to wait around and take pictures, so I pressed on hard against the river, hoping to reach the treeline before nightfall.

Mercifully, I escaped the open tundra and made it back into the forest just as the sun began to set. At least here there was ample wood for a fire, shelter from the chilling winds, and no polar bears—or so I hoped. I set up my tent in a patch of reindeer moss beside some tamaracks and, overcome with millions of blackflies and mosquitoes, dove into my little nylon sanctuary for the night just as the sky unleashed more rain.

BY THE END of the first day of my upriver battle, I had covered sixteen kilometres. Fearing the onset of hypothermia again, I realized that wading through the river all day—sometimes in water deeper than my waist—was too dangerous. The early mornings were too cold for it—I had no choice but to wait until the sun warmed things up a little before plunging back into the frigid water.

Despite the shortened schedule, I covered another sixteen kilometres on my second day—pushing as hard as I could and not taking any time to stop for lunch—instead, I just consumed beef jerky, granola bars, and dried fruit on the march. That night, I made camp beneath an ancient black spruce, around which I found a multitude of wild edibles: delicious blueberries, tiny strawberries, rather tasteless crowberries, red bearberries, orange cloudberries, and pin-striped gooseberries. I snacked gratefully on all of them—though the thought did occur to me that the abundant berries would make the area a pretty attractive buffet for black bears, which rely on berries for most of their diet. But now that I was in polar bear country, I regarded black bears with something approaching disdain—not much more than a nuisance. Even the largest black bears are usually less than half the size of a male polar bear, and not nearly as aggressive.

At any rate, I had more immediate concerns—my injured thumb. It still hurt horribly whenever I brushed it up against anything. Wearily, I sat down on some sphagnum moss and slowly began to peel off the duct tape and the bandages. It looked worse than ever: the flesh was still hanging out near the nail, and now the skin around it had turned a sickly green. I concluded that if the cost of exploring the nameless river was a lost thumb, I would accept it. With my other hand, I rooted around in my backpack for the first aid kit, dug out some alcohol pads, and gingerly cleaned the wound. If I ran out of alcohol pads, I could rely on the Lowlands' abundant sphagnum moss; absorbent and highly acidic, it was long used as a traditional treatment for wounds in both Europe and North America.

The next task was to start a fire: grey clouds were rolling in from the west, threatening more rain. The search for dry land had led me some way inland, making it a chore to hike back down to the river's banks and fetch water. My hiking boots sank into the muck as I filled a pot in the swirling waters. Nearby were some large caribou tracks. It was comforting to know that benign animal companions were at hand. It made the isolation seem less intense.

The smoke from the fire helped keep the bugs away, letting me remove my mesh bug net. My face, neck, and the area behind my ears were covered in red sores from blackfly bites. Blood smeared my beard from swatting flies and mosquitoes all day, squishing their blood-filled bodies against my face. As I waited for the water to boil, I changed into dry clothes and hung my wet ones on the crooked branches of the spruce. I didn't have the benefit of any Gore-Tex clothing, which costs a small fortune. "But," I told myself, "I'm fine without it. Explorers and fur traders did without it." Having fallen into the habit of talking to myself, I gazed out on the stunted, windswept boreal forest all around me and muttered, "People are getting soft these days."

The sky continued to look ominous, but there was no rain. A northern flicker, a type of large woodpecker, sat above me in the old spruce, keeping me company as I ate rice and drank blueberry tea. After supper, I couldn't leave my dishes unwashed—not that I cared about clean dishes, but scraps of food could attract bears. So I stumbled back down through alder bushes to the river's edge to clean them. Finding myself too exhausted to move my plastic food containers very far from camp as I customarily did, I instead carried them only five metres away and sat them beside a small tamarack. My theory was that if a black bear came across my camp, it would leave me undisturbed and content itself with raiding the food rations.

That last task accomplished, I brushed my teeth and finally crawled into the tent, which now seemed like the most comfortable place in the world—a tiny sanctuary where I could escape from the torment of the mosquitoes and blackflies, the biting wind and rain, and the toils of the day. I spread out my sleeping bag and arranged all my accoutrements just as I liked them: the shotgun along one side, the hatchet, old hunting knife, and pocket flashlight on the other. I placed my hat above a makeshift pillow of extra clothing stuffed into my jacket and tucked my compass and matches into the mesh pocket of the tent. The GPS and satellite phone were stashed inside a waterproof bag at my feet. One consolation of being abandoned by Brent was the extra space I now had inside the little tent. Here in the Lowlands, dry ground for campsites was unusual, and by necessity I was often forced to sleep on slopes, undulated terrain, or in soggy patches of reindeer moss. With a partner it was necessary to choose who would sleep where—one side of the tent generally being preferred over the other. Now at least I had the pick of the best side and could therefore rest more comfortably.

With the last remaining rays of clouded sunlight, I had just enough light to look over the maps and dig out my journal from my tattered pack. It was the same journal that I had carried with me barely two months earlier in the jungles of the Amazon. It felt strange to think that some of the insect bites on my legs came from a different continent. Flipping through the water-stained pages, my eyes fell upon an entry that read: "Saw a tarantula on a palm leaf while doing a night transect, many ant bites on legs. Large insect bite on thigh looks infected." I scribbled some notes, recorded my coordinates, and noted the weather. Then, all my muscles aching, I stretched out in my sleeping bag. The pitter-patter of rain hitting the tent lulled me to sleep; as always, a tree root was jabbing at my back beneath the tent floor.

A NOISE FROM SOMEWHERE in the darkness roused me. On the other side of the paper-thin wall, something was noisily crashing about. I dashed out of my sleeping bag and crouched in the centre of the tent—my knife out and ready to lunge. Ignoring the instinct to remain silent, I began shouting to scare off what was probably a black bear. Any moment, I expected a bear to burst through the tent. The noise outside ceased. I switched on a flashlight, though this would allow whatever was out there to see me. Light in hand, I unzipped the tent door and peered out.

"Hey!" I shouted, startling something that tore off in the direction of the river. It plunged into the shallow waters as I shone the dim light after it. A thick mist concealed the river, but I could hear the animal wade across to the far side then crash through the forest on the opposite bank. Whatever it was, I had apparently scared it off. Replacing my knife with the shotgun, I went to investigate. My concern was that a bear had raided my food rations and, with its powerful jaws, ripped open one or more of the watertight plastic barrels. Cradling the gun, I tiptoed over to where I had stowed them. They appeared untouched.

Back inside the tent, I laid down. It was 2:17 a.m. Finding it hard to get back to sleep, and adhering to my habit of imagining the worst case scenario in order to fortify myself, I recalled some of the most gruesome black bear attacks that I knew of. I had an excellent stock of them, thanks to many an evening spent reciting such tales to fellow campers. There was the time in 1978 when a black bear stalked, killed, and partially ate three boys in Algonquin Park. That story always seemed to make an impression on audiences. Then there was the notorious incident in 1991 when a perfectly healthy male bear defied everything the textbooks said about black bear behaviour and turned man-eater in Algonquin. The ferocious bear stalked two adult campers, swam out to an island they had camped on, broke their necks, and afterwards consumed their corpses. Interestingly, Cliff Jacobson had reported that the expert consensus was, contrary to what might be expected, that the most dangerous black bears are the wildest ones with little or no previous contact with humans—presumably the kind of bears that live around unexplored rivers. Suddenly, a branch snapped outside the tent. My body went tense. Maybe it was only a red squirrel. Having waited another ten minutes and heard nothing further, my exhaustion overcame any lingering concerns and I fell asleep again.

THE IMMORTAL GODS of ancient Greece, perched in their palace on Mount Olympus, took a perverse pleasure in tormenting mortals, sending them fair weather and favourable winds one moment, then hurling down terrible fury the next, just to remind mortals of the order of things. On my third day travelling upriver alone, I received a lesson in the caprices of the gods. The day had been glorious: I made excellent progress and stopped for the night on a beautiful stretch of river with wide open grassy banks. At last, it seemed that fortune was smiling upon me. The weather was so idyllic and the sun felt so warm that I actually bathed for the first time in two weeks. Refreshed from a brisk swim in the river, I then caught two speckled trout and gathered some wild berries for supper. I decided to treat myself to an open campsite near the water rather than hike back into the forest as I normally did.

But just as twilight faded to darkness, the wind changed ominously. A tremendous gust blew the coals of my campfire into a red glow. Seemingly out of nowhere, storm clouds crowded the sky. The wind howled savagely, bending trees to the breaking point. With dread and with anticipation, I rushed to prepare for the coming storm. I tied my overturned canoe, which was resting beside the tent, with rope to the nearest shrubs, fearing that it might otherwise be blown away. I had to act quickly—any moment the heavens were going to open up—so I grabbed as many rocks as I could, piled them around the edges of my tent, then dashed inside just as a bolt of lightning struck the far bank. It was followed by the loudest burst of thunder I had ever heard.

The storm raged all around me, the tent swayed violently, and each burst of thunder seemed to shake the very ground beneath me. The rain pounding the tent was as deafening as anything I experienced in the Amazon. The open ground and metal tent poles left me dangerously vulnerable to lightning. It felt as if this hurricane of a storm would carry me off in the tent like Dorothy in *The Wizard of Oz*. Instead, the tent just came crashing down on top of me. Water began to accumulate inside from the lashing rain. I sighed: it was going to be one of *those* nights.

Squirming around inside the ruined tent, I somehow managed to avoid the accumulating pools of water. There was no hope of fixing the tent in the storm—I couldn't risk getting my dry clothing drenched. So, powerless against the elements, I resigned myself to sleeping in what felt like a body bag, with the collapsed tent on top of me. As for the possibility of getting struck by lightning, I'd just have to hope for the best.

IN THE EARLY MORNING, I awoke to the sound of splashing in the river. I stuck my head out of the collapsed tent and saw three caribou, a mother with two young calves, swimming across the water. Moments like this made it all worth it.

That day, the fourth since Brent quit, I paddled, lined, waded, and poled my canoe up the Sutton. By early afternoon, I reached "the meeting of the waters," as I called it, the junction of the Sutton and Aquatuk Rivers. From here I would leave the familiarity of the Sutton and head into unknown territory. Scant published information existed on the Aquatuk. The explorers D.B. Dowling and James Edwin Hawley had only briefly mentioned it in their notes. There was a dry geological paper published back in 1971, H.H. Bostock's *Geological Notes on Aquatuk River Map-Area, with Emphasis on the Precambrian Rocks*, that shed some light on it. But Bostock focused on rocks, not canoeing, and his work had been done mostly via helicopter. Other than that, I knew of two recent scientific studies in the general area: an aquatic survey that had been carried out a few years earlier on various lakes had also sampled the headwaters of the Aquatuk, and a botanical study that had been conducted the previous summer in the vicinity of the nameless river, a tributary of the Aquatuk. But these studies said little to nothing about the waterways.

Conversations with a couple of old-timers I had tracked down before leaving on the expedition had been more fruitful. An aged aboriginal man from Peawanuck told me that the Aquatuk had "a lot of pike." Another veteran of the north, a retired cartographer, told me that he had worked on a survey some forty years earlier that, in winter, went along part of the frozen Aquatuk. One thing seemed clear: only a handful of people had ever previously ventured up this river. Rope in hand, wading with my canoe in the dark, swirling waters of this new river, I felt a mixture of trepidation and excitement as I left the Sutton behind and strayed into the unknown.

NAMELESS RIVER

The unknown is generally taken to be terrible, not as the proverb would infer,
from the inherent superstition of man, but because it so often is terrible.
He who would tamper with the vast and secret forces that animate the world
may well fall a victim to them.
—H. Rider Haggard, *She*, 1887

THE FOREST HUMMED with the beating wings of millions of mosquitoes. I had never seen such an eerie landscape—a wilderness of crooked spruce and tamaracks, contorted and twisted by the unforgiving winds, their branches draped with cobwebs of hanging lichens, and the forest floor cloaked in green moss. The grey skies and drizzling rain added to the general gloom. Most of the stunted trees stood little taller than me—though here and there were comparative giants, centuries-old black spruce that rose like ghostly sentinels above the land. The uneven ground was laced with foul pools of black water, breeding grounds for legions of mosquitoes. It was undisturbed, ancient forest with no signs of humanity.

Having journeyed some ways up the Aquatuk, I made my lonely camp on a slight prominence, beneath some spruces. As I moved through the woods, it was with a vague feeling of uneasiness, as if I shouldn't disturb this primeval place. Perilous as my journey up the Sutton had been, it had an air of familiarity about it, and I had the work of past explorers to guide me. In contrast, the Aquatuk looked and felt like virgin territory, a place untouched by the outside world. Its waters were swift, surprisingly deep, and guarded by rapids larger than anything I had encountered on the Sutton. In some places, the shoreline was thickly treed with palisades of black spruce. They seemed to frown upon me as I fought my solitary way upriver. In other stretches, sandbanks rose high above the river, crowned with scraggly trees. Though I saw many birds—eagles, sandpipers, waterfowl—I saw neither caribou nor moose, and, as a consequence, was left with an intense feeling of isolation. Nowhere did I find any trace of a human predecessor—not a chopped stump, ashes from a long-ago campfire, or so much as a hatchet blaze. Old Terry O'Neil, if he could have seen me now, would doubtless have shaken his head and deemed it all "God's country."

I found myself glancing over my shoulder every so often, as if I half-expected some supernatural thing to be stalking my steps. For the first time, the silence began to weigh on me. I tried to break it by talking to myself, but that didn't help. The sound of my own voice echoing against the immutable silence of the wilderness seemed like a violation of an unwritten law. So I kept quiet and trod lightly, feeling almost as if I had entered the confines of some ancient temple, where to disturb anything was to awaken an unnatural power.

That evening, I made a smoky fire from wet wood, since the forest was sodden from the rains. Sitting by my sputtering fire in the fading light, I could well imagine the unholy terrors aboriginal people believed inhabited the northern forest. A "thing" scarcely spoken of, and only then in hushed tones, was said to prey upon solitary wanderers who dared venture into these remote lands. I had heard whispers of it on my travels and read about it in old explorers' journals—a hideous, giant man-like creature, called the *Witiko*, or wendigo. It could, so it was said, possess the minds of lonely travellers, making them slowly turn mad, and finally overwhelm them with an insatiable craving for human flesh. For centuries, explorers and fur traders had noted their native counterparts' fear of this grim monster. In 1790, Edward Umfreville, a Hudson's Bay Company trader, confided in his journal that "there is an evil Being" that natives call the "Whit-ti co.... They frequently persuade themselves that they see his track in the moss or snow, and he is generally described in the most hideous forms." In the 1930s, the woods-man Grey Owl had warned that "The Windigo, a half-human, flesh-eating creature, scours the lake shores looking for those who sleep carelessly without a fire, and makes sleeping out in some sections a thing of horror."

As I watched the shadows cast by the flickering light of the fire, the memory of my first "encounter" with a wendigo years earlier came to mind. Wes and I were canoeing the remote and challenging Otoskwin River, some 400 kilometres north of Lake Superior. After a fortnight in the wilderness, we reached the isolated Ojibwa reserve of Neskantaga, population 265—a place accessible to the outside world only by airplane or a long and perilous canoe journey. As it was, our journey had been plagued by singularly adverse weather—incessant rain, unseasonably cold temperatures, lightning, and hail storms. Our appearance on the remote reserve created something of a stir—visitors of any kind were rare, and for two youths to have canoed there alone was unheard of.

The long-suffering community was beset by alcoholism and astonishingly high rates of suicide. Despite the grim conditions, we received a warm welcome. One individual, a man in his thirties named Randy, took a particular interest in us. He invited us to accompany him into the woods one night to howl for wolves.

The pale glow of a half-moon illuminated the old trail we followed that night through the forest, casting eerie shadows against the moss-cloaked ground as we trudged onward. Randy led the way over several thickly forested hills and down into a sort of level plain filled with pine, poplar, spruce, and birch trees.

"This is where the pack usually hunts," he whispered to us as we neared an ancient pine that had toppled over. The three of us halted beside the pine, while Randy glanced around. "We'll try howling," he whispered. "Usually they respond to the howls pretty good."

Wes and I watched as he cupped his hands around his mouth, pointed his head toward the moon, and howled loudly.

"You guys howl too," Randy whispered, motioning to us to do the same.

Wes and I had howled for wolves before, so we readily tossed our heads back, cupped our hands to our mouths, and howled at the half-moon. For the next minute, we all howled together, then paused to await a reply.

Just when it seemed that no wolves would be heard on that night, a chorus of wild cries that sent shivers down our spines echoed from out of the darkness. Randy smiled and said, "The pack has arrived."

When the wolves' howling abruptly ceased, we responded with more of our own, which encouraged the unseen animals to venture closer. They responded with yaps and more howls. This exchange continued for several minutes before the pack apparently lost interest in us and moved on through the woods.

As we turned to leave, Randy, who had taken a keen interest in our journey, asked something peculiar. "Did you ..." he began, before hesitating a moment, "see anything strange on your journey here?"

"We had some unusual weather. Hail storms, lots of thunder and lightning," I replied.

Wes, sensing that Randy had something else in mind, added, "We found a dead bald eagle."

In the silver glint of the moonlight, I could see Randy's face react to this revelation as if it had some special significance. "Did you do anything with it?" he asked gravely.

"No," we answered in unison.

Randy nodded grimly. "That eagle was put in your path for a reason."

Wes and I, rather bewildered by this comment, made no reply. Neither of us at the time had thought much of a mouldy carcass of a dead eagle washed up on a lakeshore. After some remarks about eagles and omens, Randy delved into what was evidently weighing upon his mind.

"The reason I asked if you saw anything strange," he said in the sort of hushed whisper that comes naturally when speaking in the gloom of a night-time forest, "is that I saw something *very strange* out here recently." His words were uttered with such seriousness that there was no doubting his sincerity. After a pause he continued, "I was walking along this trail, and when I came up over that ridge there, I saw something moving slowly down below in the trees. It was dark and at first I wasn't sure what it was. It looked like a big man or something. But as I watched, I saw it was no human … it was huge, seven-feet tall, all black and hairy, and walked from there to there," he motioned to the spot in question. "I was terrified," he whispered, and by the light of the moon, I could see the fear in his eyes was real, "I froze, scared half to death. People around here tell stories about such things, but I never believed them … till now."

Wes, not easily frightened, turned as white as a ghost. He had always harboured a healthy respect for native lore and mysterious terrors. On the other hand, I was practically salivating with fascination. I didn't believe in such creatures per se, but they were real enough as cultural constructs, and figuring out the origins of such legends intrigued me.

"What do you think it was?" I blurted out.

"I don't know … it wasn't human."

As we hiked back along the trail, I badgered Randy with questions. Later that night, back at the reserve, I asked Wes what he thought of the story.

Wes shook his head. "If I had heard that story beforehand, I'd never have come here."

"What? Are you kidding me? Didn't it just make you want to come all the more?" I said excitedly.

"No," Wes said shaking his head again. "It makes me wonder about some of those noises we heard in the night. What do you think Randy saw?"

I shrugged. "Probably he had too much to drink and saw a black bear on its hind legs, or somebody wandering around in a dark coat."

Wes scoffed at these explanations. He slept little that night.

LATER I SCOURED the archives, digging up everything ever written about the subject, and found that Randy's tale matched stories that dated back centuries. There were, as the anthropologist Alfred Irving Hallowell noted in 1951, two distinct wendigo traditions: "The first comprises actual persons who have turned into cannibals.... The second consists of mythical cannibal giants." In the historical records, I found ample references to both variations on the legend. As the Cree elder Louis Bird explained:

> Wihtigo. It was something that happened among humans. It means an other-than-human was created from an ordinary human—and sometimes maybe not. There is a question there. There were many kinds. There is a wihtigo that was created by starvation—humans starved, went crazy, and ate human flesh.... Other wihtigos are not understood—it is not known where they came from.

Presumably, this meant the giant kind, which Randy claimed to have seen in the forest that night.

The French encountered wendigo stories among northern tribes when they arrived in the New World in the seventeenth century. Father Jérôme Lalemant, a Jesuit missionary, witnessed "the deaths of some Indians" who were killed "by the other savages, because they were seized by a mental disease which rendered them ravenous for human flesh." Rather than dismiss such tales as mere superstition, the French explorers were inclined to take them seriously—as they had their own traditions back in France of humans transforming into violent beasts. As Lalemant explained, "It is a sort of werewolf tale."

Over a hundred known cases exist in the historical record of "wendigo possession," in which aboriginal persons were said to be transformed into wendigos and driven insane with a murderous urge to eat human flesh. The act of cannibalism supposedly gave these deranged persons superhuman strength and turned their hearts to ice. Such individuals could only be killed by special means—they had to be decapitated and their bodies cut into small bits, lest they should rise from the grave. Some tribes even appointed a "wendigo slayer," usually a shaman, whose task it was to kill such psychotic individuals—not unlike werewolf hunters in medieval Europe. Well into the late nineteenth century there were wendigo trials in Canada, in which individuals accused of murder defended themselves by claiming that what they had killed was not human but instead a wendigo.

The most detailed description ever furnished of the other sort of wendigo—the less human, more monstrous variation of the legend—was offered by Joseph Guinard, a missionary among the Atikamekw natives in northern Quebec in the 1920s. The anthropologist Richard Preston summarized Guinard's depiction of the wendigo, which was based on Atikamekw elders' accounts:

The Witiko ... are solitary, aggressive cannibals, naked but impervious to cold, with black skin covered by resin-glued sand. They have no lips, large crooked teeth, hissing breath, and big bloodshot eyes, something like owls' eyes. Their feet are more than two feet long, with long, pointed heels, and have only one big toe: "This is the way his tracks appear on sand and snow." Fingers and fingernails are "like the claws of the great mountain bears." The voice is strident, reverberating, and drawn-out into howls, and "his food was rotten wood, swamp moss, mushrooms, corpses, and human flesh." Witiko has extraordinary strength and is invulnerable. He is a nocturnal hunter of men; when he is close, his heart beats twice as quickly with joy, sounding like the drumming of a grouse. They can fly and also swim under water, making large waves to capsize canoes. They have foreknowledge of their victims' location.

It was, in other words, not a creature a traveller would wish to cross paths with alone in the northern forest.

The cannibalistic wendigo was explained easily enough—it was based on actual cannibalism, a horrific temptation in the harsh subarctic, where starvation could be a fact of life. Like European tales of werewolves or vampires, the wendigo legend served as a cultural taboo against cannibalism. In this sense, it was a very real cautionary tale of how violence debases those who commit it—mortals turned into fiends through bloodlust. More enigmatic was the other side of the legend—the giant monsters that were said to stalk the remotest parts of the wilderness. Even the Cree elder Louis Bird had said that these creatures were a mystery. What cultural function could belief in scary giants fulfill? Unless it was meant as a warning against straying too far from the beaten path, out into the unknown swamps. It was cause for reflection as I sat in the dark by my fire beneath the spruces swaying and creaking in the wind. That night I slept with my knife close at hand.

THE FOLLOWING DAY, paddling hard against the current up the Aquatuk in the rain, each stroke plunging me deeper into the unknown, I rounded a bend and caught sight of the mouth of a small tributary. I paused and fixed my eyes on the magical sight before me—this was it—the start of the nameless, unexplored river. It was about sixteen metres wide at the mouth and flanked by tall black spruces. The waters were swift, dark, and full of jagged rocks. No one, as far as I could ascertain, had ever explored this waterway. My excitement at having finally reached the river overcame any concerns about the difficulties and dangers that lay ahead. I beached my canoe on the muddy shore and jumped out to double-check the maps. I was anxious to be certain that this was the river I had been looking for. When I had confirmed beyond any doubt that this was indeed the river I had come to explore, I took a moment to set up my camera on a makeshift tripod fashioned out of the plastic barrels stacked together and photographed myself holding the Society's flag beside the water. As I did so, I noticed freshwater clam shells lying along the banks, likely eaten by river otters.

The dark skies, steady rain, and cold temperatures could do nothing to dim my enthusiasm as I began my battle upriver.

Swift as the current was, I managed to paddle a short distance before I had to plunge overboard and begin wading. It was a thrill to think that I was probably the first person this river had ever had wading through its clear, pristine waters. The forest on either side was centuries-old black spruce, which rose to a height of some ten metres or more. Rising out of the water in places were large granite boulders, looming up like icebergs. Sandbars appeared near bends, and the river had the occasional small rapid. Like on the Aquatuk, there was no sign of any past human presence, and as I penetrated deeper into this unexplored territory, I felt what an archaeologist must feel when opening some ancient tomb no person has peered into for centuries.

The rain and the water running off my pants and boots as I climbed in and out of the canoe slowly filled the vessel. I had to halt every so often to bail out the water. Canada geese with their broods of goslings swam in the river—it seemed as if this unknown waterway was some secret of theirs that I had discovered—when they saw me, they scurried off into the woods. Soon I crossed paths with larger game: around another bend, I caught hold of a magnificent sight—a majestic female moose standing together on the bank with a young calf. They seemed surprised and stood motionless, staring at me, doubtless wondering what this bizarre animal was. I photographed the mother and calf while waist-deep in the river, before the mother decided that this was enough attention for one day, and sauntered off into the forest. The baby moose took another curious look at me, then trotted off after her.

Pressing onward, I passed several small brooks that joined the river and a decent-sized creek. The rain continued sporadically, and for the odd moment I was treated with sunshine peeking through the clouds. An abundance of wildflowers covered the banks: yellow cinquefoils, dwarf fireweed, wild rose, and purple *Lobelia kalmii* (which the Cree used medicinally to treat a variety of ailments). Growing in the water near the shore were arrowheads, an aquatic plant named for their green, arrowhead-shaped leaves. The tubers of this plant are quite palatable: early explorers called it "Indian potato." There were also plenty of strawberries and gooseberries. I regretted that I couldn't identify more of the flora I saw, but much of the plant life in the Lowlands remains unfamiliar even to specialists—previously unrecorded species are still being discovered. Botanist John Riley noted that the Lowlands is "perhaps five times larger than the floodplain forests along the Amazon River" and "one of the least populated regions in the Western Hemisphere and one of the last regions of North America to have its flora and vegetation documented." In other words, plenty of territory for undocumented species to remain hidden.

My first notable geographical discovery was a small island that didn't appear on existing maps. It was a little isle in the middle of the river covered in grass, willow bushes, and cinquefoil flowers. Just beyond the island was a picturesque "S" bend, with two sets of rapids at either end of the "S" and a beautiful little pool in between. On the western bank overlooking the bend was a small hill crowned with spruces and tamaracks. It was about as pretty a spot as I had ever seen in the Lowlands, and an ideal place to rest for the night. I made camp in a sheltered grove of trees on top of the hill. After supper, I cleaned and oiled my gun, rebandaged my thumb, and fixed one of the tent's poles that had broken in the storm. That night, I slept soundly and contently, untroubled by any thought of wendigos, supremely happy in the knowledge that I had at last reached a place unknown to the world—a nameless river that it wasn't possible to learn about by simply picking up a book or consulting Wikipedia. It was a place I had seen many times in my dreams, a wilderness without a footprint, where I was the only living soul.

THE VICTORIAN EXPLORER Sir Richard Burton, who dared to enter the forbidden city of Mecca and sought the source of the Nile, remarked: "Of the gladdest moments in human life, methinks, is the departure upon a journey into unknown lands." Trekking farther along the meandering course of the nameless river, I was inclined to agree with him. The thrill of the unknown lured me around each river bend, while clear skies and warm weather quickened my pace. The current, however, was so strong that it nearly knocked me over in a few places, especially when I had to fight my way up rapids. In more tranquil stretches, as I sloshed along, I would spook pike and schools of minnows hiding in the weeds. Along the banks were wood frogs, northern leopard frogs, the occasional American toad, and butterflies that fed on the plentiful wildflowers. The forest thinned out upriver, and at places almost gave way entirely to open muskeg. A short distance beyond the riverbank, the trees mostly disappeared and were replaced by vast impassable bogs.

The smooth, pink granite boulders that loomed out of the water looked like the rounded backs of hippos, wading in some African river. Plenty of signs of real wildlife were visible. Beaver, moose, and caribou tracks lined the muddy banks, and across the mouth of a tributary stream stood an impressive metre-and-a-half-tall beaver dam. At midday, a northern harrier soared high above me, hunting for squirrels or snowshoe hares, or perhaps waterfowl. I noticed the bark had been stripped off a spruce growing along the bank where a bear had sharpened its claws. Encouraging as all this wildlife was, and as much as I relished the challenge of the adventure, it was wearisome work, and at times when I was cold, wet, shivering, and attacked by hordes of blackflies, I wished Brent had stuck around. Miserable as he had been, I missed his company. Still, I pressed on, eventually making camp in a spruce grove for another night on the river.

In the fading light, lying exhausted in my tent, I was startled by a haunting bird call echoing from out of the woods. The strange cry rang out several times. I scrambled outside the tent to see if I could find what bird was producing the noise. I considered myself pretty good at identifying bird song, but whatever made that peculiar cry left me stumped. It was unlike anything I had heard before—a most unnatural sort of wailing howl. Not all mysteries are meant to be solved.

THE RIVER'S MEANDERING COURSE snaked approximately ninety-six kilometres to its headwaters. The first day making my way upriver, I managed to cover about eighteen kilometres. The second day, I travelled thirty kilometres, or roughly three kilometres per hour, with ten hours spent travelling. So, after two days, I was already halfway there. If I could cover twenty-four kilometres a day for the next two days, I would arrive at the headwaters and then be free to paddle back to the Aquatuk with the current.

This knowledge spurred me on with renewed energy. After a breakfast of oatmeal and hot chocolate, I travelled all day without interruption. The river bottom was normally lined with skull-sized rocks, though in places I came across gravel and sand. Small rapids barred my path at times, but I pulled my faithful canoe through without too much trouble. With Brent gone, I had taken to talking to my canoe, whom I christened *Avalon*, after another vessel I had once owned. She had been quietly proving herself a worthy companion on our journey, and now bore many battle scars from running shallow rapids and being towed up rocky stretches.

In one spot, the river widened out into a sort of lagoon, with dark green lily pads on the surface of the water that reminded me of the Amazon. But onshore were what looked like ornamented Christmas trees—tamaracks with bright red seed cones. Farther along, the river meandered in oxbows, so that at times it felt almost as if I were going around in circles. In a few places, these oxbows were so extreme that the river had cut itself a new channel, leaving behind a crescent-shaped pond from the old channel that was no longer connected to the river. One gloomy stretch had an area of considerable deadfall, where most of the trees adjoining the river had toppled over from storms.

That night, after my third day journeying upriver, I camped on a bend that was thinly treed and well-elevated. The oxbow bend meant that the river was on either side of my tent at a distance of no more than four metres. As I was moving the plastic food barrels away from the tent for the night, I caught sight of something white half-hidden beneath some ferns. Puzzled, I bent down and parted the ferns. It was the bleached skull of a moose, broken into several fragments. The empty eye sockets seemed to stare up at me. The moose had likely been killed by wolves and its head carried off by a scavenger, perhaps a wolverine.

AS I EXPLORED my way upriver, I gathered a few rock samples for my geologist colleagues, recorded the flora and fauna I came across, and documented my journey through hundreds of photographs. I also took the GPS coordinates and notes I would need to map the river. I completed the final leg of my journey up the nameless waterway on the fourth day, battling cold temperatures and steady rain the whole way along the river's winding course. Exhausted, shivering with cold, wet, hungry, and alone, it was becoming hard to concentrate on much of anything other than keeping one foot in front of the other, sloshing forward in the current. The monotony of the days and the swamp forest made things seem almost as if I was in a hazy dream. Regardless, nothing could deter me from completing my quest. The river grew smaller and shallower the farther up I ventured. Thankfully, the nearly incessant rain of the past fortnight had raised water levels enough to make wading possible—otherwise it seemed doubtful that this small river would be navigable.

Finally, by late evening on the fourth day, practically staggering in the shallow water, one hand on the rope attached to the canoe, the other holding a paddle for balance, I laid eyes on the river's source. It was not quite the sight that greeted John Hanning Speke at the headwaters of the Nile or Sir Alexander Mackenzie at the tidewater of the Pacific, but to my eyes the lake at the headwaters was paradise. When the flush of triumph had worn off, I realized that all that greeted me besides the lake was more swamp, muskeg, and hordes of blackflies and mosquitoes that happily feasted on human blood for the first time. If wendigos did exist, I imagined that this would be a good place for them. Nevertheless, it was with a deep and quiet sense of satisfaction that I pitched my tent that night on the driest patch of ground available. The next day, I would be free at last to canoe the nameless river, rather than wade through it, back to the Aquatuk and out to the salt water of Hudson Bay—where I would face an adversary far more deadly than even the wendigo—the great white bear.

[8]

BACK TO THE COAST

Going up that river was like travelling back to the earliest beginnings of the world, when vegetation rioted on the earth and the big trees were kings. An empty stream, a great silence, an impenetrable forest.
—Joseph Conrad, *Heart of Darkness*, 1899

I T TOOK only half the time—two days—to paddle the name-less river back to the Aquatuk. It was with a feeling of immense relief that I was able to sit in my canoe and paddle with the flow of the river rather than laboriously drag it behind me all day. The rain, however, continued unabated. My lonely progress downriver was sped along by an encounter with a northern goshawk. The powerful raptor had been perched high above the river in a spruce. When it spotted me, it instantly swooped down, shrieking angrily at me as I paddled along. Presumably, it had a nest somewhere in the trees. Renowned for its fierceness, this impressive bird of prey will fearlessly defend its nest from fishers, wolverines, bears, and any human that should happen to stray into its territory. It was no accident that Attila the Hun had an image of a goshawk engraved on his battle helmet.

I was amazed by how far the goshawk insisted on following me down the snaking course of the river, shrieking and circling high above the whole way. Its shrill cry piercing the silence of the wilderness was unnerving—as if the forest itself was warning me to leave. With the goshawk trailing me, I felt a bit like a trespasser fleeing a forbidden realm. The message seemed to be that my presence had been tolerated long enough and I was now overstaying my welcome.

In total, I had found some half-dozen islands along the river, including a nicely forested one, dozens of small rapids, various tributaries, picturesque pebble beaches, and plenty of wildlife, but no wendigos. However, I still had to come up with a name for the river. To be honest, I liked the romantic appeal of a river with no name, and I felt some reluctance to be the person who stripped that bit of mystery from the world. But once it was explored, it had to be named. If someone had to name it, it might as well be me.

An idea for a name presented itself when I saw a dark silhouette—an owl—flying against the grey sky at noon on my last day on the river. I managed to snap a photograph of the owl before it disappeared from view. Magnifying the picture on my digital camera, I saw that it was a northern hawk owl, which unlike most owls, hunts during the day. It had made such an auspicious appearance above the river that calling the waterway the "Owl River" seemed fitting. But since I knew an Owl River already existed, and that the Geographical Names Board discouraged name duplication, I figured "Little Owl River"—it was a small river, after all—was a better name. Henceforth, in my notes the "nameless river" became the "Little Owl River."

After six days of exploring, I left the Little Owl River and returned to the Aquatuk. It seemed as spooky and eerie as it did when I last left it. Steady rain, dark skies, and cold temperatures—it was only a few degrees above freezing—left me shivering. I began to feel the onset of hypothermia again and was forced to make camp above a high bank overlooking the water. The ground was covered in white reindeer lichen and Labrador Tea shrubs, their leaves a glossy dark green with a rusty brown underside. Needing to warm up, I built myself a fire in the rain, made some hot soup, and boiled some Labrador Tea leaves for a hot drink. Fortunately, I was surrounded by numerous blueberries, so I feasted on them as well.

WHEN THE GREEK HERO Odysseus returned home disguised as a beggar after years of war, wandering, and many adventures, he was unrecognizable to all except his faithful dog, Argus, who, "lying there lifted up his head and pricked up his ears ... he wagged his tail and dropped his ears, though he lacked the strength now to come nearer to his master." The sight of his old dog brought tears to Odysseus' eyes. Captain Meriwether Lewis, on his epic crossing of North America, was accompanied by his prized Newfoundland dog Seaman. Lewis named a creek the expedition explored in his dog's honour, and after their triumphant return had inscribed on his collar: "The greatest traveller of my species. My name is SEAMAN, the dog of captain Meriwether Lewis, whom I accompanied to the Pacific ocean through the interior of the continent of North America." The great Swedish explorer of central Asia, Sven Hedin, wrote of how bitterly he felt the loss of his dog, Dovlet, who perished while they were exploring the glacier-fed Yarkand River near the western border of China. Heartbroken, Hedin buried his dog beside the riverbank and had one of his companions, a priest, say a prayer over his grave.

Alone in the wilderness my thoughts drifted, but what often occupied my mind was the memory of my dog, Riley, and the adventures that we had shared. I was still not over the shock of his sudden death. To all appearances he had remained in his prime—a lovable, good-natured dog with a curiosity to explore that mirrored my own. For eight years he had prowled the woods at my side, following wherever I might lead. Right to the end, he could chase down rabbits with ease. But in truth he was a gentle-hearted animal who seldom hurt anything. He loved nothing better than to sit at my feet and have me stroke his glossy black fur or else nuzzle up against me as we sat round a campfire, sharing a meal. When I thought of him, I remembered a passage from one of my favourite children's books, Wilson Rawls' *Where the Red Fern Grows*, when the hero's dog, Old Dan, saves him from a mountain lion: "He wouldn't leave the tree, for in his veins flowed the breeded blood of a hunting hound. In his fighting heart, there was no fear." I would silently repeat the line, "In his fighting heart, there was no fear," whenever I faced any challenge, as a sort of epitaph for Riley and as a means to steel myself. They were words I would soon have much need of.

The rain lasted all night, soaking my tattered tent. Morning brought no respite—the day dawned with unfriendly grey skies threatening more rain. A fierce wind blew against me, so that at times it felt like I was actually still paddling against the current. On the bright side, I was no longer being tormented by any insects—it was too windy and rainy for them. I ran the river's whitewater rapids without much difficulty, though the canoe grazed a few rocks here and there.

When the weather finally cleared the following day, terns, sandpipers, ducks, and bald eagles were everywhere. In the distance, flying low over the grassy shoreline was a long-tailed jaeger, a dark-grey seabird with streamers on its tail like a child's kite, and long, elegant wings. It was hunting for fish, or perhaps small mammals, as jaegers are a predatory species that will feed on mice, lemmings, and even other birds. Little was known about the jaeger's presence in the Lowlands—the ornithology field guide I was carrying noted: "This jaeger may be a regular migrant along the coast of Hudson and James bays, but its presence there is not easily confirmed owing to the region's inaccessibility to human observers." Quietly watching a jaeger soaring over the landscape was one of the privileges of exploring the isolated Lowlands.

Wading through some river grass was an unmistakable shorebird with a long, curved bill like a new moon—a whimbrel. Not far from the whimbrel was another specimen, a Hudsonian godwit, a medium-sized shorebird that nests in the Lowlands. Little is known about the nature of their nests—the ornithology field guide noted: "breeding areas are so remote that we have only a vague idea of how many nest ... and where." Such nebulous descriptions are common for birdlife in the Lowlands, which like much of the local plants, remains enigmatic. As I watched the Hudsonian godwit stalk through the water with its long, skinny legs, I felt a strange kinship with it, as it migrates annually all the way to the tropical rainforest of South America—where I might have crossed paths with it only months earlier. In fair weather, the godwit makes the over seven-thousand-kilometre migration in a single nonstop flight. When I had mentioned this fact to Brent, he had sighed and muttered, "just thinking about it makes me tired."

Hopping along the shoals and pebble shorelines were a variety of sandpipers—spotted sandpipers, pectoral sandpipers, semi-palmated sandpipers, least sandpipers, as well as both greater and lesser yellowlegs. Most of these birds nest out in the impassable muskeg and come to the rivers to hunt small fish, insects, and crustaceans. The greater yellowlegs, acting as sentinels for a flock of birds, would bob their heads and cry out to warn the others of approaching danger whenever they spotted me in the canoe. The little least sandpipers would then echo the warning with their high-pitched "peep, peep" calls. The spotted sandpipers, looking rather striking with their white chests and dark spots, exhibit an unusual reversal of the animal kingdom's gender norms. The females defend the territory, mate with multiple males in a single breeding season, and leave the males to look after the eggs. Such inverted behaviour is observed in less than one percent of the earth's estimated ten thousand bird species.

Gliding up the river were a pair of arctic terns, beautiful birds with black-capped heads, bright orange beaks, grey wings, V-shaped tails, and a graceful flight. The arctic tern is the greatest migrant of all, travelling from the Arctic to the Antarctic annu-ally—one study estimated some terns cover over ninety thousand kilometres in a single year—far greater than any other species. They are also remarkable for their longevity; their average lifespan is about twenty years, but some have lived to over thirty. The terns' harsh, raspy cries rang out over the river, then faded away as the birds disappeared around a bend.

I saw more familiar species too. A pair of Canada geese swam near the riverbank with about a dozen goslings in tow. Unlike the spotted sandpipers, Canada geese mate for life. The geese fled the water at my approach and scurried up a steep embankment into some trembling aspens. I wished I could have told them there was no reason to run—all I was after was some fresh fish. That evening, I caught a northern pike and ate it for supper along with some freshwater clams that I had gathered.

IN ANOTHER TWO days' time I had made it back to the wind-swept plains of the tundra and nearly completed the descent of the Sutton. It was late afternoon, sunny and fairly warm. My adventure was almost over, my thumb was starting to heal, and the cold I had picked up from Brent had passed. As for the pinched nerve in my back, it had not given me any trouble—in fact, I had forgotten about it. It seemed my difficulties were a thing of the past. I expected to arrive at the mouth of the river, near the old goose hunting shack, within an hour or so. The following day, weather permitting, the pilot would arrive to meet me. The sandpipers hopping around on the rocky shorelines and the terns soaring overhead raised my spirits. I had successfully explored the river, and I could bask in the satisfaction of a journey that was almost finished.

Then, in the distance, I spotted what looked like several white boulders on the shore of an island. When I paddled closer, I realized that the boulders were in fact a polar bear. The bear was stretched out and lying in the sun, apparently half asleep—beautiful to behold, magnificent, and utterly lethal. As I took another stroke of my paddle, it suddenly sprang to its feet—seemingly surprised to see me—and ran off into some alder bushes on the island. The bear didn't appear to be terribly threatening, given that it ran off at the first sight of me. I felt more excited than scared to see it. Still, just to be cautious, before paddling any farther, I loaded the shotgun and set it near my feet in the bottom of the canoe. What happened next is something I will never forget.

After I'd paddled onward for some minutes more, the bear appeared to have vanished. That is, until I came around a bend and laid eyes on another peculiar white boulder looming out of the river in the distance like an iceberg. By this point, I would have assumed that any white boulders were polar bears—but this one was clearly too massive to be anything other than an enormous rock. However, in my experience, rocks generally don't move on their own accord. When this boulder began to migrate across the river, it dawned on me with awful certainty that it was a colossal male polar bear. Whether it was the same bear I had spotted in the distance on the island I couldn't tell—that bear had vanished before I was close enough to get a good look. But this one was a monster—it must have easily weighed over a thousand pounds. Probably it was the same animal I had seen earlier, which had likely circled unseen through the maze of alders cloaking the island to plunge into the river downstream of me. It was still a fair way off, several hundred metres at least, and seemed to be swimming across the river.

Glancing down at the loaded shotgun, I remembered my earlier resolution never to fire on a bear unless it was a matter of life and death. I continued paddling, cautiously keeping my eyes on the bear in the distance. I assumed that it would reach the shore and run off—but it didn't. Instead the bear, originally with its back facing me, turned around and started *swimming upriver in my direction*. This was rather alarming; unlike the black bears

I had met with, it was clear that shouting was not going to intimidate this giant. The river here was about twenty metres wide between the left bank and a long island. The bear was closer to the left bank, so I decided, prudently, to give the bear the right-of-way and head toward the island. The island's jungle of alder bushes concealed anything lurking onshore, so I was wary not to paddle too near the island. After all, another bear could be prowling only metres from the bank, unseen in the thicket.

The river's swift current was pushing me downriver in the canoe, while the bear was steadily coming upriver. It was now only twenty metres away. At this point, I hastily set down my camera and unsheathed my belt knife, resting it on the barrel in front of me in the canoe. As I did so the bear reached a shallow pool and rose out of the clear waters to stand on all fours, revealing its impossibly huge size. Fixing its black eyes on me, the bear moved closer in my direction and snarled. With shaking hands, I took up the shotgun and pressed the walnut butt to my shoulder, peering down the barrel at the finest specimen of the world's largest land carnivore—a bear that kills and eats other bears, and evidently had no fear of me. The bear snarled and growled, displaying fearsome teeth that could crush a man's skull like a goose egg. It was now within thirteen metres and gaining on me.

My trembling index finger switched the safety off on the gun.

The bear inched closer, growling menacingly in the river, staring straight at me. I swallowed hard, trying to calm my nerves, gripping the gun tighter and resting my finger on the trigger. The bear was in my sights, but my aim was unsteady.

With no one to steer, the canoe was drifting aimlessly in the current. My heart was pounding. If the bear were to charge across the shallow river, no more than knee deep, it would be on me in a blink of an eye. If I missed, I wouldn't have a chance to reload. And one shot would not stop this bear. It looked like the king of bears, the king of all the North. The bear growled and glared at me—it was so close that I could see the breath from its nostrils, but still I wouldn't fire. The standoff continued; seconds seemed like minutes, minutes like hours. The canoe continued to drift downriver; when I had drifted about thirty metres away from the bear, I set the shotgun down and grabbed a paddle. I cautiously paddled away while the bear watched me unflinchingly for a while, then slowly moved off in the other direction.

A few minutes paddling brought me to the island with the old goose hunting shack. I had originally planned to pitch my tent onshore, but after my encounter with such a large and aggressive polar bear, I resolved at once to fortify myself inside the shack for the night. Of course, I knew that the bear could plow through any obstacles I could erect without the slightest difficulty. But I at least wanted to create a psychological barrier. I hauled my gear up from the river to the shack, made a quick fire, then climbed onto the cabin's roof to scout out the surrounding area. In the distance, a lone caribou was wandering across the tundra. With my binoculars I could see whitecaps on stormy Hudson Bay. Scanning in all directions, I saw no sign of the bear—but clusters of spruce and willow on the tundra were ideal hiding places.

That night, expecting as I did to find that the shaggy, white-haired giant had come for me, there would be no sleep. In the dark, I sat perfectly silent in the centre of the cabin with my gun in hand, straining my ears to hear the sound of anything stalking

up to the missing door of the shack, which I had barred the best
I could with one of the metal mattress frames. I could hear the
wind rustling through the alder bushes, the ripples of the current
in the river, and a red squirrel scurrying along the cabin roof.
These noises grew familiar until they were interrupted by sounds
of a struggle in the river—a frantic honking of geese, beating
wings, wild splashing, then silence.

Around midnight, a storm struck; lashing rain, screaming
winds, and violent bursts of thunder now made it impossible to
hear any movement outside the cabin's thin walls. If a bear were
to sneak up, I would never hear it. My lonely vigil lasted all
night—I dared not sleep knowing such a formidable and fearless
bear was in the vicinity, and with no door on the cabin, how
easily it could burst upon me should I drift off. Exhausted, I
would sometimes momentarily nod off, only to have visions of
a snarling bear charging through the door snap me awake. A
flicker of lightning illuminated the inside of the cabin—I caught
a glimpse of Brent's carving on the wall, "By endurance we
conquer." The morning could not come fast enough.

WITH RELIEF, I welcomed the dawn, though the sky remained
filled with dark storm clouds. I had contacted the pilot with the
satellite phone the day before, and he was due to arrive by noon.
In the rain, I packed up my gear and paddled downriver to meet
him. Waiting onshore with my gun, I kept an eye out for polar
bears. Finally, after waiting several hours, I heard the drone of a
distant engine. The float plane soon sliced through the dark
clouds and landed in the middle of the river. The bearded pilot in
the cockpit was the same old-timer who had flown Brent back

to civilization. He steered the plane over to where I stood on the bank and brought it to a halt. Opening his door, the first thing he said was, "There's a huge polar bear just upriver! I saw it as I flew in."

I nodded. "I saw it yesterday."

"That's a man-eater that one," the pilot said wide-eyed, "one of the biggest I've ever seen. It's strange to see it inland like that, normally they're by the coast. He probably caught wind of you."

We wasted little time in strapping the canoe onto one of the plane's aluminum pontoons and loading the gear. The engine roared back to life and we were soon airborne. From the co-pilot's seat I watched endless green swamp, labyrinthine muskeg, and snaking black rivers unfold below us—and dreamed of exploring them all. It was both comforting and frustrating to think about the thousands of waterways below—even if I devoted the rest of my life to exploring them, I could never hope to cover more than a fraction. In the meantime, I welcomed the thought of a hot shower and a good night's rest.

Some six hours later, with one stop midway on a lake to refuel the plane, we were back in Hearst, the small frontier logging town. The next day, on my drive home, a wild idea entered my head—the thought of turning off the highway and heading straight for the Again River. The thought of exploring it still haunted me. And now, flush with the confidence of my solitary triumph, I knew that if need be I could do it alone.

[9]

NEW HORIZONS

It is absolutely necessary, for the peace and safety of mankind,
that some of earth's dark, dead corners and unplumbed depths be left alone.
—H.P. Lovecraft, *At the Mountains of Madness*, 1936

O NCE I RETURNED to civilization, the work of the expedition wasn't over. The difference between an adventurer and an explorer is that an explorer publishes new geographical knowledge and documents findings. I had to write my official report for the Royal Canadian Geographical Society and submit my photographs and film footage. Furthermore, as part of the Society's public outreach and education mandate, I was due to speak at schools, libraries, and other venues. But before I could bring myself to complete these tasks, I was seized by the urge to set off on another adventure. My father and I went on a short exploration of some lakes near the northern boundary of Algonquin Park. Early one misty morning, paddling in one of our cedar-strip canoes, we found a moose skeleton lying on a lakeshore. The small antlers on the skeleton were the perfect size for knife handles, so I sawed one off with the intention of crafting a new handle for my hunting knife.

In the fall, while polishing off the expedition report, I accepted a position teaching survival and woodcraft to students at a wilderness academy. The students seemed to pick up fire-making faster than Brent had, and I was impressed by their willingness to sleep outdoors in temperatures below freezing. But, never having been a Boy Scout or attended a summer camp myself, it was hard to feel much like a kindred spirit with my fellow instructors: they tended to enjoy loud conversations, campfire songs, and strumming on acoustic guitars. When the other instructors would gather around the nightly campfire to sing and socialize, I'd usually slip away into the forest to examine animal tracks and any wildlife I could find. Still, there are worse jobs than teaching wilderness skills, and it was with reluctance that I left to embark on a number of speaking engagements.

Like an itinerant preacher, I spoke at a wide variety of venues— hunter and angler associations, environmental organizations, local libraries, public and private schools, retirement homes, universities, literary festivals, conferences, and museums. I shared photographs from my expeditions, discussed exploring the Lowlands, and emphasized the importance of preserving wilderness for the future. At the end of each presentation, a forest of hands would shoot up, but the first questions were always the same: "Are you and Brent still friends? *Are you still on speaking terms?*"

Brent and I remained friends much the same as we had before. I genuinely liked Brent, and despite the fact he had abandoned me in polar bear territory, I found it impossible not to forgive him. But he never went into the wilderness again. Based on his experience, Brent quickly concluded that he was not cut out to be an explorer. Whatever he was to amount to in life, it would have nothing to do with wilderness.

Meanwhile, the Geographical Society and *Canadian Geographic* offered me a position on a new project: creating an eleven-by-eight-metre historical map of North America. As appealing as I found cartography—I'd been in love with maps since I was a child—there was yet time to squeeze in another adventure before the map project started. Oddly enough, the taste of solitude I had after Brent quit the expedition had whetted my appetite for more. Thus, with three weeks on my hands, I decided to set off alone into the mountainous wilderness of British Columbia. My objective was to track down and study petroglyphs—ancient rock carvings thousands of years old—in preparation for my doctorate, which I planned to begin in the fall.

TO EARLY EXPLORERS, the distant mountains on the far side of the continent were a foreboding place of dark legends, rumoured to be inhabited by strange tribes and all manner of monsters. Long before Europeans reached the mountains, they heard fabulous tales of what lurked there. In the 1660s, the French missionary Claude-Jean Allouez reported that his native guide had "made mention of another nation, adjoining the Assinipoualac, who eat human beings, and live wholly on raw flesh; but these people, in turn, are eaten by bears of frightful size, all red, and with prodigiously long claws." Other explorers heard similar tales when they sailed along the uncharted coastline of the Pacific Northwest. In 1792, the Spanish explorer José Mariano Mociño recorded what may be one of the oldest "sasquatch" stories:

I do not know what to say about the Matlox, inhabitant of the mountainous districts, of whom all have unbelievable fear. They imagine his body as very monstrous, all covered with stiff black bristles; a head similar to a human one but much greater, sharper and stronger fangs than a bear; extremely long arms; and toes and fingers armed with long curved claws. His shouts alone (they say) force those who hear them to the ground, and any unfortunate body he slaps is broken into a thousand pieces.

The tribes along the coast that Mociño met with lived in permanent villages with large cedar houses, elaborate artwork, totem poles, wooden armour, and huge ocean-going war canoes. They looked upon the mysterious tribes of the interior as primitive, half-savages that wandered the forests in small bands like animals. They called these uncouth wanderers "*sésqʼɔc*," a Salish word meaning "wild man." In English, "*sésqʼɔc*" later became sasquatch. These traditions were garbled up with tales of the grizzly bear—a huge, shaggy-haired creature that stands up to three metres on its hind legs—to create the legendary sasquatch. At least, not believing that such a thing as Bigfoot exists, this was the theory I had formulated based on an examination of archival explorers' journals and research on aboriginal oral traditions.

One of the more intriguing sasquatch accounts that I came across was in the pages of David Thompson's journal. Thompson, an explorer with few equals who mapped more of North America than any other person, penetrated the Rockies from the east in 1811. In the dead of winter, he recorded a singular experience:

January 5: ... we are now entering the defiles of the Rocky Mountains by the Athabasca River ... strange to say, here is a strong belief that the haunt of the Mammoth is about this defile ... I questioned several (Indians), none could positively say they had seen him, but their belief I found firm and not to be shaken.... All I could say did not shake their belief in his existence ...

January 7: Continuing on our journey in the afternoon we came on the track of a large animal, the snow about six inches deep on the ice; I measured it; four large toes each of four inches in length to each a short claw; the ball of the foot sunk three inches lower than the toes, the hinder part of the foot did not mark well, the length fourteen inches, by eight inches in breadth, walking from north to south, and having passed about six hours. We were in no humour to follow him; the men and Indians would have it to be a young Mammoth and I held it to be the track of a large old grizzled bear; yet the shortness of the nails, the ball of the foot, and its great size were not that of a bear, otherwise that of a very large old bear, his claws worn away; this the Indians would not allow.

Thompson's encounter likely reflects the grizzly bear contribution to the sasquatch legend, as he himself seemed to believe. Other explorers made similar observations about strange tracks, unknown noises in the night, and legends of monsters prowling in the mountains. I found a hint of the other side of the myth— the stories of "wild men" high up in the mountains—in the diary of Paul Kane, an artist and explorer. Kane noted in his March 26, 1847, journal entry:

> When we arrived at the mouth of the Kattlepoutal River, twenty-six miles distant from Vancouver, I stopped to make a sketch of the volcano, Mt. St. Helens, distant, I suppose, about thirty or forty miles. This mountain has never been visited by either whites or Indians; the latter assert that it is inhabited by a race of beings of a different species, who are cannibals, and whom they hold in great dread ... these superstitions are taken from the statement of a man who, they say, went into the mountain with another, and escaped the fate of his companion, who was eaten by the "skoocooms".... I offered a considerable bribe to any Indian who would accompany me in its exploration but could not find one hardy enough to venture there.

Still, such stories were cause for reflection, and I knew more than a few individuals—aboriginal elders, hunters who had spent a great deal of time in the wilderness, and even a couple of mavericks with PhDs in zoology—who doggedly insisted that the sasquatch was a real animal in the flesh, surviving unknown to science in pockets of unexplored wilderness.

AFTER FINISHING MY RESEARCH on petroglyph sites in southern British Columbia, I decided to head north to the Great Bear Rainforest, the earth's largest temperate rainforest, which cloaks the islands and mountains of the northern Pacific coast up to the

Alaskan panhandle in a mantle of old-growth forest. Concealed within this mist-shrouded landscape are more than just weathered totem poles and mysterious stone carvings. Lurking in the forests are mountain lions, wolves, the world's densest concentration of grizzly bears, and the otherworldly Kermode or "spirit" bear, a rare subspecies of black bear with snow-white fur. A four-hundred-kilometre flight north of Vancouver would bring me to the isolated aboriginal settlement of Bella Coola, home to some six-hundred members of the Nuxalk First Nation. The community is situated in the heart of the Great Bear Rainforest and is the site of ancient petroglyphs. On this trip, I would go back to basics: no gun, no bear spray, no GPS, no satellite phone, just myself alone in the mountains with a knife and the bare essentials.

From the airplane window I gazed down on endless mountains capped in eternal snow. Some of these peaks had never been scaled, and no one could know how many unexplored caves remained hidden in the mountain fastness. After miles of snow and ice, a narrow ribbon of greenery loomed into view—it was our destination, the valley of the Bella Coola River, enclosed by towering mountains on either side. Stepping onto the airstrip I surveyed my surroundings. To the west lay the lush temperate rainforest of the Pacific coastline, to the north, east, and south were mountains beyond counting. Just across the tarmac I could see the swirling waters of the Bella Coola River, the very river Sir Alexander Mackenzie paddled on the final leg of his epic crossing of North America in 1793. Downstream of where I stood, Mackenzie reached tidewater on the Pacific Ocean, becoming the first explorer to cross the continent north of Mexico, beating

Lewis and Clark by thirteen years. The wilderness here had changed little in the more than two hundred years since his journey.

I hiked into Bella Coola along the road winding through the narrow valley. First, I would make arrangements with a local guide to visit the known petroglyph sites, as it was prohibited for outsiders to visit these sacred sites without a Nuxalk guide. Then, I planned to head into the mountains to seek the unknown.

I was not the first explorer attracted to the valley's mysterious stone carvings. Before he won fame for his Kon-Tiki expedition across the Pacific, the Norwegian explorer Thor Heyerdahl had come to Bella Coola in the 1940s to examine petroglyphs. Heyerdahl was convinced that the carvings were linked to ones he had seen in the distant South Pacific, considering them as evidence for his theory that people in the Americas had colonized Polynesia thousands of years ago. In town, when my interest in petroglyphs became known, I was shown black-and-white photographs proudly kept in old family albums of Heyerdahl in Bella Coola as a young man.

My guide was a Nuxalk man in his twenties named Nils. We met the following morning on the outskirts of town. Nils drove us in an old pickup truck to a small stream named Thorsen Creek, where we set off on foot up a meandering mountain trail. Climbing steadily, we passed over smooth boulders and carpets of green moss and beneath towering hemlocks, cedars, and firs. Along the trail grew skunk cabbage and devil's club—an aptly named large shrub whose sharp spines produce a painful rash when brushed against. To our left was a steep ravine, at the bottom of which roared the clear waters of Thorsen Creek as it tumbled out of the mountains on its way to the Bella Coola River. The mosquitoes were surprisingly thick, considering that it was only mid-April.

"Just a bit farther," said Nils as he led the way along the steep trail. I could hear the roar of falling water ahead—a small waterfall ran down the side of the gorge into Thorsen Creek far below us.

"Beautiful," I said, pausing to inspect the fall. I dashed over a boulder to stand on the edge of the precipice, then lay on my chest to hang over the side and photograph the waterfall.

"You're crazy!" cried Nils.

I glanced over my shoulder to see Nils staring open-mouthed at me perched on the cliff edge. "What? Are you afraid of heights?" I said puzzled.

Nils nodded, seeming to see me in a whole new light.

"Oh, I didn't realize … anyway, are the petroglyphs near here?"

"Yeah, this way."

The first of the petroglyphs were simple circles engraved in sandstone outcrops. Beyond them, on other large sandstone slabs and boulders were snarling faces, stylized birds, frogs, owls, mountain lions, mythical beasts, grotesque shapes, and indecipherable designs. The carvings formed a sort of mural—vaguely sinister looking—and are believed to have been used in secret, shamanic rituals for thousands of years.

"This is a sacred site, and in the old days if a white man was found here, he'd be kissing his life goodbye," explained Nils.

I nodded, "I see."

The oldest petroglyphs at this site are believed to be about three thousand years old, making them about as old as the Trojan War or Egypt's New Kingdom. Nils, however, pointed out one carving that dated to the nineteenth century, which was engraved using a steel tool rather than stone. I carefully photographed each carving.

"Are there any petroglyphs that depict sasquatch?"

"Sasquatch?" Nils looked at me blankly for a moment. "Yeah, that one does," he said, pointing to a hideous, snarling face etched in weathered sandstone.

I inspected it closely and photographed it. "Do you know anyone who has ever claimed to see a sasquatch?"

Nils nodded, "My grandfather has seen them. Lots of people have."

"What do they look like?"

"Like people, only with more hair."

"Where do they live?"

"High up in the mountains," said Nils. "In places humans can't get to. In caves on steep cliffs and on glaciers."

"Anywhere around here?"

Nils nodded, "Yeah, come here." He motioned for me to step closer to the edge of the ravine, where the trees opened up enough to allow for a view of the encircling mountains. "You see that big mountain over there?"

I nodded.

"No one goes up that mountain. Sasquatch live up there."

This revelation struck me as keenly interesting, and I at once began to brood over the idea of hiking up the mountain Nils had pointed out. I had no alpine gear with me, but I could explore the forested slopes at least as far as the snowline. As we returned down the trail, I continued to ponder the petroglyphs and ask Nils about local legends.

After a few days milling around Bella Coola, investigating more rock carvings and archaeological sites, I made arrangements with a wildlife lodge operator to drive me to the base of the mountain Nils had pointed out. After my last expedition, I wanted to return to my roots and head into the wilderness with as little gear as possible.

My driver quizzed me as we drove along a bumpy mountain road hemmed in by thick forest on either side.

"Do you have a satellite phone?"

"No."

"GPS?"

"Just a compass. I prefer the old-fashioned way."

"A gun?"

"Nope."

"Bear spray?"

"No."

"Well, it sounds like you must know what you're doing," he shrugged as he steered the truck around a fallen tree branch that blocked part of the narrow road. "So, I'll meet you here at the end of the road in a week?"

"That'd be good."

The road came to an end at the base of the mountain. There was an old trail that led some way up the mountain slope, and I planned to follow it. "Good luck," said my driver, as I exited the truck and strapped on my backpack.

"Thanks," I replied.

"Keep an eye out for grizzlies," he advised, before driving away.

My first task was to find myself a sturdy walking stick that I could sharpen into a spear if the need arose. That accomplished,

I started along the narrow trail into the dark woods. I hiked without stopping until mid-afternoon, when I arrived at a fine moss-carpeted glade a fair way up the mountain that seemed perfect for a base camp. There was a small pond nearby where I could fetch water and plenty of dead trees around for firewood. An inspection of the area revealed no signs of bears, but a short distance from where I pitched my tent was some mountain lion scat, with the tiny hooves of an unfortunate young mountain goat in it. But mountain lions rarely attack humans, so I wasn't troubled. My plan was to camp in the glade and explore more of the mountain over the following days.

The next day, I started climbing the mountain, scrambling over boulders and steep slopes. At one point, a pine marten chasing after red squirrels scurried across the wooded slope below me. As I climbed higher, I encountered several caves, but they appeared to be unoccupied by anything other than spiders. Finally, I made it as far as the snowline, where I had a spectacular view of the sheer, snow-capped mountains that framed the valley. The highest peaks stood some three thousand metres above sea level. Cloaked in a mantle of snow and ice, it was easy to see why people imagined the formidable heights as home to all manner of monsters.

In the late afternoon, when I returned to my camp, I met with a startling sight: large claw marks sunk into the bark of a cedar tree near my tent. Uneasy, I clenched my spear and looked quickly in all directions. Inspecting the ground did not reveal any tracks. But there could be no doubt that grizzlies were in the area, hungry after the lean winter. Bears often mark their territory by scratching trees, and these claw marks couldn't have been more than a few hours old.

Sleeping in a tent suddenly lost much of its appeal. To protect myself from the possibility of a bear attack at night, I decided to build a more secure shelter to sleep in. The only tools at my disposal were a hatchet, my knife, and a folding saw, along with some rope and paracord. With these tools I could fashion a sleeping platform between four trees a safe distance off the ground. Of course, bears can climb trees, but I would be much better protected on an elevated platform than in a tent on the ground. Working quickly to beat the sunset, I had to shinny up each tree and lash together the strong sticks I had cut to create a platform between four hemlocks. After the frame was finished, I cut sticks that I would bind to the rectangular platform, creating a solid floor to sleep on. For protection against the rain, I made a roof out of my tarp and enclosed the sides with hemlock boughs. To make the floor more comfortable, I laid moss and more hemlock boughs over the platform. My shelter finished, it served as a rather cozy abode for the next five nights.

Few things encourage reflection quite like fresh mountain air and utter solitude. Over the following days, as I continued to explore the mountain, my old obsession, the Again River, weighed on my mind. Four years had elapsed since the day when, brooding over maps in my cluttered study, I had first learned of the river's existence. After the aborted attempts to explore it, first with my father and later with Wes, the Again had remained at the back of my mind as a nagging ambition left undone—it was the one that got away. Now, sitting alone on a mountain slope, staring off at distant snow-capped summits, I quietly resolved to myself that no matter the cost, I would explore the Again that year, alone if need be.

"THOSE PORTAGES CAN'T be done alone," said Wes. "There's no way to carry the canoe through that forest by yourself. It's a jungle, you need a machete just to get through there."

"So you'll come with me then?" I asked.

Wes thought for a moment. "Maybe ... I have to think about it."

Back home from my adventures in the mountains, there was little time to dwell on whether Wes would come with me to explore the Again River. In addition to my work on the map for the Royal Canadian Geographical Society, I had committed myself to an archaeological excavation at a site along the Niagara River, where I would be busy five days a week doing a different sort of exploration—digging into the earth. I was also under a deadline to finish a story for *Canadian Geographic* about a canoe trip I had undertaken through the Minesing Swamp, a wetland near Lake Huron. Thus, there was little time to think of northern rivers: I spent my days digging in the dirt and my weekends and evenings working on the map. When July arrived, I was on Parliament Hill in Ottawa with a team from the Geographical Society to officially unveil the map. There, beneath the gaze of the gothic turrets and gargoyles of the Parliament Buildings, I first mentioned to one of *Canadian Geographic*'s editors my plans to explore the Again River. It was readily agreed that I would produce a few articles for the magazine's website on my expedition.

"You must be busy preparing for it then?" asked the editor.

"I haven't had a chance yet, but I'll be ready."

"Who's going with you?"

"I'm not sure yet."

"Tell me you're not thinking of doing this alone?" She looked alarmed.

"If need be," I said.

"Adam!"

Once the map unveiling ceremony was over, I departed immediately for Ohio, where I was to join another archaeological dig on an Iroquoian site. It was while in Ohio—standing in a cornfield under a blazing sun examining prehistoric stone projectile points—that I received a call from Wes. He told me that he couldn't explore the Again River that summer. Maybe, he suggested, he would be available next year. But that to me was unthinkable—to delay for a day longer, let alone a year, was likely to drive me as mad as Captain Ahab.

"No," I said to Wes on the phone, "I can't wait. I'll do it by myself if I have to."

"That's crazy," replied Wes.

My frenzied schedule and lack of any partner meant that there was little time to prepare for the expedition. I had no chance to review my old notes on the Again or even to obtain new topographic maps. The old charts from three years earlier with Wes had become water-stained and illegible. There was neither time nor money to replace them. But like the explorers of old, I had canoed many rivers without maps and could, if need be, create my own. All I had was a single 1:50,000 scale map of the most important part of the route supplemented with a few sketchy printouts from satellite imagery—more than sufficient, I thought, to find and explore the river.

Flushed with confidence and practically half-mad with a long-suppressed desire to pry open the secrets of this obscure waterway, I could barely permit myself a moment's rest until I had reached it. The Ohio dig finished, I drove back to Canada without delay, packed up my gear, and set off to finally free myself of an obsession that had long vexed me—a river that no known person had ever fully explored.

10

TRAILBLAZING

In the beginning was the forest. God made it and no man knew the end of it.
It was not new. It was old; ancient as the hills it covered. Those who
entered it saw it had been there since the beginning of habitable time.
—Hervey Allen, *The Forest and the Fort*, 1943

TERRY O'NEIL MET ME at the old train station in Cochrane, Ontario, on what was a glorious summer day. The air smelled of freshly cut timber from the logging operations that were the mainstay of the local economy. We had breakfast at the station's restaurant before I drove the two of us out of town on the mining road to the starting point for the expedition.

"You're going to do this alone?" asked Terry, incredulous.

"Yes," I said.

"Couldn't you convince someone to go with you?"

"No such luck."

Terry shook his head, "Adam, this is a risky thing to be attempting alone. Did I ever tell you about the last people, besides you, I shuttled out to the Kattawagami?"

"Yes, only one came back alive."

"That's right," Terry nodded, "and just this summer I shuttled a guy who was going to attempt the Kesagami River, and he had to call search-and-rescue on his satellite phone."

"What happened?"

"He was canoeing on James Bay and got stranded on an island. You can't drink the water in the bay; it's salty, as you know. And he ran out of fresh water and couldn't get off the island because of stormy weather. They had to rescue him with a helicopter."

"Well, no one is coming to rescue me," I said.

In about two hours' time we arrived at the bridge over the Kattawagami River, passing several black bears along the way. Unlike in past years, when I had started by exploring Hopper Creek, dry weather dictated that this time I would embark directly from the Kattawagami.

"The water levels are very low," said Terry, looking down from the bridge. We had parked the car to take a look.

"You're right," I replied.

"It's been a very dry summer. I can't remember a summer so dry," said Terry, who had just celebrated his seventy-second birthday the day before I arrived.

"Well, rain has a way of following me," I said.

I hoped it would rain—the dry conditions made forest fires a lethal hazard, and here, in the southern part of the Lowlands, there was more forest cover to burn, so escaping from any fire would be more difficult than farther north. According to the most recent Ministry of Natural Resources fire report, over a hundred active fires were burning across the North, including one not far from the area I would have to pass through.

"I'll keep your car safe at my place," said Terry, as I handed him my keys.

I had about finished carefully packing my canoe—the same vessel, *Avalon*, that had braved the perils of the nameless river with me. My gear consisted of one outfitter backpack, a watertight plastic barrel, two paddles, and a fishing rod—no shotgun, as the nearest polar bears were over a hundred kilometres north of my route, though I did pick up some bear spray for the black bears.

"Well …" said Terry, looking at me for a while and wondering, it seemed, whether he was going to be the last person to see me alive. "Good luck, Adam. Be smart out there, and don't take any unnecessary risks."

"I never do," I replied.

Terry waved goodbye, and I tipped my brown fedora at him, under which I wore a mesh bug net to keep off the relentless attacks of the blackflies and mosquitoes. Then I stepped into my canoe, pushed off from the shore into the swift current, and launched myself once more into the wilderness. I was keen for the challenge and paddled hard, eager to encounter the first of what would be hundreds of whitewater rapids. I didn't have long to wait. Soon the first sizable rapid roared ahead. "Here we go," I said to myself as I zipped up my lifejacket, tossed off my hat, and strapped on my helmet—ready for battle. I had equipped the canoe with a floatation device—an inflated bag made of flexible PVR that was fitted and secured into the stern behind my seat—which hopefully would keep the boat buoyant if raging whitewater rapids submerged it.

These first sets of rapids proved shallow and rocky, but usually with a deep enough passage in the middle that I could squeeze through. Water levels, as Terry had observed, were remarkably

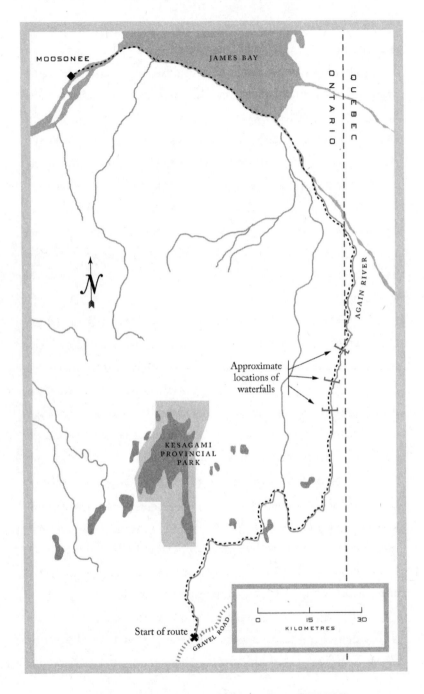

AGAIN RIVER EXPEDITION ROUTE

low—about a metre and a half lower than the last time I paddled the Kattawagami in 2009. This was worrisome news—low water levels could mean dry creek beds and render the route I was planning on following to reach the Again's headwaters vastly more difficult, if not impossible.

Some of the rapids were so shallow that I was forced to get out of my canoe and wade rather than risk damaging the hull by scraping over jagged rocks. As I was wading, guiding the canoe down a narrow passage between several boulders, I glanced up and was startled to see a black bear sitting on the grassy river-bank. It was less than thirty metres downriver, munching contently on some aquatic plants. The bear, preoccupied with its food, had its head down and took no notice of me. It was a large black bear, but sitting on its haunches eating, it looked more like Winnie the Pooh than anything threatening, so I felt comfortable photographing and filming it. It was only when I spoke on camera, mentioning that a bear was just downriver, that the bruin finally noticed my presence and slowly shuffled off into the forest, as if my intrusion at breakfast was unpardonably rude.

Later that day I passed through a tranquil stretch of river, where the woods on either bank had been charred by a forest fire. Young jack pines and juniper bushes sprang up from the ground, which suggested that the fire had taken place a few years earlier. The dead spruces and tamaracks, burnt black from the fire, stood like tombstones over the ravaged land. It was a stark reminder of the hazard that hung over my solitary journey—both the Again River itself, and the nameless streams I would follow to reach it, were far too small to offer any escape from a forest fire. Even if I could somehow evade the searing heat, there would be little hope of avoiding the suffocating smoke.

That night I made camp on the riverbank, outside the burnt area. Here, the forest was more cheerful, with whiskey jacks, boreal chickadees, and dark-eyed juncos singing and chirping in the trees, and plenty of wild berries about. I spotted a snowshoe hare, rusty brown in its summer coat, near my camp, and during the course of the day I had seen eagles, geese, ducks, and three river otters. Such wildlife kept me in good company and dispelled any feeling of loneliness.

THE FOLLOWING DAY, hours of long, hard paddling coupled with much wading through shallow boulder fields and rapids brought me to the weedy lake, the same body of water that I had visited years earlier with my father and later with Wes. Beneath a half-moon, I camped on a sandy stretch of shoreline for the night.

At dawn, the sounds of a whimsical birdcall echoing from across the mist-covered waters woke me. Intrigued, I stood at the water's edge, staring across a lake that was as smooth as glass. I squinted at the far shore, half a kilometre away, thinking I could make out two large animals in the shallows. They were apparently producing the peculiar calls. When I grabbed my binoculars and pressed them to my eyes, I had to do a double take: I saw a pair of giant prehistoric-looking birds. Standing four feet tall and with a seven-and-a-half-foot wingspan, the enormous grey birds could only be sandhill cranes. The cranes' grey feathers accentuated a blood-red band around their eyes that looked something like a costume ball mask. Here in these austere northern forests, a land of gloom and shadow, the cranes seemed out of place, though in fact they are found across much of North America's wilderness.

I got underway early, paddling out of the lake and back onto the Kattawagami River, eager to begin the process of leaving its watershed behind and penetrating to the Again River. It was a hot, sunny day; waterfowl were abundant, eagles soared overhead, otters and the occasional beaver swam in the river, and an osprey dove for fish—the only spectators to my attempt at making a modest contribution to exploration history.

Rapids and large boulder fields straddling the river slowed my progress. In these stretches, the canoe had to be carefully towed as I waded ahead and tried to avoid scraping it on the rocks as much as possible. The dry summer had left the river so low that I scarcely recognized it as the same waterway that I had previously paddled. The lack of water also alarmed me because of what it boded about the Again River—knowing as I did that the Again was a smaller river, I had to wonder whether it would be possible to paddle it at all. No matter how careful I was, shallow, rock-infested rivers would be sure to scrape and gouge the canoe terribly. And if the canoe was punctured beyond repair, crossing the seas of James Bay at the end of my journey would be all but impossible. But I had resolved to explore the Again River no matter the obstacles, and so I proceeded, expecting the worst and hoping for the best.

By noon I had reached the tributary that I was seeking—a small river that drains into the Kattawagami. Four years ago, I had explored this then-nameless tributary with my father as the first step in reaching the Again. Lined with tamaracks, I had taken to calling it Tamarack Creek. Its meandering, rock-strewn course led through swamp and forest to a beautiful lake. Paddling and wading up it had been arduous enough with another person. Doing it in low water and alone would make it little short of a nightmare. The lack of water meant that I had to drag and portage the fifty-two-pound canoe and my ninety pounds of gear and provisions for considerable stretches. But I was so impatient to reach the Again that I threw myself into the creek when paddling proved no longer possible, dragging the laden canoe behind me through the rapids that blocked the way forward. The blackflies and mosquitoes swarmed around me as thick as storm clouds, but this only motivated me to move faster. The creek bottom was a treacherous mix of crevices and sharp rocks, where twisting an ankle was all too easy. In other places, the drought had left the creek little more than a trickle, which made dragging the canoe impossible. Here, I had no choice but to carry the canoe over my head, balancing it on my shoulders, and then portage the remainder of my gear up to the next stretch of water deep enough to resume paddling and wading. Luckily, I received help from an unexpected source—beavers. To compensate for the lack of rain, the beavers had built several dams on the creek, which by holding back water, created deep stretches that I could paddle up with comparative ease. The engineers of the wilderness, beavers are extraordinary in their capacity to modify the environment to suit their needs—minutely adjusting water levels on their ponds to just the right amount to keep their lodges safe from predators and allowing themselves to swim under the ice come winter.

By evening, I had left the creek behind and arrived at a large, picturesque lake that was its headwaters. For a few more hours, I paddled along the lake, passing sandy beaches framed by dark woods while listening to the haunting cries of loons echoing from across the blue waters. That night, I sipped herbal tea and feasted on fresh pike, arrowhead roots, and wild berries, mulling over the challenge that awaited me in the morning—the start of the gruelling portages through forbidding swamp forest. The trackless morass of alder swamps that lay beyond the lake's northern shores was as far as my father and I had reached four years ago. The next summer with Wes, I had sought to avoid the worst of the swamps by striking off farther south, blazing kilometres of trails with the rising sun as our guide to a chain of several lakes before time ran out and forced us to turn around. It was imperative that I find the old blaze marks Wes and I cut in the forest three years ago. Failure to find our old trail would mean a delay of at least several days, in which I would have to laboriously blaze my way through the forest again, navigating across a monotonous landscape clogged with bloodsucking insects.

THE FIRST PORTAGE was approximately two kilometres one way, a trek that would have to be done in three stages: the first with my backpack and fishing rod, the second with the watertight barrel and paddles, and the third with the canoe. So, in total, counting doubling back, I had ten kilometres to cover on foot to reach the next lake, assuming that I managed to maintain the correct course and never lose my way in the forest. Wes, knowing the difficulty of carrying the canoe across the open bogs and almost impenetrable forest, doubted the feasibility of my doing this alone. But the iron law of necessity makes many things possible.

I soon located the spot where Wes and I had camped on the lakeshore three years earlier, and from there scouted the forest until finding a few of our old blaze marks on the straggly tamaracks and spruces. The sap, which had oozed out of the trees when struck with a hatchet, had since hardened on the bark and stained the once white blazes a yellowish hue. There was, properly speaking, no trail to follow, for the ground remained covered in saplings, shrubs, lichens, moss, and swamp pools. But it didn't matter—the important thing was that I had found the faded blazes and could follow them to the next lake.

In the forest, the blackflies and mosquitoes were appalling— far worse than on the breezy lakeshore, and I was soon sweating heavily from the labour of carrying my gear over the uneven terrain, which made walking exhausting, sinking as I did into the soggy, moss-covered ground. Parts of the portage cut through fairly open forest of stunted tamarack and spruce, but the middle section passed through an alder swamp, where finding the old blazes was difficult and my boots were soaked in the stagnant waters. Frequently, I had to set down my load and scout ahead until I refound a blaze mark and could safely continue. As I staggered forward under the hot sun, I snapped off branches to make a more visible trail and added a few new blazes with my knife. After the first two loads were across, I brought the canoe. I dragged it most of the way over the swampy ground rather than attempting to carry it over my head, which would never work in the thick forest, given how closely spaced the trees were. At any rate, it would be impossible to follow the blazes with a canoe over my head. Panting heavily, I had to continually flip the canoe on its side, slide it between some trees, then readjust it again to avoid the next obstacle blocking the way forward. It felt something like playing a game of Twister, where the challenge was to somehow move my thirteen-foot canoe between ranks of small trees that at times grew so close together they resembled prison bars.

It took six hours to complete the portage—encouraging progress. When I reached the lake on the far side, I quenched my thirst in its waters, then paddled against a strong headwind to its far end, where another gruelling portage awaited. This time, the start of the portage was right in the middle of an alder swamp, and once more I had to search for the old blazes to find the way forward. The alders were nearly impenetrable, entangling me as I attempted to hack a way through with the heavy pack on my back while balancing on little clumps of dry moss in the morass of foul black water. The bugs were as fierce as ever, and if I failed to pay attention for a moment, I would lose my way in the jungle of alders that was so thick it felt almost suffocating. It was impossible to see more than a few feet in any direction.

Eventually, I crossed the alder swamp and emerged in a more pleasant wood on the other side with tall trees festooned in old man's beard. The ground here was carpeted in green moss with clusters of bright red mushrooms, creating the vague impression of a fairy-tale forest—an effect that was enhanced by the croaking of a wood frog. I halted to eat some wild raspberries and blueberries and satisfy my thirst. Birds sang in the trees above me. Growing in a shadowy patch nearby were some Indian pipes, a type of white herb shaped remarkably like a tobacco pipe. They reminded me of home—Indian pipes grew in the forests that surrounded my family's house and had been one of my favourite things to search for in the woods as a child. Refreshed from the drink and the berries, I pressed on, passing through

more thick brush before finally reaching the shore of a picturesque little lake with shining blue waters enclosed by dark green
woods. Near the shore were bright-coloured, carnivorous pitcher
plants, a sort of northern Venus flytrap that feeds on insects and
frogs, trapping them in its "pitcher," from which they never
emerge.

It was still hot and sunny, so I pressed on further once this
portage was completed, heading out onto the lake. Three years
ago, this lake had reminded me of Temagami, a rugged region
of rolling hills, waterfalls, and beautiful lakes in central Ontario.
In my journal I had named it Temagami Lake. The forest
surrounding it boasted the biggest trees I had yet seen on my
journey: ancient spruce and tamarack that grew to a large size
owing to better soil. The ground in this area was less swampy
and in places included actual hills, a rarity in the Hudson Bay
Lowlands, though I was still somewhere near the southern
boundary between the Lowlands and the more rugged Canadian
Shield. A short paddle brought me across the lake to its thickly
treed eastern shore. A few hundred metres into those woods and
over a steep hill lay another nameless lake, which three years ago
I had called Last Lake, because it was the last lake before the
final forbidding portage to the Again River's headwaters. Too
agitated with anticipation to stop for the night, I decided to
keep pushing on, first hacking my way through the thick brush
and forest, then dragging my canoe up the steep hill and down
to Last Lake on the other side. The sun was setting, but I
managed to finish off this third consecutive portage of the day
and canoe to the lake's far shore, where I made camp. It had
been a thirteen-hour day of continuous labour, in which I had

portaged some sixteen kilometres and paddled several more. And the next day, I would have to do it all over again.

This lake was as far as Wes and I had reached three years ago, and as close as I had ever come to the Again River. When we made the decision to turn back, we had been blazing a trail through swamps beyond the lake's northeastern shore. This time I decided to pursue a different course to another lake that my map assured me lay several kilometres away—I would head east, into the rising sun, rather than attempt to follow the non-existent course of a stream that appeared on the map but did not in fact exist, which had led Wes and me astray last time.

That night, exhausted as I was, sleep proved difficult—the anticipation of the critical next day kept me awake. I looked upon the portage to the Again's headwaters as the make-or-break of my entire enterprise. There was simply no way to know in advance if I could locate the headwaters, let alone portage my gear and canoe there. From what I could gather from the satellite images, a vast morass of muskeg barred the way forward. Early explorers had judged the muskeg of the Lowlands as an impassable barrier to overland travel. The woodsman and writer Grey Owl furnished one of the best descriptions of it:

> In places the forest dwindles down to small trees, which, giving way to moss and sage brush, thin out and eventually disappear altogether, and the country opens out into one of those immense muskegs or swamps which makes overland travel in whole sections impossible.... These consist mostly of stretches composed of deep, thin mud, covered with slushy moss, and perhaps sparsely dotted

with stunted, twisted trees. Bright green, inviting looking fields show up in places, luring the inexperienced into their maw with their deceptive promise of good footing. These last are seemingly bottomless, and constitute a real danger to man or beast.... There are holes between hummocks that are filled with noisome stagnant water, which would engulf a man.

But as I finally drifted off to sleep in my tent, visions of bottomless muskeg on my mind, I told myself that I would find a way, no matter what.

I AWOKE AT the crack of dawn—the day's labours would require all the daylight I could get. After a hurried breakfast of oatmeal and tea, I struck off into the gloomy, dew-covered forest, carrying only my hatchet and compass. This time, there were no old blazes from three years ago to follow—I was starting from scratch. Therefore, it was impractical to attempt carrying anything across on this first trip, when all my physical energy and mental powers would be devoted to navigation and trailblazing. I was excited and a little nervous. I was really in the unknown now—a place where every sight was new to me, and each step carried me deeper into unexplored territory.

My cargo pants were soaked by the dew on the shrubs and trees as I trudged into the dark woods, but things appeared promising at first. The ground sloped upwards—a welcome sign, as it meant no immediate muskeg, but it quickly led into impenetrable brush, where spruce and tamarack branches clawed at my face as I tried to hack a way through. It felt claustrophobic in the deepest thickets, where the sunlight never penetrated beneath the gloom of the thick, entangling trees. It was vital to blaze a set of marks on both sides of the trees—which, like Hansel and Gretel's bread crumb trail or Theseus' ball of thread in the labyrinth, would allow me to find the way back. I relied on both my brass surveyor's compass and the sun—when I could see it—to navigate. Eventually, I emerged from the thicket into more typical Lowlands forest—sparsely treed, swampy moss and lichen covered ground, and plenty of dark pools and little hummocks that turned walking into an exhausting ordeal. Each step would cause me to sink down into the moss, and in a few places, I had to leap across swamp holes, all while swarmed by clouds of blackflies and mosquitoes.

The forest seemed to go on forever. At times my mind wandered—I would begin doubting myself, wondering if I was heading in the right direction and if there was any lake to be found. Maybe, for all I knew, it was just a quagmire. But then I would give my head a shake, banish all such doubts, and trudge deeper into the woods.

In a shady grove, I caught sight of a dash of red moving along the ground—a spruce grouse. The docile bird seemed to hardly notice my presence, pecking and scratching at the ground like a domestic chicken. As much as I hated killing anything unnecessarily, I was awfully hungry. Almost in spite of myself, I unsheathed my belt knife, crept closer to the grouse, then threw the knife at it. The bird gave a cackle and flew into the branches of a big spruce. I sighed—but then I remembered the hatchet gripped in my other hand and tossed it tomahawk-style at the bird in the tree. It narrowly missed the grouse's head.

Lunch would have to wait. I collected my weapons and resumed the portage.

Finally, after four and a half hours of hiking and blazing through what felt like an endless swamp forest, I laid eyes on what to me was the most splendid and thrilling sight—an expanse of dark, misty water in the distance—*the lake*. Columbus must have felt the same intense excitement when he first glimpsed land in 1492. All my doubts dissipated, all my restless anxiety evaporated, and what was left was the exhilarating satisfaction of a scheme revealed to be possible. The fact that several hundred metres of open muskeg, denuded of nearly all tree cover, separated me from the lakeshore barely put a dent in my enthusiasm. All that mattered at the moment was that the lake appeared to exist, and that I appeared to have found it.

It took nearly an hour to return through the forest to my camp on the other side. I had left my tent up and my gear unpacked in the event that I ran into difficulties blazing a way across, in which case I imagined spending another night in this spot. But that was now unnecessary, so I quickly packed up my gear, strapped on the watertight barrel, and headed back into the gloom of the woods. I did the portage in stages—taking each load halfway across, then returning for the next load. By late afternoon, I had transported my backpack and plastic barrel, as well as the paddles and fishing rod, to the end of my blazes, which was still nearly three hundred metres short of the actual lakeshore—which remained beyond the open muskeg.

I now hiked all the way back to fetch my canoe—the last and most difficult thing to transport. I pulled it behind me, but it constantly wedged between trees, forcing me to push and heave to get it through and slowing my progress to a crawl. Rain began to fall in the evening when I was still only about halfway across. Reluctantly, given the fading light and steady rain, I knew I had to give up my hopes of finishing the portage that day. As things stood, it looked like I was in for a miserable night, not having had the chance to make camp yet or find any dry ground to pitch the tent on. Leaving the canoe behind me in the forest, I headed to where I had left my other gear to rest for the night.

The whole area near the lakeshore was a soggy sea of muskeg. In the rain I searched for a patch of solid ground big enough to pitch my tent on—not finding anything, I settled for rigging up a tarp between a couple of scraggly tamaracks to keep the rain off. Camping as I was in the middle of muskeg in a rainstorm, I assumed that it would be a wet night no matter what I did. But somehow, I managed to stay more or less dry inside my tent beneath the rain tarp, and on the bright side, the muskeg was quite comfortable to sleep on.

IN THE MORNING I put on my wet clothing, skipped breakfast, and resumed my portage in the sodden forest. Just walking a few feet through the rain-soaked brush further drenched my already wet cargo pants, boots, and socks. The sky above me remained grey and overcast, offering little hope of drying anything. But the Again's headwaters were near at hand, and within a few hours I had completed what I had failed to do three years ago with Wes: I successfully carried the canoe and all my gear across the last terrible portage, which, counting all the doubling back, totalled nearly fifteen kilometres. The final stretch—the remaining three hundred metres or so across the muskeg—was the most difficult of all. I loaded my canoe with everything aside from the plastic barrel, which I strapped onto my back, and began dragging the whole assemblage forward. As I sloshed onward, the ground visibly sank beneath me, causing pools of cold water to form around my feet. But the sight of what lay before me—the mysterious mist-shrouded headwaters of my long-sought river—gave me the strength to finish the task.

When I reached the marshy lakeshore, I pushed the canoe into the water and hopped into the stern. A thick mist made it impossible to see the far shore, or much beyond the canoe's bow. The water was shallow—that much was plain from the green rushes sprouting up from the lake. It was still a large body of water, though, probably more than a kilometre across, and as such I was wary about venturing too far from land into the mist, for if a storm were to strike, my shallow vessel could easily swamp. By paddling off into the misty lake, I had crossed my Rubicon—there could be no retreat now. The idea of attempting to portage back was unthinkable—no matter what the Again River contained, I was irrevocably committed to continuing.

11

RIVER OF MYSTERY

*Fearlessness is better than a faint-heart for any man who puts his nose
out of doors. The length of my life and the day of my death were fated long ago.*
—*Skirnir's Journey*, Ancient Norse Myth

I PADDLED THROUGH THE MIST to the far side of the lake and
then skirted its shoreline, searching for some sign of the Again
River. At first there seemed to be nothing but an uninterrupted
shore of cedar and spruce trees. Had I made some mistake and
come to the wrong lake? Anxiously I kept paddling through the
mist and rain, trying to find an outlet somewhere. At last, I spotted a black stream, little more than a creek, flanked by alder bushes
and swampy woods on either bank and covered in lily pads,
arrowheads, and rushes. *This was it*—the start of the unexplored
river that I had dreamed about for years. I had stared at its vague
outline on those old maps, trying to picture what it looked like
and what it would be like to paddle. Even now, I half doubted
that I had really found it—it was hard to believe that after so
many false starts, *I had finally made it*.

The river itself, despite the ancient forest on either bank, could
have been one of the creeks I had paddled in the countryside

where I grew up. I actually imagined that the hardest and most dangerous part of the journey was now over—that the challenges ahead were nothing compared with the navigational complexity and sheer endurance required to complete the trailblazing portages. So, despite the fact that the skies in all directions remained one unbroken mass of unfriendly grey clouds, I felt sanguine. I paddled downstream in the drizzle, unfazed by a swarm of mosquitoes buzzing around my head. If I had known what awaited me down-river, I would not have been quite so confident.

Soon I encountered large beaver dams, which I had to lift the canoe over, but I did so with relative ease. The dams were of such solid construction that I could stand right on top of them while hoisting the loaded canoe up and over. More problematic were shallow, sandy stretches of river that required wading and dragging to get the canoe through—but they were nothing unusual. The river seemed to be an untouched sanctuary for wildlife—beavers, otters, muskrats, moose, and waterfowl were all around. A king-fisher glided low over the water before disappearing into the woods. Freshwater clams were scattered along the river bottom, a good meal should I need it.

The river's meandering course passed through several weedy lakes, which I paddled across in the rain, hoping that the water-way would grow bigger and spare me from more canoe dragging. These lakes were of considerable size, spanning several kilometres. Nevertheless, after passing through another big lake, I found that the river remained little more than a rocky creek, hemmed in by lush cedar trees and too shallow to paddle. The only way forward was to carefully wade in the swift current and drag the canoe behind me with a rope. But as I slogged along, cautiously balancing in the rushing water, my hopes were dashed—ahead the river vanished entirely. Instead of flowing water, all I saw was a dry creek bed covered in rocks. The river, I soon realized, was still there, flowing beneath the rocks as little more than a trickle. I had no choice but to do another exhausting portage, carrying the canoe over my head and all my gear forward until the river re-emerged.

Fortunately, a pool lay just beyond the dry stretch, only a hundred metres away. Beyond that, the river remained deep enough to either paddle or wade. In a few more hours I had navigated through a calm stretch that resembled a small lake, and then squeezed through another narrow gap no wider than my canoe that was choked with a rock-strewn rapid. Beyond this rapid the river transformed again—it now flowed into one of the prettiest lakes I had ever seen: clear blue water studded with spruce- and cedar-covered islands with yellow sand beaches. The islands were so picturesque that they seemed almost surreal—compared with the muskeg and swamp, they were an enchanted paradise. I made camp on a beach on one of the islands, the moon rising above me in the twilight. Taking it all in, it felt as if I had stepped into the frame of a Group of Seven landscape painting and left the nightmarish swamps far behind.

PEOPLE OFTEN ASK me, "Aren't you afraid, going out into the wilderness all alone? Don't you worry about something bad happening?" There are no easy answers to such questions. As William "Doc" Forgey, the guru of wilderness first aid and a veteran of many canoe journeys, once explained of his own experiences:

Somehow on long trips, the uncertainty of the next day's travel, the food supply, the amount of time, all seem to gnaw at me.... Perhaps I'm not cut out for wilderness travel. I asked Sigurd Olson one day about this. He laughed and said he'd put the same question past Camsell at the Explorer's Club one day. Camsell replied that he'd spent most of his adult life exploring the bush and had been scared during nine-tenths of it.

That would be *the* Charles Camsell, founder of the Royal Canadian Geographical Society and a man born and raised in the wilderness of the Northwest Territories. If a man like that was afraid nine-tenths of the time, there surely could be no shame in admitting to feeling fear. On the other hand, William Hunt, better known as "The Great Farini," an explorer of Africa and a daredevil tightrope walker, said of his many adventures, "I have never known fear." With others, such a claim might ring hollow—but with Farini, few could doubt it. A farm boy from the backwoods of Upper Canada, in 1860 Farini walked across Niagara Falls on an amateurishly rigged tightrope with no safety line while performing all sorts of stunts in the middle of the rope. In 1885, bored with life, he plunged into the wilds of southern Africa to explore the Orange River, scrambling and climbing over sheer cliff faces and around waterfalls with the same serene indifference he exhibited above the torrent of Niagara. If Farini had merely been an adventurer, his fearlessness could perhaps be explained away as the exuberance of a rash man with more brawn than brain—but Farini was no fool. Fluent in seven languages, he presented his expedition findings to both the

Royal Geographical Society and the German Geographical Society, addressing the latter in fine German. He patented several successful inventions, authored books on such esoteric topics as techniques for growing geraniums, and despite his death-defying exploits, lived to the ripe old age of ninety.

As for myself, I am too in love with adventure and the allure of the unknown to let fear stand in my way. So, while I certainly have felt fear in the wilderness, most of the time, I ignore it. Or when I can't ignore it, I embrace it. Fear just adds to the adventure. At least, that is the sort of thing I tell myself when I'm in a tense situation—such as when a bear is outside the tent, I'm paddling a raging rapid, or I'm caught out in the open in a lightning storm. But on the Again River, things were slightly different—I was so possessed by a mixture of curiosity, ambition, and excitement that little room was left for fear.

When the next morning dawned and I awoke on the island's sandy shore, it was not with any sense of foreboding about what might await me downriver. After a breakfast of oatmeal, I packed up my camp and set off into the lake, heading for the distant shore. I paddled hard into a stiff headwind, riding over sizable waves and scanning the dark woods with my binoculars in search of the river's outlet from the lake. At first nothing was visible— the shore appeared to be one unbroken wall of grim black spruce. This was puzzling—surely the river had to flow out somewhere. It took half-an-hour to paddle across the lake, battling the wind. Only then did I discover that the river's outlet was hidden from view behind high weeds that shot up from the water. As I nudged the canoe into the reeds, an arctic tern soared above me—the first tidings of the salt water that lay to the north on stormy

James Bay. I took a last glance back at the lake as the tern glided away. This was the final lake on my journey—from here, the Again River flows uninterrupted through the Lowlands, to where it eventually joins the much larger Harricanaw River, which in turn drains into James Bay. My hands were cut and scraped from the portages, my body was riddled with blackfly bites, a rash had developed on my feet from the constant wetness, and that morning the handle had broken off my water purifier, rendering the device useless. But, staring ahead at the unexplored river that awaited me, a smile lit up my face, and not for anything in the world would I have wanted to be doing anything else.

I pulled my paddle through the water, drawing the canoe into the current of the river, eager to see what lay beyond the next bend. There was, it turned out, a nearly endless stretch of rocky rapids. I ran as many as I dared, but more often than not I had to climb out of my canoe, plunge into the water, and guide the boat forward with rope to get around jagged rocks. Sometimes I would be in ankle-deep water, only to take another step and find myself waist-deep in a hidden pool. In places, I had to lift the canoe over serrated rocks, and my hiking boots would sometimes become wedged in crevices concealed beneath the dark water. By the afternoon the sun had disappeared behind rain clouds, which didn't trouble me much, as rain would raise water levels and help spare my canoe from the rocks that lined the river bottom. Hopefully, it would also put out any nearby forest fires.

The river was strikingly different from the Little Owl River I had explored the year before, or even the Kattawagami. It had a more southern character, with a greater variety of trees and higher banks. At places the landscape resembled Algonquin, with granite rock outcrops along the shore covered in caribou lichens and blueberries, as well as juniper bushes and wild rose. The tall jack pines that overlooked the river reminded me of one of Tom Thomson's paintings. In more tranquil stretches, beavers swam in the river and noisily slapped their tails on the surface of the water as I passed, a warning to their friends that a strange intruder was drawing near.

That night I camped on a slab of granite overlooking the river beside a large rapid. The blackflies were atrocious until I got a fire going to keep them away. Beyond the rock outcrop, the forest was thick with spruces, their spindly branches interlocking to form a barrier that precluded hiking inland. In the middle of the night, I awoke to the sound of a violent thunderstorm, which made me rather uneasy. I was surrounded by tall trees, and there was not much I could do to minimize the risk of a lightning strike. I simply had to hope my luck would hold—it was, after all, the thirtieth or fortieth thunderstorm I had endured in a tent.

IT WAS A cold, miserable day with steady rain. Clad in an old army rain jacket and wearing a helmet, I spent all morning running whitewater rapids and occasionally wading through dark, swirling water. Grey boulders the size of small cars loomed out of the river, which I weaved around in the canoe. The river was narrow most of the time, less than forty metres wide, and while it included the occasional deep stretch, most of it remained shallow. Small hills and, in a few places, granite cliffs enclosed its course. I shivered as I paddled along, chilled from frequently wading in the water and pulling the canoe to avoid damaging it on the rocks. Given how shallow the river was, it appeared that I wouldn't encounter any terribly dangerous whitewater.

Ahead, the river curved sharply around a narrow bend. I edged along the left bank, trying to see what lay beyond the bend—more small rapids, from the look and sound of things. Cold and tired, I paddled into the bend. Suddenly the current became extremely swift—propelling the canoe into a frothing set of rapids, beyond which seemed to be a larger drop. It was too late to try to backpaddle, and I couldn't grab hold of anything on the shore of slippery granite rocks. I plunged through the first set of rapids unscathed—but now I found myself hurtling toward the larger drop, which looked like a big, steep rapid. I was on my knees in the canoe, ready for white-water, my muscles tense and my paddle angled like a rudder to steer the canoe.

An ominous, almost deafening, roar from downriver struck fear in my heart. Something big was beyond that first drop, and I was racing toward it. In a flash, I plunged over the first chute, managing to keep the canoe upright as the bow vanished beneath the furious waves and the vessel filled with water, but directly ahead the river disappeared entirely.

A waterfall.

In an instant the flooded canoe and I were flung over the fall. In the drop, the vessel pivoted sideways and dumped me into a frothing cauldron of wild water, sucking me down under. I was tumbled and pulled in all directions, as if I were trapped inside a washing machine. The crushing force of the falling water held me under, despite my lifejacket, for what felt like an eternity. I was running out of oxygen—but at last my head broke the waves and I breathed in a life-giving gulp of air while I was swept along downriver in thunderous rapids.

Out of the corner of my left eye I caught a glimpse of the canoe, lying overturned in an eddy, apparently destroyed. But I had no time to worry about that or digest what had just happened. Farther downriver my gear—the backpack and plastic barrel—were being swept away through more rock-studded rapids. Gasping for air and weighed down by my drenched clothing and boots, I swam to shore as quickly as I could. I had to recover as much of my gear as possible. Once on the slippery rocks, I immediately dashed along the shoreline, leaping precariously from wet boulder to wet boulder, racing downriver in an attempt to salvage what I could.

My waterlogged backpack snagged on some rocks in the middle of a rapid; I threw myself back into the river to grab it as fast as possible. It seemed to weigh a ton, but I pulled it out and tossed it onshore before running after the barrel, which was still being borne downriver. A desperate dash back into the swift water brought me to it; I quickly scooped it up and got back onshore. I managed to recover my paddles too. Then, dreading what I might find, and panting heavily, I turned around and sprinted back upriver to fetch my canoe.

My heart sank when I saw it—it was floating in an eddy upside down, the hull crushed in. I scrambled over some boulders down to the river's edge, waded into the water, reached out and grabbed hold of the overturned canoe, and hauled it onshore. I flipped it over to inspect the damage. The oak gunwales were shattered, the front seat was broken, a few bolts had popped off from the side leaving gaping holes, the bow was damaged, and the hull was pressed in and misshapen, but not punctured. My fishing rod, a pair of moccasins that were sitting in the canoe, and my hat—the old fedora I had worn for years—were gone, swallowed up by the river, never to be seen again. Fortunately, when I went over the waterfall, I had been wearing my helmet and, unlike the canoe, I had emerged without injury—other than my wounded confidence.

Once I had a chance to take a good look at the waterfall, I saw that it consisted of an upper and lower drop squeezed in a narrows between granite rocks. The upper drop, where I had managed to keep the canoe upright, was only about a metre and a half high, but the second drop was about six metres, and in that fall my already flooded canoe and I had toppled over sideways. The river narrowed at the waterfall to only seven metres wide, which concentrated all the water into one raging, seething torrent and created a deep, frothing pool at the bottom.

Despite this unexpected mishap, I wasn't going to abandon the exploration of the river. To quit—to accept defeat, to admit the river had beaten me—was out of the question. I would paddle a raft of logs all the way to the ocean if I had to. But determined as I was to continue, the shock of being swept over an unknown waterfall did not leave me unfazed. I had to face the reality of the situation—if my head had been smashed on a rock, my leg wedged underwater in a crevice, or my body pinned under the flooded canoe, it would have been game over. Realizing how close I had come to disaster, I made two vows as I stood shivering on the riverbank beside the roar of the water-fall. First, I vowed that if I survived this journey, never again would I go alone on an expedition into unexplored territory. It was just too risky. Second, I vowed that once I had the canoe repaired, I would proceed downriver with extreme caution, no matter the delays this would cause. I would stop to carefully scout all whitewater and restrain myself from attempting to paddle any large rapids. These vows reassured me and soothed my anxiety about the days ahead. As it happened, I would eventually break both vows, but I didn't know it at the time.

Cold, wet, and shaken, I set about to repair the canoe. I could do little about the shattered gunwales or the broken seat, but I hammered and kicked the hull more or less back into shape and used duct tape to patch the holes in the side where the bolts had been. The canoe wasn't a pretty sight, but it seemed serviceable enough. The repair work finished, I figured it was best not to dwell too much on what just happened, so I repacked the canoe and resumed paddling downriver—alert for more surprises.

Downriver from the waterfall, a forest fire had charred the area, transforming once-lush woods into a desolate wasteland of barren rock hills that overlooked the waterway, a scene made even bleaker by dark skies and rain. While the river had a few calm stretches, myriad whitewater rapids remained the order of the day. At one point, a narrow canyon enclosed the river, which was churned into a fury of impassable rapids that I didn't dare try to paddle in the battered canoe. Protruding from the middle of this seething cataract was a small rock island, waves crashing loudly against it. I paddled to the shore just above the canyon's entrance, resigned to yet another arduous portage. The route overland was blocked by charred deadfall, which I had to scramble over with my gear and the canoe.

Within a few hours of being swept over the waterfall, my patience for wading through cold, rushing water and portaging around chest-high deadfall was exhausted, and in spite of my vow, I took to paddling larger rapids again. This may have been risky, but without risks an explorer is unlikely to make any progress. Fortunately, the damaged canoe didn't leak and I paddled the rapids without much trouble.

After a last spate of rapids, the river's fierce current slackened and I entered a wide, calm stretch that allowed me to relax for the first time in hours. Half-hidden in some tall alder bushes onshore was a young moose. It was reaching down toward the water's edge with its long neck to eat some shrubs. The moose looked at me for a few minutes as I photographed it while drifting in the canoe, but it seemed more interested in its leafy food than me.

The tranquil stretch of river didn't last long. Shortly after passing the moose, I thought I could hear a distant roar. Was it the wind? I cocked my head to the side and listened as I continued to drift downriver—it *was not* the wind. There was no mistaking the noise now—it was the sound of crashing water; a terrifying roar that chilled me to the marrow after my last encounter with an unexpected waterfall. When I rounded the next bend, I looked ahead and saw the river disappear over a vertical drop.

This time, no rapids concealed the waterfall, and I paddled as close as I dared before putting into shore and climbing out to inspect what awaited me. The ancient forest here had escaped the path of the forest fire, and I was back in a green world of towering spruce and tamaracks, swaying and creaking above me in the wind. After climbing onto the bank, I tied my canoe to a nearby spruce, then set off to investigate the waterfall. The thickness of the woods along the riverbank forced me to hike inland up a blueberry-covered hill, until I found an opening in the brush where I could push through to glimpse the waterfall.

It was a spectacular sight—a roaring, mist-shrouded cascade some eight or nine metres high that hurled furious waves of destruction against boulders and rocks. I doubted I could have survived a plunge over this violent fall. I stood there, in the rain, almost spellbound—mesmerized by the sight of a nameless waterfall that in all likelihood no other living person had ever seen.

When the government cartographers had created their maps of the Again River in the 1960s, they hadn't marked any waterfalls on its course. That was because they had neither canoed the river nor explored it on the ground. Those imperfect maps had been created on the basis of grainy black-and-white aerial photographs, snapped high above this vast wilderness, in order to make a rudimentary survey back in the 1950s and 1960s. Evidently, the aerial photographs had been too limited to reveal the river's waterfalls. Google Earth's low-resolution satellite images—which unlike better-known locations, were all that existed for this obscure and forgotten piece of geography—were likewise too indistinct and blurry to distinguish waterfalls. Here they had remained, hidden away unknown to the outside world. Back in 2008, when I first began my study of the river, I had suspected that it might contain some waterfalls, and now I took pleasure in finding this to be true—even if I had found out the hard way.

Arresting as the sight of a previously undiscovered waterfall was, it meant another difficult portage through thick woods to safely transport the damaged canoe and my gear to the other side. To reach the water beneath the fall, I had to scramble down a steep embankment and over wet, slippery boulders with the canoe. This portage was made even more difficult by my wet boots and clothing.

After completing the portage, I decided to press on downriver, navigating more rapids before stopping for the night. Unfortunately, there was virtually nowhere I could pitch my tent—the whole area was a criss-crossed pile of fallen trees, felled by a fire that had cleared the forest as far as I could see. I had to settle for sleeping on a comfortless rock outcrop beneath a few ghostly cedars.

THE AGAIN RIVER had hidden its secrets well. As it turned out, more waterfalls were waiting to be discovered. But reaching them was no easy matter. The river flowed through a kaleidoscope of different rapids of all sizes and descriptions—cascades, smooth ledges, abrupt drop-offs, foaming cataracts, rocky rapids, staircase-like steps, and impassable channels. I portaged around the rapids that couldn't be paddled safely, snacking as I did so on the wild berries that flourished in the direct sunlight—a result of the fire that had levelled most of the surrounding trees. At one place, the river forked around an island with steep rock faces—on one side was a cascade waterfall splashing over a sloping granite crag and on the other was a narrow channel of ferocious whitewater. Neither side could be navigated in the canoe, so I gingerly paddled above the falls, putting to shore at the rocky island, where I would have to scale the steep granite sides and hoist my canoe up and over them.

Immediately beyond this island, the river squeezed through what looked like a narrow S-bend laced with rapids. Given the strenuous and time-consuming work of portaging over the island, I had no wish to portage any more than was strictly necessary. At this rate, exploring the river would take an inordinate amount of time—just how long I had no idea. The adventurer in me reasserted himself, and once more I threw caution to the wind in order to run rapids. Standing on the island's shore, I could see whitewater directly ahead, but the danger seemed minimal as long as I managed to reach the shore after the first two sets of rapids, before the sharp curve in the S-bend—around which it was impossible to see.

I paddled through the first rapid easily enough, but the second one turned out to have a steep chute like a miniature waterfall, with a metre-and-a-half vertical drop. The canoe's bow vanished beneath the foaming water at the bottom of the chute, filling the vessel. But the canoe remained afloat, and with furious effort I was able to paddle the half-sinking craft against the swift current to the shore, where I flung down my paddle and caught hold of some tree roots to prevent the canoe and me from being swept around the bend.

Soaking wet from the wild ride through the rapids, I climbed up the rocky riverbank and pulled the canoe onshore, where I dumped the water out. Since I had no idea what lay beyond the river bend and was somewhat wary of more excitement, I decided to hike ahead on foot to get the lay of the land. What I saw astonished me.

IF I HAD EVER doubted it, I learned that even in our age of satellite technology and high-tech gadgetry, no substitute exists for the pure, simple pleasure and honest rewards of being in a remote, unknown place. The hours I had spent studying the grainy old aerial photographs and blurry satellite images of the Again River could never have prepared me for the reality of this place. I found myself in a land of unsurpassed beauty, standing beneath red pines, lush cedars, and white birches on a sandy cove nestled between massive granite boulders that had come to rest here as if tossed by the hands of some giant. Across the clear blue stream, roaring and rushing with rapids, was a small mountain, rendered nearly barren by a forest fire, that looked like some otherworldly mirage. Beyond the mountain was a narrow canyon framed on one side by sheer cliffs of pinkish granite and on the other by a rocky hill. Small trees and shrubs clung tenaciously to the cliffs. Just before this canyon was a deep, tranquil stretch of water. It seemed to me like the sort of place the ancient Greeks or Vikings would have consecrated as a sacred pool of the immortals.

I picked my way over deadfall from a past forest fire, pushing past young spruces that had sprung up in the years since the fire. I hiked up the rocky summit, hopping at times from one fallen tree to another to avoid the difficulty of constantly climbing over the obstacles that barred the way forward. The ground beneath me was cloaked in blueberries and raspberries, which I ate happily. The sun was shining above me as I reached the peak and scanned my surroundings in all directions. I could see that beyond the swirling waters of the narrow canyon, the river snaked around again and emerged in a wide, calm stretch that resembled a small lake framed by rocky cliffs and small mountains. In the far distance, I could see the glimmer of moving water, where the lake emptied into a raging torrent.

The little peninsula with the sandy cove covered in lush cedars and white birches had somehow escaped the forest fire's path, and was one of the most beautiful places I had ever set foot in—it was a place that no dream could have improved, aside from the blackflies and mosquitoes. But the insects scarcely bothered me, so taken was I with the spot. I decided to gather as much dry cedar and birchbark as I could. These items I regarded as among the most precious treasures in the world, invaluable as they are for starting fires—especially in a land where such trees are rare. I was tempted to rest on the narrow peninsula for the night, near the sandy cove. The river curved in such an extreme bend that it flowed on either side of the peninsula at a distance of no more than ten metres. But I had a schedule to keep, and I had no way of knowing what surprises might lay ahead. To delay could be fatal to my enterprise, and it would be foolish not to take advantage of a rare day of fair weather.

Thus, with reluctance, I banished any thought of stopping early for the day in this pleasant spot and returned to fetch my gear for what would be a lengthy and arduous portage over the rocky, deadfall-strewn hills, around the canyon, and out to the little lake, where the water finally calmed enough to resume safe travel.

Rock climbing along the steep sides of the canyon was necessary to complete the portage, which was, I suppose, only slightly less hazardous than paddling the rapids themselves. In fact, this portage was so difficult, blocked as it was in every which way by chest-high fallen trees and thick emergent spruce saplings, that for a moment I contemplated running the canyon with the empty canoe rather than attempting to portage it across. But after methodically studying the rapids, I reluctantly concluded that the lapping waves were too high for my shallow canoe's sides and would spill over and flood it again.

There was nothing to do but try to carry the canoe over the rocky hills and the barricades of deadfall. Fatigued and sweaty from the first two loads, I replenished my water bottle directly from the river and quenched my raging thirst. Since I had lost my hat in the waterfall, there was nothing to keep the sun's rays off, as all I had to wear now was my helmet. Under the hot sun, swarmed by bloodthirsty insects, I lifted the canoe up and started the portage. Exhausting as it was getting up the rock hill—the canoe had to be painstakingly lifted over chest-high deadfall that blocked my path every few steps—the hardest part was the end of the portage. I had to climb down an almost vertical rock slope with the canoe to reach the end of the canyon.

When the portage was over, I reloaded the canoe and explored the little lake, which was really an exceptionally wide and calm stretch of river. It was hemmed in on one side by a towering rock face that rose nearly fifty metres straight out of the water and on the other by forested hills. Beyond this expanse of calm water were more dangerous rapids, which I paddled through in the canoe, navigating them with all the skill I possessed. At one place, the river narrowed to a mere three metres wide before plunging over a small chute into a wider pool. Surrounding this part of the river were more scars of an old forest fire—some dead trees were still standing, sparsely spaced; others had toppled over, and between them grew tight ranks of young spruces.

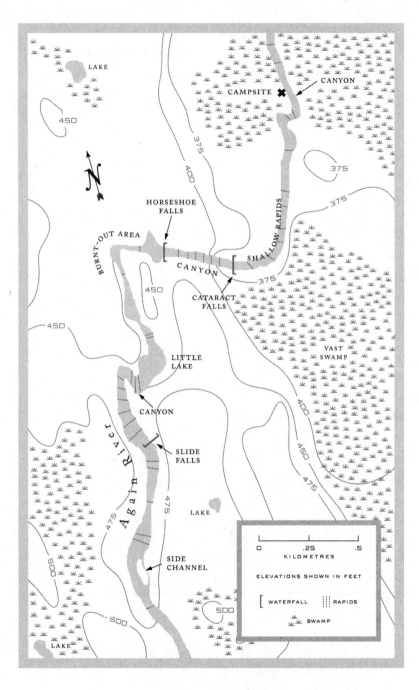

AGAIN RIVER

I lifted the canoe around the chute, which couldn't be paddled, and then entered the pool with great caution. Ahead I could see a vertical drop of what was unmistakably another waterfall, and beyond that I had a view stretching to the distant horizon of endless wilderness.

[12]

ADRIFT

Come what may, all bad fortune is to be conquered by endurance.
—Virgil, first century BC

INSIDE THE POOL above the waterfall was an island, which I paddled around, hugging the rocky shoreline until I found a place I could safely land. The waterfall was a beautiful six-metre-high curtain of golden water, falling straight down in the shape of a horseshoe. It was the prettiest of the waterfalls I had seen so far. Beneath it was a wild canyon laced with lethal rapids squeezed between narrow walls of ancient granite. The river rapidly descended through these spectacular cataracts before widening at the canyon's exit and plunging over another rocky fall. Beneath that final waterfall were more rock-studded rapids, and beyond that the river curved around a bend and disappeared from view. This canyon was the largest I had come across and covered nearly half a kilometre in length, all of which would have to be portaged.

This portage would be an undertaking of considerable difficulty—more than ever, a partner would have been useful.

There was no easy path forward; the ground on either side of the canyon was a jumble of fallen trees, effectively blocking any passage forward except by the most determined effort. I would have to climb steep cliffs and rocky hills while hacking through the young, thick spruces that had emerged since the old fire and pull the canoe either under or over the overlapping dead trees that lay like roadblocks in every direction.

The Again River was proving a tough adversary—my hands were becoming more scraped and cut daily, my face was sunburnt, my right knee near the joint had somehow been cut up (I was unsure how it had happened), the rash on my feet from the constant wetness had spread to my legs, my back was sore from carrying the heavy loads, and all over my body were small bruises and scrapes. But I bore my battle scars with pride and remained confident that nothing could stop me in my quest to explore the river.

I was now somewhere near the artificial provincial boundary between Quebec and Ontario, so I knew that I wasn't the first person to explore this wild canyon. A small team of government surveyors who had charted the boundary line must have passed through this area on a north–south axis in the late 1920s. Of course, they weren't here to explore the river, let alone attempt to paddle it. But emerging from the forest, they must have been struck by the awesome incongruity of these towering rock hills, crags, and gorges compared with the typically flat and swampy terrain. It was certainly a rare departure from the muskeg and swamp that covers nearly all of the Lowlands.

When I reached the roaring cascade at the end of the canyon, I saw that it split around a barren rock island, forming another small waterfall on one side. A few hours of hard work enabled me to transport everything to the base of this little waterfall. I could not see what lay beyond the bend outside the canyon, but more rapids were certain. As much as I wanted to, an impenetrable barrier of deadfall and thick brush onshore made travelling ahead on foot to scout what lay beyond the bend impossible. The only option, risky as it was, was to repack the canoe and paddle more or less blindly downriver. As a precaution, I would stick as close to the shoreline as possible, in case another dangerous waterfall or cataract was hiding around the next bend.

I repacked the canoe and cautiously paddled forward around the bend, the swift current propelling me on. As I suspected, no shortage of dangerous cataracts and enormous rapids were waiting ahead. For the next kilometre or so, the whole river was a wild, ungoverned fury of whitewater, with inconsequential stretches of less violent water in between. The river snaked in a hairpin curve at one spot, flowing into yet another canyon. The rapids in the apex of this bend were impassable; their giant waves would swallow my canoe if I dared try to paddle through. To arrive inside the canyon's walls, I had no choice but to perform another extremely tiring portage over some of the thickest brush and deadfall I had faced. I made camp for the night beneath these rocks, in a spot that was otherwise pleasant, with good access to the water for cooking and plenty of firewood. I set up my tent beneath a few live cedars, and that night fell into a deep, exhausted sleep.

THE NEXT DAY, I paddled hard without interruption, running every rapid I encountered and, for once, having no portages. As a result, I made great time and managed to canoe the remainder of the river, which was about half of its entire course (or roughly fifty-four kilometres), aided greatly by hundreds of swift rapids and a strong current. Throughout the day the river's appearance changed frequently and dramatically, so that at times it was hard to believe I was still canoeing the same waterway. After the last canyon, granite rocks gave way to grassy sandbanks and lime-stone cliffs. Much of the route along the river was burnt out by a forest fire, though some portions remained cloaked in undis-turbed old-growth forest. In places were stands of large birch and poplars as well as beautiful forested islands. There were no more canyons or waterfalls, and while I paddled through endless rapids, they could not compare with the ferocity of the upper part of the river. Throughout the day, I came across a variety of waterfowl, as well as beavers.

By the evening, I had reached the end of the Again River, where it emptied into the vast waters of the Harricanaw River. The Harricanaw was nearly a kilometre wide—strewn with gravel sandbars, shoals, and rapids. I made camp on a high bank in thick woods overlooking the junction of the two rivers.

While my journey wasn't over, that evening I treated myself to a cup of cranberry tea to quietly celebrate the fulfillment of my long-cherished ambition to explore the Again River. I had pried open its long-guarded secrets, seen things no other mortal eyes had ever seen, trod in untouched places, and gained knowledge of the previously unknown. I had discovered at least five unmapped waterfalls—more if I counted smaller "split" falls around islands. I had navigated rapids no one else had ever paddled, and in the process, I had become the only person on record to canoe the Again River in its entirety, right from its swampy headwaters down to its outlet on the Harricanaw. Perhaps one day I could look forward to seeing my name added to a monograph listing river journeys, such as *Canoeing North into the Unknown*, under an all-new entry for the Again River. But, in the foreseeable future, I neither expected nor cared to receive any accolades for my achievement—after all, this had not been a Geographical Society expedition but a personal quest. And as a personal quest, I had received all the recompense I could desire from what I had seen and experienced. Surely, for the rest of my life, the memory of the roar and sight of the Again's waterfalls will remain vividly imprinted on my mind—much as I imagine Livingstone was haunted by the roar of Victoria Falls to his dying day or John Muir by the sight of Yellowstone's geysers.

THE NEXT MORNING I bade farewell to the Again River and set off down the Harricanaw. I thought I could detect a hint of sea air on the morning breeze, but it was a good thirty-four-kilometre journey down this new river to reach the salt water of James Bay. The Harricanaw was an impressive sight, with big trees and enormous islands on its wide course. In addition to the familiar tamaracks and black spruce, balsam fir, poplar, birch, and cedar grew above the river's high muddy banks. Several bald eagles soared overhead, hunting for fish.

As peaceful as the Harricanaw appeared, the river conceals a dark, violent history. In the eighteenth century, the Hudson's Bay Company had established an isolated outpost near the Harricanaw's mouth on James Bay. This tiny fur trade post, cut off from the rest of the world in the wilderness of the Lowlands, was manned mostly by aboriginal people. On January 20, 1832, a group of about a dozen eastern Cree arrived at the post and were, according to an eyewitness, "in a Starving and Naked State." They begged for food and other provisions, which the post's commander, a Métis man named William Corrigal, gave them. Two days later—apparently as secretly planned—the group returned, burst into the post, slaughtered its inhabitants in cold blood, and plundered it of furs and supplies. Corrigal, his native wife, and seven other Cree who were occupants of the post were killed. Four survivors managed to escape the massacre. They embarked on a desperate trek to seek help at Moose Factory, a larger post about sixty-five kilometres away on the Moose River. There, a posse of men was quickly assembled to hunt down the murderers. They eventually succeeded in tracking the killers down, five of whom were summarily executed.

The remains of the Hudson Bay's post are long gone, and near the Harricanaw's mouth, where it once stood, is now only silent forest. As I scanned the area, it was easy to imagine that ghosts still haunted this unhappy place. According to Cree legends, ghosts haunt many islands and old campsites around James Bay. The only animal I saw in the vicinity was a small black bear, scurrying along the riverbank.

On the opposite side of the river was a small clearing with a cluster of wood buildings. This was Washow Lodge, established two years earlier by the Moose Factory band council in a novel attempt to alleviate unemployment problems by stimulating adventure-tourism in the region. The Harricanaw, after all, was a large river without any substantial portages that could be navigated with relative ease by experienced canoeists. It had never amounted to a major trade route in the heyday of the fur trade, but in the twentieth century various adventurers had been attracted down its five-hundred-kilometre-long course, including the young Pierre Trudeau. Float planes could land on its mouth to transport canoeists and other guests, and motor boats could access the river from across James Bay.

When I reached the muddy shoreline near the lodge at low tide, I could distinctly smell the sea air on the breeze. The lodge had no dock of any kind, so I was forced to wade to shore and drag my canoe and supplies across mud flats, sinking down into the muck as I attempted to reach solid ground. The lodge was situated above a grassy bank in a half-acre clearing. It looked deserted—the buildings were locked and the area around them was rather untidy, with equipment and rubbish strewn about. I couldn't help but think that attracting tourists to this area wouldn't meet with much success. The swampy Lowlands aren't what most people have in mind when they picture majestic wilderness. Nevertheless, I admired the idea—perhaps if the Moose Cree could succeed in making people see the Lowlands as a wilderness with intrinsic value, the land could be preserved from industrial exploitation—to my mind, a welcome change.

One service the lodge offered was transport via motorboat across stormy James Bay to the Moose River, on the western side of the Bay, where I could catch the Polar Bear Express train south to Cochrane. As much as I enjoyed ocean canoeing—something I had done many times—my frail little craft, only thirteen feet long and about half the depth of a standard canoe, was inadequate for the open sea. It had served me well on the portages through thick forest, but the inevitable trade-off was limited utility and safety on open water. A shuttle would spare me at least several days—possibly more if the weather was stormy—of hard paddling on James Bay in my battered canoe. I decided to wait around to see if a boat would arrive at the deserted lodge—biding my time sketching landscapes and with my binoculars watching for the elusive Eskimo curlew. But no boat or plane appeared, and I began to suspect the place received few visitors.

The next day, I used the satellite phone to call the lodge's office in Moose Factory to see if it was possible to arrange a shuttle. That was a challenge in itself—it was a rainy day, and the satellite phone wasn't waterproof. I had difficulty picking up a signal, and when I finally made a call the phone cut out. I thought that I heard a voice over the crackling line say that weather permitting a boat would arrive sometime in the next few days.

The following day it rained furiously and high winds gusted ceaselessly off James Bay. I collected rainwater in my cooking pot, tea mug, and water bottles—the water at the mouth of the Harricanaw was too salty to drink. Given the weather, it seemed unlikely that any boat would arrive that day. But that evening I was surprised to hear the sound of a distant engine. On the horizon, a small boat equipped with an outboard motor appeared—somehow it must have made it through the storm. Two men were on board, clad in yellow rain pants and jackets. When they arrived at the lodge, it was high tide, and they came ashore in hip waders. I assumed that the three of us would spend the night camping and head to Moose Factory in the morning.

Instead, the two men, Mark and Tyler, were eager to leave as soon as possible. They were both members of the Moose Cree First Nation. We chatted briefly about my journey, and I asked if either of them knew of the Again River. Mark, the elder of the two, was vaguely familiar with its outlet on the Harricanaw but knew nothing else about it. They both seemed rather surprised that I had travelled all this way alone.

"It's rough out on the Bay," said Mark, who looked about thirty. "We had a tough time crossing—big waves out there."

Tyler nodded. He appeared to be in his early twenties. We briefly waited onshore to see what the weather would do—the wind remained fierce, and it continued to rain sporadically. But Mark and Tyler felt that we could safely make the journey back to the Moose River. So we loaded my canoe and gear onto the boat and shoved off into the river. I waded into the cold water then climbed on board. Neither Mark nor Tyler had lifejackets.

The boat was a fibreglass vessel about twenty feet long, with a high prow to handle the rough waves of the open sea. Mark operated the motor while Tyler and I sat on a loose bench placed near the front of the boat, with the canoe stashed behind us. Mark revved the engine and we headed full speed downriver toward a vast expanse of open water. Roughly the size of Lake Superior, James Bay is a southern extension of Hudson Bay and, as such, is usually classified as part of the Arctic watershed. All the islands within the Bay, even small ones only a few kilometres offshore, are part of Nunavut. Notoriously prone to storms, even today no accurate marine charts exist for much of this sea. Many small craft have foundered and sunk on its murky, storm-tossed waters, taking mariners and canoeists to a watery grave.

In 1984 four American canoeists, after completing a six-week descent of the Albany River, the largest river in the Lowlands, attempted to paddle along the desolate James Bay coastline south to Moosonee. None of them were ever seen alive again. Storms were so severe during the search to find the missing canoeists that rescue aircraft had to be grounded for four straight days. They were all presumed drowned.

One of the larger vessels to fall victim to James Bay was the *El Dorado*, a fur trade supply ship. In 1903 the *El Dorado* struck a reef and sank near James Bay's eastern coast. When the survivors reached the shore, they didn't receive the welcome they had anticipated. None of the isolated fur trade posts on the Bay had enough provisions to provide for the *El Dorado*'s survivors through the winter. The castaways were bluntly told that they had a choice—starve to death or try to reach the nearest settlement, more than five hundred kilometres away. They chose the latter. In the words of one of the survivors:

> [We] left the Moose River on the 22nd [of September] and set out on our fearsome journey of what we expected to be at least 300 miles overland to reach civilisation. We met many very bad rapids, and had several narrow escapes.... [T]wo canoes overturned in one great rapid, and it was all we could do to save their passengers from drowning. We had to go up to our necks in water to reach the capsized canoes, and, of course, we lost most of the food they contained, which made our plight terrible.

Ragged and starving, they staggered on with their grim journey, realizing that most rapids were too dangerous to navigate:

After this accident it was arranged that we should carry the canoes as much as possible where the waters were too dangerous.... Carrying a canoe in such a place is awful work. There was no path by the riverside ... often men had to go first and cut away trees.... Then, also, the ground was so undulating that only two men could possibly support the canoe, one in front and one behind. The banks were sometimes almost perpendicular, and thick with trees.... We camped in flimsy tents at night, but our clothes were always wet through, even before we lay down. Then it was piercingly cold, and everything froze on us.

The Cree guides from Moose Factory who were leading the party soon became lost and admitted they had no idea what lay ahead. They abandoned the group and headed back the way they came. The survivors continued alone, and after another arduous week, they arrived at an isolated frontier settlement. As far as shipwreck survivors on James Bay went, they were lucky—others never lived to tell their tales. According to Inuit oral tradition, Europeans shipwrecked in the nineteenth century on the Belcher Islands, which lie north of James Bay on Hudson Bay, were massacred.

THE BOAT RIDE was extremely rough. Tyler and I were tossed violently about on the bench as the prow flew clear out of the water when we crashed over large waves at top speed. The land was barely visible—we were some six or seven kilometres offshore—which meant that if we were to capsize or swamp, we would have no chance of reaching land before hypothermia killed us. I began to wonder if it might not have been safer to paddle across the Bay in my canoe. After half an hour battling fierce waves on the open sea and steady rain, Mark yelled from the stern that conditions were too rough, and that we had to turn back. He piloted the boat around, and we sped off to seek the safety of the Harricanaw's mouth.

We returned to the lodge to wait out the storm. The sun was setting, and I figured we would wait until morning before attempting a second crossing. But in another half hour the storm seemed to have slackened a little, so Mark and Tyler, in spite of the fading daylight, resolved to try again. Back out on the ocean the waves seemed nearly as rough as before, and we banged about in the boat as Mark gunned the engine full throttle. At one point, Tyler pointed to a white dot barely visible on the muddy sea—a beluga whale.

We were cruising far offshore, smashing over the large waves, for about two hours when suddenly the engine sputtered—then died. Bewildered, Tyler and I pivoted round on the bench to see what the problem was—only to see Mark in the stern looking equally puzzled. He yanked on the engine's pull cord in an attempt to restart the stalled engine. It sputtered, then died again. This wasn't the time or place to experience engine troubles—we were pitching about in sizable waves, five or six kilometres offshore. The sun was setting on the horizon; in less than an hour darkness would cover the sea. Mark swore and pulled on the engine's cord again. This time nothing happened at all—not even a tentative sputter. He removed the engine's cap and inspected the motor.

"What's wrong with it?" asked Tyler.

"Don't know," replied Mark. "Got plenty of gas. It just died."

After a few more futile attempts to restart the motor, Mark accepted that he could do nothing further. We were at the mercy of the elements, adrift on the ocean in a small boat, with no fresh water and only one lifejacket between the three of us. The sun had nearly disappeared, the temperature was dropping, and we were a long way from any help. But none of us panicked. Mark and Tyler were my sort of people—calm in the face of trouble.

Fortunately, Mark had a satellite phone—a much better, more expensive model than the one I had rented for my expedition—and he now attempted to call Moose Factory. Over the phone Mark explained our situation to his boss, the person in charge of Washow Lodge. She was understandably alarmed and said that another boat would be sent at once to find us. With his GPS, Mark gave her our coordinates. But it seemed doubtful the other boat would find us at all. We were drifting in big waves, and it would be dark by the time any boat could arrive in the general area. To make matters worse, the wind was blowing offshore, which meant we were drifting farther and farther from land, which was now hardly visible.

"I guess we'd better try to paddle to shore," Mark grimly suggested.

The boat was equipped with only one oar for an emergency, and the big, clumsy thing was not much use for paddling. Luckily we had my two paddles, which we used along with the oar to try to paddle to safety. The nearest island—a windswept spit of mud and grass—was about two kilometres away, and we headed toward it as best we could. The boat was difficult to paddle—it was not designed for that purpose—and given the large waves, we were making little progress. Though we kept up the effort, it was obvious we would never reach the island. I could see, or thought I saw, some sort of white object erected on it.

"What's that white thing on the island?" I asked.

"A cross," said Mark.

"A cross?"

"Yeah, ten years ago a family drowned here when their boat swamped in a storm. So a cross was put on the island."

"I see," I said.

This news wasn't very encouraging. It was nearly dark, and we were just a small speck adrift on the immensity of James Bay. Growing a little desperate, Mark moved to the front of the boat and began throwing the anchor overboard in the direction of the distant island, then dragging the boat toward it, repeating the process over and over. It was painfully slow-going, and though he made a valiant effort, he was soon exhausted and gave up. As we pitched about on the boat, I gave Mark and Tyler a couple of granola bars from my plastic barrel.

The moon had risen above us and cast an eerie glow over the surface of the sea. We drifted aimlessly in the dark, bobbing along with the waves. I shivered in my wet boots and rubbed my legs to keep warm. The boat was not equipped with lights, and neither Mark nor Tyler had a flashlight. I had two small pocket flashlights—we would have to rely on these to try to signal the other boat.

After several tense hours spent drifting in the dark, I thought I saw something glimmer on the horizon. "Look!" I said, pointing at a faint light in the distance.

"It's the other boat!" shouted Mark.

The light was a long way from us, so far that we could not even hear any sound of an engine. The faint light would temporarily disappear then reappear. We attempted to signal with the flashlights, but their weak light gave little hope that we would be seen.

"I don't think they'll ever spot us," said Tyler.

"Be patient," replied Mark as he continued to shine a flashlight in the direction of the other boat. Eventually, we heard the sounds of their engine and the light grew bigger. At last they had seen us.

The rescue boat was identical to our own, except that its motor seemed to work just fine. On board were two men from Moose Factory, Thomas and Jeff, good friends of Mark and Tyler. We transferred everything from the disabled boat to theirs, except for my canoe. With rope, the disabled boat was fastened to the working one and towed behind as we headed for the Moose River in the dark. Our rescuers used a GPS to navigate because nothing could be seen in the dark and there were many hazardous rocks, shoals, and sandbars. Towing the other boat further reduced our speed, and we chugged along at a slow pace. As it was, we would be lucky to arrive in Moose Factory before the sunrise.

The wind had died down, and now the surface of the sea was fairly calm. I shivered in the cold night air. Exhausted from lack of sleep—it was well past midnight—I nearly nodded off. Meanwhile, my on-board companions spoke of strange things. They discussed their experiences with unidentified lights in the night sky above James Bay—which they thought might be alien ships—and some enormous tracks found sunk in the moss onshore near an isolated creek, apparently left by some unknown creature.

Suddenly, the boat struck something and we all lurched forward in our seats.

"We're snagged on something," said Thomas, from the other boat.

Mark and I jabbed paddles over the side into the dark water. To our surprise, it was only knee deep—though the shore was still several kilometres away.

"We're on a sandbar," said Mark.

The boat's propeller had struck the bottom. Thomas lifted the engine out of the water and the rest of us jabbed with paddles to push the boat into deeper water. But when the engine was started again, we found we were still snagged.

"It must be the engine on the other boat," said Thomas. "It's hit the bottom."

Thomas, Jeff, and Mark plunged overboard in their hip waders. It was a strange sight—the five of us somewhere on the immensity of James Bay—struggling to free a stranded boat in the moonlight, with nothing but black water visible in all directions. Thomas, Jeff, and Mark stood nearly knee-deep in the water and attempted to raise the other boat's engine off the bottom, but its hydraulics weren't working and they couldn't free it from the sandbar.

"We need a screwdriver to get the engine off. It's the only way to free it," said Jeff.

Neither boat had a screwdriver, but I had my old Swiss Army knife—a thoughtful gift from my grandparents for my third birthday, which had served me well ever since. With the Swiss Army knife's slot-head screwdriver we were able to unscrew the engine, raise it out of the water, and at last free ourselves from the shallows.

It took us several more hours to reach the mouth of the Moose River. The Moose had been a major artery of the historic fur trade, since it connects directly with dozens of other waterways that reach into the heartland of the Canadian Shield. Just as the first faint streaks of orange sunrise appeared on the horizon, we arrived at Moose Factory—a small Cree community situated on an island some eighteen kilometres upriver from James Bay. We were all exhausted from our journey and eager to get home to sleep. I was left at the band office, which also functioned as a sort of museum, where I was told I could make myself comfortable. I curled up on a metal bench near an exhibit of a stuffed polar bear, and I found that I slept soundly beneath the snarling gaze of this deceased predator.

WHEN I AWOKE several hours later, I still had the feeling that I was bobbing on the boat. For breakfast (or rather brunch), I met with a retired trapper, Sinclair, who had spent a lifetime in the wilderness around Moose Factory. He had heard I was in town and was keen to meet me. We sat down opposite each other at the only diner on the island, located inside the band-owned co-op building. After introductions and small talk, I began to tell Sinclair about my journey. His reticence melted away and he became rather excited as I showed him pictures of black bears, canyons, rapids, and waterfalls on my camera.

"That's a big bear!" Sinclair said, looking at one of my photographs. "You did this all alone?" he asked incredulously, shaking his head.

"My last partner bailed on me, so I've become used to travelling alone," I explained.

"I've never known anyone to canoe the Again River," said Sinclair. "My family used to trap on the Corner River. Do you know it?"

"Yes," I nodded, "but I've never canoed it." The Corner was a small waterway near the Kattawagami—one of hundreds in the area.

"What made you want to canoe the Again?" asked Sinclair, sipping his coffee.

"Because no one I knew of had ever canoed it."

"There's usually a good reason for that," he laughed.

I nodded. "The river is full of rapids and falls, and the upper part is mostly too shallow to paddle."

The revelation that even Sinclair had never heard of anyone canoeing the Again River was significant. Unlike the dozens of other people I had spoken to about the river—bush pilots, prospectors, trappers, canoeists, old-timers—most of whom had never heard of it, Sinclair was an aboriginal elder with plenty of experience in the area. The fact he had even heard of the river was a testament to his considerable knowledge. But given the thousands of waterways in the James Bay watershed, no one person could know them all. While the lack of written documentation about the Again River had been the basis for my exploration of it, hearing this news from Sinclair made my journey feel a little more special.

After brunch, I wandered around Moose Factory, exploring the town and looking at rusty old cannons lying half-forgotten in an overgrown patch of grass near the river. They were relics from a bygone era, when a Hudson's Bay Company fort had stood on the island and served as a major centre of the fur trade. As I stood there on the riverbank, I thought to myself with satisfaction that while the glory days of the fur trade were past, the age of exploration was not yet over.

[13]

CHANGING THE MAP

But his soul was mad. Being alone in the wilderness, it had looked within itself and, by heavens I tell you, it had gone mad.
—Joseph Conrad, *Heart of Darkness*, 1899

T HE AGAIN RIVER had haunted me for years—a nagging obsession that frequently dominated my thoughts. I had expected, or rather hoped, that after I had finally explored this mysterious river, I could banish it from my mind and seldom think of it again. But I found that its spell over me had not yet been broken—not even by canoeing the entire river.

Unanswered questions vexed me. For one thing, I had not resolved the puzzle of how the river got its unusual name, nor had I located the old surveyors' records from the 1930s. More problematic was the question of the waterfalls—I had supposed that upon my return home, I would be able to determine their precise locations with the use of satellite imagery, given that I now knew they existed and their approximate positions—which would allow me to add them to a map of the river.

But the available satellite images were too poor to pinpoint all the waterfalls, including the one I plunged over in my canoe.

I could only detect with confidence the horseshoe waterfall in the canyon and the furious cataract at the end of the same canyon. Even a trip to the National Air Photo Library in Ottawa, where I dug up the original black-and-white aerial photos of the Again River from the 1950s, proved of little use. The old, grainy images revealed no more than the newer satellite ones. And so it began to seem, almost against my better judgment, that if I wanted to precisely map the Again River, I would have little choice but to canoe it again.

The irony of the river's name was not lost on me. Difficult and hazardous as it had been the first time, and eager as I was to move on to new challenges, like a moth to a flame I seemed irresistibly drawn back to it. No sooner had I returned from the wilderness than I began making preparations for a return journey into the Lowlands.

My intention was that a second trip to the Again River would not be a hasty, last-minute venture to satisfy personal curiosity like the mad quest I had pulled off in 2012. Instead, it would be a carefully planned expedition complete with gear that I had previously lacked. Hopefully, I could also recruit a partner, which would make it safer and easier to carry the extra equipment. For the return expedition, besides the equipment that I would need to survey waterfalls, I planned to invest in a tripod and a better camera to obtain high-quality photographs. This time, I would also forgo my woodsman's preference for traditional navigation and instead carry a GPS, so that I could plot each waterfall's exact location. After all, much as I disliked electronic gadgetry, this was a chance to literally change the map by adding waterfalls to it—a fine feather in the cap of any explorer. But more than that, there was something deeply alluring about the thought of mapping unknown waterfalls.

Ever since the Belgian explorer Louis Hennepin's awestruck description of Niagara Falls first appeared in print in 1683, explorers' tales of finding unknown waterfalls have captivated imaginations. In 2003, for example, the rediscovery of a single waterfall in a park in northern California made headlines in *National Geographic*. According to *National Geographic*'s story, a park ranger "discovered a giant waterfall that had languished unseen for decades because of rugged territory and inaccurate maps." The waterfall in question was not entirely unknown— rumours of its existence had circulated for years, and it was even marked, albeit inaccurately, on an old map from the 1960s. That map had led the park rangers on an initially futile search for the phantom waterfall. Undeterred by their failure to find it, they next turned to aerial photographs, which revealed a white blur about a kilometre from the spot marked on the map. A second hike into the remote area finally revealed the long-lost waterfall. The ranger and his colleague were credited with the discovery, even though they reported that the area around the waterfall had been logged decades earlier. But the loggers and other occasional hikers in the area had never properly documented the falls, and at least according to geographers, documentation is the essence of exploration and discovery.

In contrast, the multiple waterfalls hidden along the Again River's torturous course were infinitely more obscure than the California waterfall. There was never any logging anywhere near the Again River; no maps of any kind had ever shown waterfalls on the river's course; and the river was not part of an easily accessible park where hikers need only stray a few kilometres off established trails to glimpse a hidden waterfall. Accustomed as I was to travelling hundreds of kilometres from the nearest road or town, it seemed ironic that the unknown California waterfall was located a mere three kilometres from an existing trail and only twenty-four kilometres from the park's headquarters—all of this in a state that is home to thirty-eight million people. But the rediscovery of the California waterfall is a testament to how even in the twenty-first century, rugged wilderness and thick forest can conceal all sorts of features as well as the fact that the world has not been as thoroughly explored as many might assume.

The Royal Canadian Geographical Society's Expedition Committee was quick to approve my plans and offer me funding for a return to the Again River. The Committee knew that there was something special about finding unmapped waterfalls, particularly on a river in the Hudson Bay drainage basin where waterfalls are much less common than in mountainous terrain. In the Rockies, for example, undoubtedly dozens of unknown falls are located on isolated streams waiting to be discovered. The objective for the new expedition was to carefully photograph the waterfalls, measure their height, and record their precise locations. I would get underway the following summer, when the Lowlands would be free from the grip of its long, harsh winter.

In the meantime, I was busy speaking at schools and other venues about exploring, snowshoeing around the woods in preparation for a winter expedition I was planning, and tracking down explorers' papers as part of my doctoral research. My quest for old explorers' records, which took me far and wide, at last bore fruit. I found buried in some tedious records the secret I had been looking for—the origin of the Again River's peculiar name. I had finally located the surveyor's account from the 1930s—which was, as far as I knew, the only written description of the Again River in existence beyond my own.

The description was made in 1931 by Shirley King, an Ontario Land Surveyor, who along with his Quebec counterpart J.M. Roy, had led expeditions to survey the northern part of the provincial boundary in the summers of 1930 and 1931—something that had never been done before. Their challenge was to survey a perfectly straight line through difficult terrain and unexplored wilderness all the way to tidewater on James Bay. King wrote of their preparations:

> As a preliminary to starting the survey, little or no definite information could be obtained from any source of the area north of Mile 140. The composite of most of the information we did obtain was that it was a great muskeg, containing areas through which it would be impossible for us to go.

Undaunted by these reports, King and his surveying party pressed on. Their route north along the artificial line was extremely difficult—especially when they attempted to paddle the rivers. King explained, "Canoes were literally cut to pieces in these shallow rapids filled with sharp angular stones." As a result, they were forced to resort to "man-hauling"—that is, carrying their equipment on foot. As they blazed their way north, they passed through forests and swamps, over creeks and rivers, and across lakes and

ponds. The party, King reported, then came upon a certain nameless river, the existence of which they had been informed of ahead
of time by a Cree trapper on James Bay. King recounted:

> At Mile 178, we were fortunate in coming upon a stream
> which more or less paralleled our line all the rest of the
> way to the Bay. This river we named the Again River
> from the fact that the native who first told us about it
> was constantly interpolating the word "again" in his talk.
> Soon Mr. Roy and his men found themselves talking of
> the Again River.

That explained the origin of the river's name. Apparently it was
conceived on a whim for a river that King and his men had only
passed over at one small point.

Unfortunately, King wrote nothing more about his native
informant, but most likely he was a trapper from one of the
James Bay communities who was familiar with the lower part of
the river, near where it joins the Harricanaw River. Whether
King and his party had managed to canoe any of the Again
River—other than where they had to cross it—was unclear. If
they had attempted to explore it at all, it was only the lower,
more tranquil half, beyond the worst rapids and waterfalls, most
of which King was unaware existed. The destruction of his canoes
and the difficulty of the terrain soon convinced King that his
entire route was impractical: "It never was a feasible route for
good travel or transport," he concluded.

Like me, King was struck by the rocky cliffs and hills
enclosing the Again. He noted:

It is composed of pre-Cambrian granite rocks, and is said to be the line of contact between the old pre-Cambrian shield and the later Devonian rocks. It is a miniature mountain range with its little valleys filled with moss and scrub growth and its 50-100 foot mountains, bald or bearing scant timber growth. The total drop of the escarpment is about 100 feet down to the James Bay coastal plain. About half a mile west of the boundary, the River Again cuts through the escarpment, in a small canyon or waterfall.

King and his surveying party never saw the various falls farther upriver—they never went upriver and passed well east of its course. King had referred to only a single waterfall, though it seemed difficult to believe that he and his men could have failed to notice the two waterfalls less than five hundred metres apart in the canyon. But waterfalls and rivers were not their concern—their objective was to survey a boundary line. At any rate, their glimpse of the Again River left most of it unexplored, and plenty of blanks to fill in.

I experienced déjà vu when I read one part of King's narrative. After King and his party had completed their survey and arrived at James Bay, they ran into difficulty attempting to cross the sea to Moose Factory. King appreciated the difficulties of trying to travel on James Bay:

Extremely low water for as much as two miles out from shore, muddy shores, tides, winds, scarcity of landing places and camping places, all combined, make for a different set-up in conditions of travel than is found on inland waters. Good seaworthy boats or large canoes and plenty of provisions are two very important things to remember in coastwise travel on James Bay. You cannot live off the country and you cannot travel when the wind whips in from James Bay. Stories were told [to] us of parties being held up for two, five, even up to twelve days on windbound points. In going across James Bay, low tide caught us on a bar, about 3 or 4 miles out from the mouth of the Harricanaw River. Two hours elapsed before tide again floated our 2 foot draught boat.

Over eighty years later, making the crossing wasn't much easier.

WHEN THE SPRING arrived and the snow melted, I was spending my days on an archaeological excavation near Lake Erie and my nights preparing for the Geographical Society expedition. Preparing by myself, that is. To my dismay, in spite of my earlier vow, it looked as if I would be going on another solo journey. Wes, who I had hoped would join me, had big news of his own—he was soon to become a father. I thought this news might be all the more reason for Wes to embark on one last great adventure, but to his credit Wes believed that it precluded him from undertaking any more dangerous expeditions. After my experience with Brent, I was reluctant to trust anyone besides Wes on an expedition. At least if I went alone, I could be certain of an absolute commitment to the expedition.

However, exploring the Again for a second time and measuring its waterfalls alone presented its own set of challenges.

Measuring the height of each waterfall would be tricky—the obvious way of doing it would be to use a theodolite to measure vertical angles, and then calculate the heights using basic trigonometry. But a theodolite is a heavy and bulky surveying instrument, and carrying one on top of all my other gear and provisions across the punishing portages and quicksand-like muskeg was not a promising option.

My father was an experienced surveyor, and when I put the task to him he came up with a lightweight alternative to a theodolite. He took a .22 calibre rifle scope and mounted it on the side of a Mastercraft Torpedo Level, a hand-held electronic measuring tool used in construction. This instrument could then be mounted on a lightweight tripod. The scope would allow me to precisely measure things from a distance by fixing the crosshairs on a given point and measuring a vertical angle. The whole contraption weighed less than one-tenth as much as a theodolite and was small enough that I could easily slip it into my backpack. Together we tested this device for accuracy against an ordinary theodolite by measuring the heights of some trees. It proved less than a centimetre off the measurement obtained with an ordinary theodolite—more than accurate enough for my purposes.

As for my canoe, reasons of economy and sentiment dictated that I would rely on my old vessel, *Avalon*, notwithstanding the damage that it had sustained from the plunge over the waterfall and the many jagged rocks. The three-decades-old craft needed extensive repairs. My father and I rebuilt the gunwales from scratch, patched the holes, strengthened the hull with epoxy, removed the damaged front seat, and added a second wooden thwart for increased stability. I also removed the foam padding from the outside of the canoe, which had lost much of its buoy-ancy from old age. It had also proved a hassle on portages. The padding would wedge against trees as I dragged the canoe through the forest, causing me lengthy delays as I struggled to free it. Since I anticipated high water levels, which would make the river's rapids more dangerous, I wanted more floatation to lash inside the canoe. But it turned out that the demand for canoe floatation devices was small, and the manufacturer no longer made them. In the end, I had to settle for an inflatable pool toy—a small raft—which I lashed inside the bow of the canoe. When the repair work was finished, I felt confident that the canoe and I could handle just about anything.

Besides the Royal Canadian Geographical Society funding, I also managed to attract some private-sector sponsorship for my expedition. An American manufacturer, Globalstar Communications, offered to provide me with its latest model of satellite phone. In the past, I had shunned such gadgets as unwor-thy of a true adventurer and had undertaken wilderness journeys without them. But Geographical Society policy dictated that they have some means of communication with me. Meanwhile, Outdoors Oriented, a local store specializing in outdoor gear, outfitted me with a new water purifier to replace my broken one, a larger watertight canoe barrel, and some other gear. The hand-held water purifier, which works with a carbon filter, is a useful device. Even in the remote, isolated rivers and lakes of northern Canada, drinking untreated water is not entirely safe, given the parasites found in wild animal urine and feces. On the other hand, I had now spent nearly a month in total drinking untreated water on my wilderness journeys, and had never fallen ill. But given all the other risks inherent in my undertakings, my preference was to minimize those hazards that I could.

Lastly, I had the unexpected backing of a private benefactor, an armchair geography enthusiast interested in my expeditions, who kindly wrote me a cheque for a thousand dollars. Victorian and Edwardian explorers, such as Sir Ernest Shackleton, often relied upon the patronage of private individuals for much of their expedition funding. In return, Shackleton offered to name his geographical discoveries in his sponsors' honour. For instance, he named a large, rocky promontory jutting into Antarctica's Wendell Sea after Janet Stancomb-Wills, a wealthy tobacco heiress who supported his expedition. I could not promise the same, since the Geographical Names Board of Canada, the government body in charge of approving names for geographical features, has stringent rules that forbid naming anything after a living person, and commemorative names for deceased persons are restricted to individuals who have made extraordinary contributions to the country.

In the midst of my expedition preparations, I was contacted by a journalist in the United Kingdom who was interested in doing a story on me. She was a budding freelance journalist and couldn't be sure whether any publications would be interested in the story, but I agreed to an interview. She said that she would shop her article around to a few media outlets to see if there was any interest. At the time, I didn't think too much about whether the interview would be published since I had already done several interviews with Canadian newspapers about the Again River, and for years my adventures had been covered by local media. Several weeks went by and I heard nothing further from her, and I soon forgot about the whole thing.

Just before I was to depart for the Again River, as a sort of warm-up, I embarked on a shorter wilderness trip with Wes, my twin brother Ben, and a mutual friend of ours. We spent three relaxing days—aside from a thunderstorm—fishing and paddling around a few uninhabited lakes in northern Ontario. But little did I realize, sitting on a granite rock beneath a white pine on a glacier-carved lake, that half a world away in the United Kingdom the freelance journalist's story had found a publisher. The article appeared in *The Guardian*, one of the United Kingdom's biggest newspapers. It became the top-viewed story of the day on *The Guardian's* website, and it sparked substantial interest on social media. Of course, I had no idea about any of this until I returned home from the wilds. Once back, I didn't bother checking my email until the following morning. When I did, I gained a new appreciation for Lord Byron's quip: "I woke one morning and found myself famous." My inbox was deluged with emails—it seemed that every media outlet on the planet wanted to inter-view me. Requests came from the BBC, CNN, Al-Jazeera, the Weather Network, and dozens of other stations as far afield as Poland, Israel, and China. It was only then that I learned the story had been published. I was at a lost for how to respond to all the interview requests—they seemed to be never-ending and, as a result, I spent nearly the whole week before my departure in a series of non-stop interviews with journalists from around the world. It felt strange that what had been a private obsession of mine for years—an obscure river virtually no one else had ever cared about—was suddenly the subject of such intense interest.

Each interview I did seemed to generate more interest. I was besieged with requests from production companies to make a TV show about my adventures. A geologist asked if I would gather rock samples for him from the Again River, which could be used for his university classes. Math teachers wanted to know the details of how I used trigonometry to measure waterfalls, in the hope that they could use this example to stimulate their students' interest in math. One enthusiastic entrepreneur contacted me to say that he had devised a fool-proof, all-organic bug repellant, which would keep me perfectly protected.

Canada's public broadcaster, the CBC, asked if it could send a team from its flagship news show, *The National*, with me to the river. I had to explain that the idea was impractical. A number of newspapers splashed pictures of me on their front pages, including the *Toronto Star*, which captioned its photo of me with the line "Canada's Indiana Jones." It seemed as if I was suddenly the world's most famous explorer—if only for fifteen minutes.

The Globe and Mail asked if one of its reporters could accompany me on the expedition. I spoke to the eager journalist on the phone.

"Have you done much canoeing?" I asked.

"Never," he replied.

"You've never been canoeing?" I asked in disbelief.

"No, but I'm keen to come with you."

I tried to let him down gently. "Maybe another time."

The enormous quantity of media requests made it impossible for me to keep up with them all, even with the help of the Royal Canadian Geographical Society's media liaison. Inevitably, like all of today's instantaneous and hastily produced news coverage, stories began to appear that were full of errors and distortions. Some of the less diligent news outlets blissfully glossed over the nuances of my work on the Again River—ignoring, for example, the difference between an unexplored river and an uncharted one. *Exploring* means journeying to a place to make a detailed investigation of it, while *uncharted* means unmapped, which the Again River was not, as it had been charted on the basis of black-and-white aerial photos. Some journalists also ignored the difference between "first on record"—I was the first person on record to canoe the Again in its entirety—and "first ever." This struck me as careless, since journalists surely understand the difference between "the coldest winter ever" and "the coldest winter on record" or the difference between "the biggest northern pike ever" and "the biggest northern pike on record."

The continual media interviews—which, understandably, the Geographical Society insisted that I do—ate into my preparatory time for the expedition. I was asked to delay my start date by several days in order to do more interviews, but I stubbornly refused. I was eager to escape from the limelight and seek solitude in the wilderness. With only an hour of sleep, I appeared bright and early on CTV's morning news show, *Canada AM*, then promptly left the studio to drive due north to Cochrane to begin my expedition.

"YOU'RE A CELEBRITY!" exclaimed Terry O'Neil, as he greeted me outside the train station in Cochrane. "I was having my morning cup of coffee, watching *Canada AM*, and the next thing I know, I see you on the TV. I said to my wife, 'I know that guy!'"

I laughed.

"You know, I was going to call up the *Cochrane Times Post*, our local paper, to let them know you were in town," said Terry, smiling broadly, "but I figured you might not like that, so I didn't."

"Thanks. I've had about all I can handle of news coverage."

"I figured as much," said Terry. Then, looking grave, he added in a sombre voice, "but I have bad news."

"What's that?" I asked, concerned.

"Adam, it's been a very rainy summer. The water's going to be high."

"That will make canoeing the shallow parts easier," I replied.

"But what about the big rapids?" asked Terry.

I shrugged and tried to reassure Terry that I would be perfectly fine. Inwardly I was a little alarmed, but I thought it best not to let him notice it.

Terry shook his head as he got into my car. Rather encouragingly, as we drove out of town and headed into the wilderness, he told me once more about the canoeist who had drowned on the Kattawagami River in 2006. I would soon find out whether my canoe and I were up to the challenge of paddling the Again in high water.

END OF A JOURNEY

We shall not cease from exploration
And the end of all our exploring
Will be to arrive where we started
And know the place for the first time.
—T.S. Eliot, *"Little Gidding,"* 1942

T HE LIFE OF AN EXPLORER is often lonely. Soldiers and sailors have their bonds of brotherhood—but explorers tend to be lone wolves, solitary sorts not given to intimacy. The more time they spend beyond the reach of civilization—in a place where life depends on cunning, and where they alone are the sole authority—the more difficult it becomes to adjust back to a normal life. Some of the world's greatest explorers—men who had endured adversity and dangers beyond counting—later found themselves forlorn, wracked by self-doubt and overcome by despair. Meriwether Lewis, lionized for his crossing of North America, was later consumed by inner demons. Spurned in love, lonely and drinking heavily, despite the fame and accolades bestowed on him, Lewis fell irretrievably into despondency. One night, unable to cope any longer, he shot himself in the head.

The bullet only grazed his skull. Grabbing another flintlock pistol, Lewis shot himself through the chest. Still, he did not die. Fully conscious, but out of ammunition, in desperation he reached for a razor. In the words of a horrified witness who burst upon the scene, Lewis was found "busily engaged in cutting himself from head to foot." Choking with blood, Lewis gasped, "I am no coward; but I am so strong, [it is] so hard to die." Only after agonizing pain that lasted for hours did Lewis—one of history's most fearless explorers—finally succumb to his self-inflicted wounds.

John Hanning Speke, after discovering the source of the world's longest river in 1858, a riddle that had been puzzled over since the days of the pharaohs—became ensnared in bitter controversies over his discoveries back in England. His fellow explorer Sir Richard Burton disputed the Nile's source, and the acrimonious debate resulted in angry polemics in journals and newspapers. Speke had braved every imaginable danger in the wilds of Africa, but he found the hounding of the civilized world insufferable. On the afternoon of September 15, 1864, shortly before he was to appear at a session of the Royal Geographical Society to debate Burton, he fatally shot himself while hunting in the English countryside.

Some explorers simply vanished in the wild, never to be seen again, their fate a mystery, such as Percy Fawcett in the Amazon in 1925 and Hubert Darrell, a forgotten hero of the Arctic and solo explorer without equal, who disappeared in northern Canada in 1910 while on a lone journey into unexplored territory. Others lived into old age only to discover that their singular experiences had rendered them unsociable and incapable of developing deeper bonds with other people. They lived out their days filled with loneliness. But not for anything, I think, would any of them have traded their wilderness explorations for a more settled exis-tence—like Faust, they could not repent, for they had seen and done things no one else had.

RAIN FELL ALMOST ceaselessly during the first seven days of my journey, further swelling already high water levels, which were at least a metre and a half higher than they had been the previous year. This meant that the waterfalls would be correspondingly shorter, as the water beneath each fall would have risen since I had last seen them. As Terry had warned, it also meant that the whitewater would be faster and more powerful. While the water-falls posed little danger as long as I remembered their locations, the river's countless rapids were unavoidable. Any one of these rapids was capable of swamping my shallow canoe—which I depended on to snake between dense forest on portages, not to handle whitewater. Even if I ran one hundred rapids flawlessly, an error on the hundred and first could prove fatal.

I got my first taste of high water levels while paddling down the winding course of the Kattagawami River on day one. Some of its rapids were transformed into frothing cataracts—one of which nearly hurled my canoe and me straight into a massive boulder that towered out of the river. I just barely managed to steer the canoe clear of the boulder as we plunged through the raging torrent. After that, I decided to make camp early for the day to rest. As it was, I was exhausted from a week spent with little sleep—and sleep deprivation and wilderness canoeing aren't usually a winning combination.

The next day, rejuvenated from a night spent on a bed of lichens and moss, I paddled hard, arriving at a large, reed-covered lake. The weather had turned cold, with temperatures barely above freezing. While I was crossing the lake in a stiff headwind, a drizzle of rain turned into a steady downpour, chilling me to the bone. I managed to escape hypothermia by spending the night holed up in my tent on a sheltered island far from shore. Despite the weather, I was as happy as could be—I was back in the wilderness doing what I loved best. In the forest on the island I felt like I was in a dream world—the cathedral of ancient trees blotted out the sky, sheltering me from the rain, while thick carpets of bright green moss covered the ground.

The portages were as demanding as they had been the year before: the forest was sodden from steady rain and the ground was even swampier. But at least I could follow my old trails and didn't have to blaze any new ones. One day, in the middle of the longest portage to the Again's headwaters, I had fallen into a sort of mental fog, staggering onward in rain through swamp forest, when suddenly a deafening crash reverberated from out of the depths of the woods. Instinctively I froze. A tree must have toppled over—something I had witnessed several times in my life—but after days of silence, any loud sound was arresting. The tree might have fallen of its own accord, or it might have been knocked over by a black bear searching for insect larvae. I waited in silence to see if a bear would appear. When none emerged, I gingerly carried on with the portage to the Again's headwaters, glancing over my shoulder every so often.

On that moonless night, I pitched my tent on a dry patch near the shoreline. More than just bears could be lurking in the darkness: wolves, wolverines, and supposedly wendigos haunted these unexplored regions. Anything out there could be silently watching me as I lay scribbling notes by the glow of my flash-light. Occasionally I heard a branch snap, the wind howl, or some unidentifiable noise rise from out of the darkness. But I slept easy—to be in the woods was to be home.

Strangely, my most dramatic wildlife encounter of the expedition took place in broad daylight. One morning I crawled out of my tent, still half-asleep, into some rare sunshine. I had camped in a burnt-out area. Short jack pines, the first trees to grow after a fire, and alder bushes were the only greenery on the charred landscape. I shuffled behind the tent into some chest-high alders to find some firewood. When I struck a branch with my hatchet I heard a sudden noise behind me—spinning around I caught sight of the fleeing backside of an enormous wolf. In a flash, it disappeared into the alder bushes. The wolf had been no more than three metres away from me. Previously in the wild, I had only caught a glimpse of wolves from a distance. I was puzzled to see one so close. But wolves, like all dogs, are innately curious, and this one, I suppose, couldn't resist investigating what strange manner of creature lived in the nylon tent.

THE HIGH WATER made the rapid-choked course of the Again River more hazardous, but this time I didn't have to worry about getting swept over any hidden waterfalls. I knew their approximate locations, and I could remember the look of the river above each fall. Several canoeists have been killed by unsuspected waterfalls in the James Bay watershed, and I didn't intend to join them. According to legend, a war party of Iroquois braves plunged to their deaths in their birchbark canoes over an unfamiliar water-fall on the Abitibi River, at a place still called Iroquois Falls. More recently, in 1993, two American canoeists had drowned when they were trapped in a furious current and swept over a waterfall on the Missinaibi River. Their deaths were attributed in part to inaccurate maps of the river, which is, nevertheless, one of the best-known rivers flowing into James Bay.

Despite the higher water levels, the river was still shallow and rocky in places, especially along its upper course, which forced me to occasionally wade and pull the canoe behind me. In these stretches, the bottom of my canoe frequently scraped over sharp rocks. Each time my canoe ground over another rock, I wondered if it would be the last straw—but somehow *Avalon* managed to hold up. In a traditional birchbark or canvas canoe, the endless sharp rocks would have made navigating the river nearly impossible—part of the reason why the Again remained unexplored for so long.

As I navigated farther along the river, it grew larger and deeper. The whitewater rapids were of considerable size with serrated rocks and boulders dispersed throughout them like the obstacles in a pinball machine, all of which I had to snake around in my canoe. I spent all day doing so, navigating one rapid after another; but something about the grey skies, drizzle of rain, ceaseless rustle of running water, and cold air lulled me into a haze. Alone with my thoughts, my mind would drift, a risky prospect when every bit of river has hidden rocks. I find staying mentally focused to be one of the most underappreciated challenges of solo wilderness travel.

In the midst of one otherwise ordinary rapid, while I wasn't concentrating on the river, my canoe suddenly smashed into a barely visible boulder, spun sideways, flooded, and bent round like a boomerang from the power of the water. When it began to fill with water, I leapt onto the boulder, while my gear was swept downriver. The force of the cascading water pinned the inundated canoe on the granite rock so that it looked as if the canoe would snap in two. There was nothing to do but attempt to free the crushed canoe from the rock and repair it onshore. I carefully stepped off the boulder into the cold, swirling water, which rose to my waist, and worked to free the canoe. It took all my strength to pull the flooded canoe off the rock and wade to the alder-covered banks to fix it. Fortunately, the repair work was easier than I thought it would be—I popped the crushed hull back into shape and it sustained little permanent damage. After retrieving my plastic barrel, paddles, and waterlogged backpack, which lucky for me were blocked from travelling far by rocks, I resumed paddling with a greater effort to avoid slipping into any further reveries.

A few days after my canoe was nearly broken in two by the boulder, I encountered more difficulty in whitewater. I had been navigating rapids along the Again all day—portaging around the largest ones, but more often than not running them. I was soaking wet from the waves, which frequently lapped over the canoe's shallow sides and forced me to halt regularly, unpack the canoe, and empty the accumulated water before continuing. But I knew I was nearing the beautiful stretch of river that ran between the rocky hills and canyons, and I was eager to arrive there soon by paddling as many rapids as possible. Though I had only been there once, the stark beauty of the place was engraved in my memory.

After a sharp bend in the river, another rapid roared ahead— foaming water was crashing noisily over a rock ledge. The drop was not much more than a foot, so I decided to risk paddling it rather than unpack everything and perform yet another portage. But when I plunged over the ledge in my canoe, the waves lapped right over the bow, flooding the vessel. For a few seconds, it seemed as if the flotation I had lashed inside the canoe would prevent the inundated craft from sinking, but the weight of the water proved too much—as if in slow motion, the canoe sank with me in it.

My lifejacket kept me afloat as I found myself swimming in rapids, gasping in the cold. I grabbed on to the flooded canoe with my right hand, while with my left I struggled to get a hold of my watertight barrel, backpack, and paddles. With my hands full trying to hold on to all my vital gear, I watched helplessly as my brown fedora—an identical replacement for the one I had lost in the waterfall the year before—disappeared into the swirling water. Kicking with my feet, I managed to swim over to a boulder in the river, beach my canoe on that, and then make several trips to shore to secure my gear. Besides my hat, I lost my fishing rod, bug spray, a few other small items, and a bag of dried apples—nothing I couldn't survive without.

THE MASTERCRAFT TORPEDO LEVEL mounted with the .22 calibre rifle scope worked like a charm for measuring the waterfalls—despite the hordes of blackflies that devoured my face and hands as I set up the instrument. My face was smeared with blood from their incessant bites. Sometimes, if I inhaled, I would cough from having swallowed a cloud of insects. Even in the rain the mosquitoes still swarmed me. Meriwether Lewis had written of the torments caused by swarms of mosquitoes:

The musquetoes continue to infest us in such manner that we can scarcely exist; for my own part I am confined by them to my bier at least 3/4 of the time. My dog even howls with the torture he experiences from them.

The early explorers in the Lowlands had learned from their aboriginal counterparts to cake themselves in foul-smelling bear grease to protect against blackflies and mosquitoes. I preferred a long-sleeved shirt, a mesh bug net, and if things were really awful, insect repellant, which was however never very effective.

The highest waterfall I surveyed measured just over six metres, or around twenty feet, which meant that at the time of my first expedition, it was probably not quite eight metres, or nearly twenty-five feet. The waterfalls on the Again River number between five and nine, depending on how one classifies "a water-fall" (no universally agreed criteria exist). The number varies based on whether one counts "split falls" around rocks or islands as one or two waterfalls, whether upper and lower drops should be counted separately, whether "step falls" (a sort of cascade) should be counted as a waterfall, and whether an exceptionally fierce, steep rapid with a considerable drop should be considered a waterfall or just a big rapid. My preference is for a conservative scale, according to which the Again River has five waterfalls. Waterfalls can be classified into over a dozen different categories, including curtain falls, plunges, cascades, fans, horsetails, slides, ledges, and punchbowls. The waterfall I went over was a ledge waterfall, where water descends over a vertical drop while main-taining partial contact with the bedrock. The horseshoe-shaped waterfall at the start of the longest canyon on the river was a plunge fall, where water descends vertically without contact with the bedrock. Two of the waterfalls, including the highest, were violent cascades, and the smallest was a "slide waterfall," where water glides over bedrock while maintaining continuous contact. I photographed, measured, and recorded the longitude and latitude of each one—something no one had done before.

As fulfilling as I found such old-fashioned explorer's work, as I paddled, waded, and portaged my way downriver, I was conscious of my desire to finally be rid of the Again. I wanted to move on to new horizons. Like a siren call, some new temptation, perhaps the promise of another nameless river, would lure me elsewhere into the wilderness. As I sat in my canoe paddling, I started to daydream of faraway places where I could explore a river no other living person had ever seen. A sudden zeal to finish my work meant that my progress on the expedition was rapid—I pushed myself hard from sunrise to sunset. When I had reached the end of the river, I paused to empty my watertight barrel of provisions and fill the barrel with a supply of freshwater. (The remaining provisions from the barrel I crammed into my worn backpack.) Then I headed down the Harricanaw River to the salt water of James Bay, where I intended to remain for a few days.

I spent my time near the mouth of the Harricanaw making short forays into the sea in my canoe—once or twice getting caught in terrifying waves far from shore that nearly swamped the canoe—and on land sketching birds, taking notes, and enjoying the solitude. But that solitude came to an end late one afternoon when I hiked down to shore to fetch some drinking water from my barrel. My eyes were greeted with an unexpected sight—a flotilla of canoes was coming downriver. I stood and stared at the canoes—it took a moment for me to appreciate that they were no mirage. There were six in total, each with two occupants. As they neared, I saw that it was a group of teenage campers, led by two adults. I stood on the riverbank, watching them as a wild animal might stand motionless and blankly stare at a passing canoe.

At the time, it didn't occur to me that the ragged appearance of a lone man deep in the wilderness, suddenly emerging from the woods, might startle them. I had neither shaved nor bathed in weeks; my mop of hair was dishevelled by the wind, my clothes were tattered, my pants ripped nearly to shreds from the portages. A hunting knife was stuck in my belt and my army rain jacket was draped over my shoulders.

They paddled up to the bank near where I stood, beached their canoes, and began somewhat timidly climbing up the slope to where I stood watching them.

"Hello!" said the first one, apparently the camp counsellor in charge. He was a bearded, jovial looking man of about thirty.

I nodded hello.

"We thought you might be a Cree trapper," he said, as his young charges followed him up the bank, carrying their packs. The other counsellor was a woman in her mid-twenties. "But you don't look like one."

"No, I'm not," I said, warming up to the idea of being around people again. "Did you canoe the Harricanaw?"

"Yeah. We're from Camp Pine Crest. I'm Matt."

We shook hands.

"I'm Adam."

"You're not here alone, are you?"

"Yes, I am."

"I take it you canoed the Harricanaw too?" asked Matt.

The campers had gathered round me in a semi-circle, curiously examining me as something of an exotic specimen.

"No," I said, "I came down the Again River."

They looked at me blankly.

"It's a tributary of the Harricanaw. Have you heard of it?"

"No," said Matt. "All alone?"

"Yes."

"Now that's something," he said nodding appreciatively. "Well, we're going to camp here tonight. You're welcome to join us for supper. We've got plenty of extra pasta."

Some of the kids looked at me expectantly.

"Thanks," I replied, "I'd be happy to join you," and, in fact, I was. As much as I like solitude, it was nice to be able to talk with people that could appreciate what I had just done.

That evening, we gathered around a campfire on what was a rather cold, windy night to eat pasta and swap stories. I regaled them with tales of my travels, unexplored rivers, hidden water-falls, and snarling polar bears. They, in turn, told me about their summer camp and their three-week trip down the Harricanaw, which they took great pride in completing. And to their credit, any three-week canoe journey is no picnic. After dinner, I was astonished to learn that on their entire trip they never once drank tea. This seemed unthinkable: tea is the traditional drink of the northern woods, and some might say it is as much a part of the wilderness experience as the haunting cry of a loon, the crackle of a late-night fire, or a silent morning paddle across misty lakes. When I mentioned that herbal tea was the one luxury I prized above all in the wilderness, the campers all wanted a cup. We boiled several pots over the fire that night. Their trip had been a vegetarian one, and the teenage boys, in particular, looking rather ravenous, were ecstatic when I gave them some bags of jerky from my own supply.

THE NEXT MORNING, the campers and I went our separate ways. They set off to paddle to Moose Factory—which in fair weather was not a problem in their large, seventeen-foot canoes. Meanwhile, I remained behind on the coast, where I was to rendezvous with some of my companions from last year and cross James Bay with them.

This time things went smoothly, without any engine troubles or unexpected delays on sandbars. We did, however, stop to gather sweetgrass, a plant used in traditional Cree spiritual ceremonies. In Moosonee, as I was loading my canoe onto one of the Polar Bear Express' boxcars for the train ride south, a man strode up to where I was standing with an excited look on his face.

"You're Adam Shoalts!" he said, shaking my hand.

"Yes," I replied, a little surprised by the attention.

"You're a legend," he exclaimed.

"Not quite," I laughed.

"I've read all about you. I've done a lot of canoeing myself, but you know, nothing like what you do."

"Where do you canoe?"

"Around here mostly, the Moose River. I live in Moosonee," he explained. "I used to be a professional cyclist, but I gave that up and moved here with my wife. I love the outdoors—hunting, fishing, all that stuff."

"That's the life," I said.

"I gotta ask you," he said eagerly, "to show me your canoe. You've got to have some awesome gear."

"Not really," I gestured to my canoe lying in the open boxcar.

A horrified expression came over the man's face. He was apparently expecting to see something state-of-the-art. "That's your canoe!?"

"Yes."

"How did you canoe here with that? That's not even an ordinary tripper canoe. It's so small. How does that thing get through rapids?"

"I bought it second-hand. New canoes are expensive," I explained.

"But you must have sponsors throwing themselves at you?"

"No," I laughed. "Not yet, anyway."

When I returned home I discovered that the media's interest in my expedition hadn't died down. I had received more requests for TV appearances, magazine stories, and radio interviews. I accepted a few, but otherwise attempted to maintain a low profile. Wes had mentioned that he and his family were heading to Algonquin Park on a camping trip, and invited me to come along. I could never refuse any opportunity to strike off into the wilderness, so I happily joined them and forgot about the interviews. At night around the campfire, I entertained his young nieces and nephew with tales of man-eating bears and sasquatches lurking deep in the woods. I taught them how to make different types of tea from various wild plants, and I found myself wishing that I could remain in the forest and forget about the other side of life as an explorer—the paperwork.

Of course, that wasn't possible. I had several hundred unread emails in my inbox, maps to create, and my expedition report and photographs to submit to the Geographical Society. In my absence in the wilderness, some outlandish claims had circulated about the Again River. Someone had claimed that the falls on the Again River were already mapped—but that proved to be a simple case of cartographic illiteracy. Another person, with no background in exploration history, geography, archaeology, or common sense, claimed that the 107-kilometre, rock-strewn, rapid- and waterfall-choked course of the Again River, which terminates in a swamp, was actually a "major trade route." Of the hundreds of rivers in the Hudson and James Bay watershed, no more than a dozen or so could be said to have ever constituted a major trade route—and they were well known. The Again was emphatically nothing of the sort.

I fully expected, and regarded as inevitable, that in an age of internet anonymity, someone somewhere would claim to have previously canoed the Again River. Of course, such a claim would make no material difference to my expedition. But, to my surprise, despite the intense media glare focused on the river, only a single person emerged who claimed to have previously canoed it—a testament to its utter obscurity. The lone individual, a seventy-one-year-old man, claimed that he had been part of a team of geologists who had canoed the Again in 1961 under contract for the Quebec government. The other geologists, he said, were now dead. When I spoke to him on the phone and asked why the Quebec government would hire geologists to canoe a river that was mostly in Ontario, he admitted they had only explored the lower, more tranquil half of the river, beyond most of the dangerous rapids and all the waterfalls. Back in 1961, he had been a nineteen-year-old summer employee, and he had only spent that one summer in the area. He explained that the group had been dropped via helicopter at the river's halfway point and that it was just one of several they canoed. His memory, after fifty-two years, was rather hazy—he couldn't remember which river the Again flowed into and didn't recognize any of the waterfalls from my pictures. However, he insisted, the expedition's leader, the geologist Jerome Remick, had documented all their findings and work in an official report. I was sure that I had read Remick's dry report five years earlier, and that it said nothing of the Again River. But, to be certain, I obtained copies of it, both in English and the original French, and reread it. As I suspected, the report made no mention of the Again River, nor did the Again appear on the maps that accompanied it. Their work had focused on the rivers in the upper part of the Harricanaw's watershed, well south of the Again. Of course, I couldn't rule out the possibility that they had canoed the lower part of the Again and for some reason failed to mention it—but this seemed unlikely. I could only speculate whether this claim was an honest mistake—after all, it had been over half a century. At any rate, it was immaterial to my expedition and made no difference to me personally. I had done what I had set out to do five years earlier when I first began to dream of the river in my cluttered, map-lined study, and beyond that, nothing much mattered.

A few months after my return from the Again, to my surprise I received notice that I had been elected as a Fellow of the Royal Canadian Geographical Society for "extraordinary contributions to geography." To be elected a Fellow was to join the company of such explorers as Sir Richard Burton, David Livingstone, Sir Henry Morton Stanley, Sir Ernest Shackleton, Sir Francis Younghusband, Percy Fawcett, and Charles Camsell—all of whom had been elected Fellows of their respective geographical societies on the basis of their expeditions. In comparison to them, I had done next to nothing to deserve such a distinction. The rivers I had explored in the Lowlands were small waterways, of no great importance in themselves, and my expeditions, while difficult and to a degree dangerous, were still only minor affairs.

I was to have the honour of presenting the Society's flag that I had carried on my expeditions to Canada's governor general, His Excellency, the Right Honourable David Johnston. At the ceremony in Ottawa, I marched down a red carpet holding the carefully folded blue flag in my hands, rows of seated dignitaries on either side, stepped onto a stage, bowed, and presented the flag to the Queen's representative, feeling a bit like an explorer from an earlier era. When he shook my hand, His Excellency mentioned that he would like to join me on an expedition—if I promised to travel at a slower pace and do most of the paddling.

Gratifying as it was to be recognized in this way, the truth is that when my exploration of the Again River was finally complete, it wasn't as if I felt a great weight had been lifted from my shoulders. I had gained the knowledge that I had sought about a river that had previously been an enigma, but many other unknown rivers remained to be explored—and I couldn't resist them. I felt nearly as restless as ever in my obsession with seeking the world's last unexplored rivers, and I still had an almost overwhelming compulsion to push myself to the limit to explore such places. The Again, like all the other rivers I had explored before it, seemed only to increase my appetite for greater challenges. And besides, I had the example of other Geographical Society Fellows to live up to. Within days of presenting the Society's flag to the governor general, I had resolved to undertake a new expedition that would surpass all of my others in terms of risk, hardship, and geographical remoteness. I had, with *Canadian Geographic*'s encouragement, set my sights on the unexplored reaches of the High Arctic—the most extreme environment on earth where canoeing is possible.

The morning after the ceremony with the governor general, I attended a meeting at *Canadian Geographic*'s office to discuss these plans. The magazine was interested in an Arctic expedition, and they thought I was the man for the job—if I wanted it, and of course I did. *Canadian Geographic* stipulated that any expedition I dreamed up take place north of the Arctic Circle—a line of latitude that runs around the top of the world. Everything north of this line has at least one day of continuous daylight in the summer and at least one day when the sun never rises in the winter. Beyond the Arctic Circle lie the vast, nearly uninhabited Arctic islands—an immense archipelago of frozen wilderness stretching over 2,400 kilometres from east to west and consisting of 36,563 islands, of which only ten are inhabited. It's a barren land of glaciers, featureless tundra, windswept mountains, and frigid lakes.

The canoe was never meant for the icy rivers of the High Arctic. The Inuit—who first colonized Canada's Arctic islands about eight or nine hundred years ago—relied on dogsleds for transportation for most of the year, and when the ice briefly melted in summer would travel in kayaks made from animal skins, which they used to skirt the rocky coastlines. It was only in the mid-twentieth century that the first intrepid explorers attempted to canoe High Arctic rivers—no easy task, given that the Arctic is actually a cold desert that receives very little precipitation. As a consequence, most rivers in the Arctic are shallow, rock-strewn streams that are unsuitable for canoeing—aside from when the snow melts in July, which transforms these streams into raging torrents. The difficulty of canoeing in such a place is appreciable: besides all the usual hazards such as drowning, smashing one's head on a rock, or getting crushed by an overturned canoe in a rapid, the icy water and cold air temperatures mean that merely capsizing or swamping in a river is liable to prove fatal. To add to the difficulties, the region has no trees to speak of, nothing in the way of natural materials like spruce resin or birchbark with which to repair a canoe, scarce shelter from the merciless winds, few wild edibles of any value, and of course, polar bears with no fear of humans. Even in mid-summer the wind chill is often minus ten Celsius, and snowstorms are possible.

As I left the meeting in the editor's office and headed back down the hallway to leave, I couldn't help but step into the boardroom to see Sir Francis Younghusband's sword mounted on the wall. Three and a half years earlier, the sight of it had filled me with an irresistible yearning for faraway, unexplored lands. And now, seeing his sword again and having just received my orders to devise a new expedition, I felt once more the inexpressible allure of the unknown, the romance of adventure, and the thrill of exploration.

AFTERWORD

He said he should prefer not to know the sources of the Nile,
and that there should be some unknown regions
preserved as hunting-grounds for the poetic imagination.
—George Eliot, *Middlemarch*, 1874

E VERY YEAR THE WORLD gets a little more crowded, a
little less wild, a little more settled. We are fortunate to still
have vast areas of wilderness and some unexplored territory. But
what remains is unlikely to last long in the face of an ever-
growing human population coupled with an insatiable thirst for
natural resources. Wherever I have ventured, from the Amazon
to the High Arctic, including even the Hudson Bay Lowlands, I
have found that the quest for natural resource extraction is never
far behind—whether it be fossil fuels, minerals, or new logging
frontiers. We are losing the natural world faster than we can
explore it. In the world's tropical forests, entire species go extinct
before they ever become known to science. When forests and
wetlands are converted into farms, shopping malls, highways,
or cities, we lose more than just the world's magnificent bio-
diversity—that bewildering blend of animals and plants that

makes our world such a fascinating place. We also lose something that's deep in our collective psyches—the vast, forbidding, but enchanting world of untrammelled wildness, those critical "hunting-grounds for the poetic imagination." It has been my privilege to experience some of these last remaining realms of mystery on the earth. I have tried to tread as gently as possible in these places; I look upon them like a pilgrim does a sacred site. It is my deepest hope that they are preserved for future generations, so that it remains possible to hear the call of faraway lands, of untouched wilderness and the unknown. We all lose when it becomes impossible to find such a place.

ADDENDUM

IN 2015, WITH Chuck Brill, Adam Shoalts returned to the Hudson Bay Lowlands to explore the western fork in the Brant River, one of the two rivers he was originally interested in exploring in 2011 for the Royal Canadian Geographical Society.

ACKNOWLEDGMENTS

T HIS BOOK would not have been possible without the help, expertise, and encouragement of many people who shared an interest in seeing the story of my adventures published. Most important of all was my literary agent, Rick Broadhead, who first approached me in the summer of 2013 about the idea of writing a book, and then deftly guided me through what to me was the uncharted territory of the publishing industry. Rick was everything a writer could want in a literary agent, and never once led me astray over any unexpected waterfalls or into any hidden rocks.

I was also fortunate to benefit from the expertise and professionalism of a great team at Penguin Canada. My editor, Nick Garrison, brought a keen eye and insightful mind to the narrative, and a sympathetic appreciation for what it is that I do. Nick also made sure to keep me on the right track when I was getting lost in the literary woods. Nicole Winstanley, Penguin Canada's president and publisher, was supportive throughout this process and made me feel at home with Penguin. I am indebted to Scott Richardson, the book's graphic designer, for the book's layout and cover. Scott also created the book's maps based off my originals. Mary Ann Blair, the managing editor for the project, kept everything on schedule and running smoothly, despite having to deal with my absence for weeks in the wilderness without contact. The copyeditor, Claudia Forgas, carefully scrutinized the manuscript and helped correct errors. I also want to thank Tricia van der Grient, who handled the publicity for the book, and Justin Stoller for his work on a number of fronts. I must also thank the Royal Canadian Geographical Society, especially for their support of my expeditions in 2011 and 2013.

I was fortunate in finding a number of friends and family kind enough to read earlier stages of the manuscript and offer comments and suggestions. In particular I want to thank Diane Moore, Sandra and Charles Durant, Frank Hummell, Alice Yi, and Elizabeth Hudson. My friends Brent Kozuh and Wesley Crowe were also supportive of this book, and I wish to thank both of them for sharing in some of the adventures retold here and for remaining my good friends throughout it all. Finally, I must thank my parents, both of whom not only encouraged and nurtured my love of literature and the outdoors, but put up with the stress of my many solo expeditions.

INDEX